Place Matters

Over the last two decades there has been increased interest in the distribution of crime and other antisocial behaviors at lower levels of geography. The focus on microgeography and its contribution to the understanding and prevention of crime has been called the "criminology of place." It pushes scholars to examine small geographic areas within cities, often as small as addresses or street segments, for their contribution to crime. The authors describe what is known about crime and place, providing the most up-to-date and comprehensive review available. *Place Matters* shows that the study of the criminology of place should be a central focus of criminology in the twenty-first century. It creates a tremendous opportunity for advancing our understanding of crime, and for addressing it. The book brings the collective knowledge of eighteen top scholars to provide a comprehensive understanding of crime at place.

Place Matters

Criminology for the Twenty-first Century

DAVID WEISBURD
Hebrew University and George Mason University

JOHN E. ECK
University of Cincinnati

ANTHONY A. BRAGA
Rutgers University and Harvard University

CODY W. TELEP
Arizona State University

BREANNE CAVE
George Mason University

KATE BOWERS[1]
University College London

GERBEN BRUINSMA
NSCR Amsterdam and VU University Amsterdam

CHARLOTTE GILL
George Mason University

ELIZABETH R. GROFF
Temple University

JULIE HIBDON
Southern Illinois University

JOSHUA C. HINKLE
Georgia State University

SHANE D. JOHNSON
University College London

BRIAN LAWTON
John Jay College

CYNTHIA LUM
George Mason University

JERRY H. RATCLIFFE
Temple University

GEORGE RENGERT
Temple University

TRAVIS TANIGUCHI
RTI International

SUE-MING YANG
George Mason University

[1] remaining authors listed in alphabetical order

CAMBRIDGE
UNIVERSITY PRESS

32 Avenue of the Americas, New York, NY 10013-2473, USA

Cambridge University Press is part of the University of Cambridge.

It furthers the University's mission by disseminating knowledge in the pursuit of education, learning, and research at the highest international levels of excellence.

www.cambridge.org
Information on this title: www.cambridge.org/9781107029521

© Cambridge University Press 2016

This publication is in copyright. Subject to statutory exception
and to the provisions of relevant collective licensing agreements,
no reproduction of any part may take place without the written
permission of Cambridge University Press.

First published 2016

Printed in the United Kingdom by Clays, St Ives plc.

A catalog record for this publication is available from the British Library.

Library of Congress Cataloging in Publication Data
Names: Weisburd, David, author.
Title: Place matters : criminology for the twenty-first century / David Weisburd and 17 others.
Description: New York : Cambridge University Press, 2016. | Includes bibliographical references and index.
Identifiers: LCCN 2015039546 | ISBN 9781107029521 (Hardback)
Subjects: LCSH: Criminology. | BISAC: SOCIAL SCIENCE / Criminology.
Classification: LCC HV6023.5 .W45 2016 | DDC 364–dc23 LC record available at http://lccn.loc.gov/2015039546

ISBN 978-1-107-02952-1 Hardback
ISBN 978-1-107-60949-5 Paperback

Cambridge University Press has no responsibility for the persistence or accuracy of URLs for external or third-party Internet Web sites referred to in this publication and does not guarantee that any content on such Web sites is, or will remain, accurate or appropriate.

Contents

List of figures	page vii
List of tables	xi
List of contributors	xiii
Preface	xvii

1	Crime Places within Criminological Thought	1
	Is the Study of Crime and Place "Criminological"?	5
	At What Specific Unit of Geography?	8
	What Is New in the Study of Crime at Place?	11
	What Follows?	14
2	The Concentration of Crime at Place	16
	Place and Space	16
	Crime Concentrations at Places	17
	A Law of Crime Concentration at Places	22
	Does the Law of Crime Concentration Apply Across Time?	25
	The Implications of Crime Concentrations	27
	The Coupling of Crime to Place	29
	Microgeographic Places and Spatial Interaction Effects	34
	Conclusions	41
3	Theories of Crime and Place	42
	Processes That Create Crime Places	42
	Two Theoretical Perspectives	43
	Opportunity Mechanisms	54
	Social Disorganization Mechanisms	58
	Applying Social Disorganization to Places	60
	Synthesis	61
	Conclusions	67

4	The Importance of Place in Mainstream Criminology and Related Fields: Influences and Lessons to be Learned	68
	The Growing Role of Microgeographic Places in Traditional Theorizing of Criminality	68
	Contributions of Place Perspectives from Other Disciplines into Mainstream Criminological Theory and Research	71
	What Can Criminology Learn from Other Disciplines about Places in the Future?	81
	Conclusions	84
5	Methods of Place-Based Research	86
	The Importance of Theory in Developing Methods	86
	The Importance of Methods	88
	Evolution to Space	90
	Spatial Autocorrelation	92
	What Is the Appropriate Cone of Resolution?	93
	The Development of New Geographies	95
	Innovative Data Applications of GIS	96
	Crime Hot Spots	101
	Predictive Techniques	104
	Computer Simulations	108
	Operational Decision Making with New Geographies	110
	Conclusions	111
6	Reducing Crime at High-Crime Places: Practice and Evidence	113
	Situational Crime Prevention at Places	114
	Police Efforts to Control Crime Hot Spots	115
	The Importance of Place Managers and "Third Parties" in Controlling Crime Places	127
	Community Corrections and Crime Places	133
	Crime Displacement and Diffusion of Crime-Control Benefits	135
	Conclusions	138
7	Crime Places in the Criminological Imagination	140
	The Law of Crime Concentration and the Future of Crime and Place Studies	141
	Broadening Theoretical Development	146
	The Importance of Intra- and Interdisciplinary Perspectives	148
	The Importance of Advances in Data, Methods, and Statistics	151
	Implementing Place-Based Crime Prevention in Practice	153
	Conclusions	158
Notes		159
References		163
Index		197

Figures

1.1 Changes in rates of microplace studies published in *Criminology* over time. *Original source*: Weisburd, D. (2015). "The law of crime concentration and the criminology of place." *Criminology*, 53(2), 133–157. Courtesy of Wiley. *page* 4
1.2 Map of the home addresses of juvenile offenders. *Original source*: Shaw, C.R., Zorbaugh, F.M., McKay, H.D., and Cottrell, L.S. (1929). Delinquency areas. A study of the geographical distribution of school truants, juvenile delinquents, and adult offenders in Chicago. Chicago, IL: University of Chicago Press. Copyright 1929 by the University of Chicago. 7
2.1 Crime concentrations by street segments in Seattle, WA. *Original source*: Weisburd, D., Groff, E.R., and Yang, S.-M. (2012). *The criminology of place: Street segments and our understanding of the crime problem.* New York: Oxford University Press. Used by permission of Oxford University Press. 21
2.2 The proportion of street segments that account for 25 percent, 50 percent, 75 percent, and 100 percent of crime in Tel Aviv-Jaffa, 2010. *Original source*: Weisburd, D., and Amram, S. (2014). "The law of concentrations of crime at place: The case of Tel Aviv-Jaffa." *Police Practice and Research*, 15(2), 101–114. Reprinted with permission of Taylor & Francis Ltd. 22
2.3 The law of crime concentration in large cities. *Original source*: Weisburd, D. (2015). "The law of crime concentrations and the criminology of place." *Criminology*, 53(2), 133–157. Courtesy of Wiley. 24
2.4 The law of crime concentration in small cities. *Source*: Weisburd, D. (2015). "The law of crime concentrations and the criminology of place." *Criminology*, 53(2), 133–157. Courtesy of Wiley. 25

2.5	Changes in crime concentration and number of crime incidents over time. *Source*: Weisburd, D. (2015). "The law of crime concentrations and the criminology of place." *Criminology*, 53(2), 133–157. Courtesy of Wiley.	26
2.6	Twenty-two trajectories of crime incidents for Seattle, WA, street segments. *Original source*: Weisburd, D., Groff, E.R., and Yang, S.-M. (2012). *The criminology of place: Street segments and our understanding of the crime problem.* New York: Oxford University Press. Used by permission of Oxford University Press.	29
2.7	Drug hot spots in Jersey City, NJ. *Source*: Weisburd, D., and Mazerolle, L.G. (2000). "Crime and disorder in drug hot spots: Implications for theory and practice in policing." *Police Quarterly*, 3(3), 331–349. Reprinted by permission of SAGE Publications.	31
2.8	Chronic hot spot street segments in Seattle. *Original source*: Weisburd, D., Groff, E.R., and Yang, S.-M. (2014). "Understanding and controlling hot spots of crime: The importance of formal and informal social controls." *Prevention Science*, 15(1), 31–43, Figure 2. With kind permission from Springer Science and Business Media.	32
2.9	Spatial distribution of trajectory patterns in southern Seattle, WA. *Original source*: Weisburd, D., Groff, E.R., and Yang, S.-M. (2012). *The criminology of place: Street segments and our understanding of the crime problem.* New York: Oxford University Press. Used by permission of Oxford University Press.	33
2.10	Neighborhood disorder, collective efficacy, and street crimes per face block, in Chicago, 1999–2000. *Original source*: St. Jean, P.K.B. (2007). *Pockets of crime: Broken windows, collective efficacy, and the criminal point of view.* Chicago, IL: University of Chicago Press. © 2007 by the University of Chicago.	34
2.11	Example of concentric circles buffers surrounding a facility. *Original source*: Taniguchi, T.A., Rengert, G.F., and McCord, E.S. (2009). "Where size matters: Agglomeration economies of illegal drug markets in Philadelphia." *Justice Quarterly*, 26(4), 670–694. Reprinted with permission of Taylor & Francis Ltd.	39
3.1	Place management and other explanations for crime concentration at places.	48
3.2	A hypothetical history of opportunity and crime at a place: a shopping mall.	55
3.3	Proprietary and proximal places.	57
3.4	Spatial concentration and spatial autocorrelation for public housing assistance. *Source*: Weisburd, D., Groff, E.R., and Yang, S.-M. (2012). *The criminology of place: Street segments and our understanding of the crime problem.* New York: Oxford University Press. Used by permission of Oxford University Press.	62

List of figures

3.5 Streets where at least 75 percent of registered voters are active voters. *Source*: Weisburd, D., Groff, E.R., and Yang, S.-M. (2012). *The criminology of place: Street segments and our understanding of the crime problem*. New York: Oxford University Press. Used by permission of Oxford University Press. 63

4.1 Map of cholera fatalities in London. *Original source*: Map by Dr. John Snow, 1854. 76

5.1 Impact of edge effects on crime hot spot surfaces. 94

5.2 Overlay of floors in Gladfelter Hall, the hot spot of crime identified within a building. *Original source*: Rengert, G.F. and Lowell, R. (2005). *Police Foundation crime mapping news: A quarterly newsletter for crime mapping, GIS, problem analysis, and policing*. Washington, DC: Police Foundation. 99

5.3 Hotspot grid with robber densities defined as number of incidents per square kilometer represented in form of a two-dimensional thematic Map (left image) and in form of a three-dimensional "information landscape" (right image). *Original source*: Wolff, M. and Asche, H. (2009). "Exploring crime hotspots: Geospatial analysis and 3D mapping." In M. Schrenk, V. Popovich, D. Engelke, and P. Elisei (eds.), *Cities 3.0-smart, sustainable, and integrative* (pp. 147–156). Sitges, Spain: Competence Center of Urban and Regional Planning, Figure 3. With kind permission from Springer Science and Business Media. 100

5.4 Risk terrain and shooting overlay. *Original source*: Caplan, J.M., Kennedy, L.W., and Miller, J. (2011). "Risk terrain modeling: Brokering criminological theory and GIS methods for crime forecasting." *Justice Quarterly*, 28(2), 360–381. Reprinted with permission of Taylor & Francis Ltd. 106

5.5 Prospective hot spot map using 50-meter grid squares. *Original source*: Bowers, K.J., Johnson, S.D., and Pease, K. (2004). "Prospective hot-spotting the future of crime mapping?" *British Journal of Criminology*, 44(5), 641–658. By permission of Oxford University Press. 107

5.6 Forecasting strategy comparison. Average daily percentage of crimes predicted plotted against percentage of cells flagged for 2005 burglary using 200-meter by 200-meter cells. Error bars correspond to the standard error. Prospective hotspot cutoff parameters are 400 meters and 8 weeks (left) and optimal parameters (right) are 200 meters and 39 weeks. *Original source*: Mohler, G.O., Short, M.B., Brantingham, P.J., Schoenberg, F.P., and Tita, G.E. (2011). "Self-exciting point process modeling of crime." *Journal of the American Statistical Association*, 106(493), 100–108. Reprinted with permission of Taylor & Francis Ltd. 108

6.1 Campbell review of hot spots policing program main effects. *Original source*: Braga, A.A., Papachristos, A.V., and Hureau, D.M. (2012). "Hot spots policing effects on crime." *Campbell Systematic Reviews*, 8(8).   122

6.2 Campbell review of hot spots policing program displacement and diffusion effects. *Original source*: Braga, A.A., Papachristos, A.V., and Hureau, D.M. (2012). "Hot spots policing effects on crime." *Campbell Systematic Reviews*, 8(8).   123

6.3 Continuum of police strategies to control crime hot spots. *Original source*: Braga, A.A., and Weisburd, D. (2006). "Problem-oriented policing: The disconnect between principles and practice." In D. Weisburd and A.A. Braga (eds.), *Police innovation: Contrasting perspectives* (pp. 133–154). New York: Cambridge University Press.   124

6.4 General theory of place management. *Original source*: Madensen, T.D. (2007). *Bar management and crime: Toward a dynamic theory of place management and crime hot spots*. PhD dissertation. Cincinnati, OH: University of Cincinnati.   129

Tables

2.1 Distribution of All Dispatched Calls for Police Service in Minneapolis, MN, by Frequency at Each　*page* 19
2.2 The Distribution of Total Demand for Police Services among Street Addresses Experiencing a Given Annual Rate of Demand in Boston, MA, for the Period 1977 to 1982　19
2.3 Summary of Crime Incident Data in New York City, 2009–2010　21
2.4 Location Quotients for the Impact of a Facility on the Surrounding Area　40
6.1 Effectiveness of Opportunity-Based Interventions at Places　115

Contributors

David Weisburd is a distinguished professor at George Mason University and Director of the Center for Evidence-Based Crime Policy. He also holds a joint appointment as the Walter E. Meyer Professor of Law and Criminal Justice at the Hebrew University Faculty of Law in Jerusalem. Professor Weisburd is the recipient of many prestigious honors and awards including the Stockholm Prize in Criminology 2010, the American Society of Criminology's Sutherland Award in 2014, and the 2015 Israel Prize.

John E. Eck is Professor of Criminal Justice at the University of Cincinnati. He has conducted research on policing, crime places, and crime prevention since 1977. He is a former research director for the Police Executive Research Forum. There, he studied investigative operations, police anti-drug strategies, and helped field test and develop a problem-oriented approach to policing. Eck's Ph.D. dissertation (University of Maryland, 1994) developed the idea of "place management." He joined the faculty of the School of Criminal Justice at the University of Cincinnati in 1998.

Anthony A. Braga is the Don M. Gottfredson Professor of Evidence-Based Criminology at Rutgers University and a senior research fellow in the Program in Criminal Justice Policy and Management at Harvard University. He is an elected fellow and Past President of the Academy of Experimental Criminology (AEC). In 2014, he was the recipient of the AEC's Joan McCord Award recognizing his contributions to experimental criminology.

Cody Telep is an assistant professor in the School of Criminology and Criminal Justice at Arizona State University. He received his Ph.D. from the Department of Criminology, Law, and Society at George Mason University, where he worked at the Center for Evidence-Based Crime Policy. His research interests include evaluating policing innovations, police legitimacy, evidence-based policy, and experimental criminology. He is the Secretary-Treasurer for the American Society of Criminology's Division of Policing.

Breanne Cave is a senior research associate at the Police Foundation. She received her Ph.D. from the Department of Criminology, Law, and Society at George Mason University in 2016. Her research interests focus on policing, crime and place, research translation, and security issues. Her research has been published in the *Journal of Experimental Criminology, Police Practice and Research,* and *Policing: An International Journal of Police Strategies and Management.*

Kate Bowers is a professor of Security and Crime Science at the University College London Department of Security and Crime Science. She has published over eighty papers and book chapters. She serves on a number of journal editorial boards and has a number of external appointments such as Acting Independent Expert for the European Commission and Expert Reviewer for the US Office of the Assistant Attorney General. Her work has been funded by the Home Office, the US Department of Justice, UK police forces, the Department for Education and Skills, and UK research councils EPSRC, ESRC, and AHRC.

Gerben Bruinsma was, from 1999 till August 2014, Director of the Netherlands Institute for the Study of Crime and Law Enforcement (NSCR) in Amsterdam, a national research institute of the National Organization for Scientific Research (NWO), and is currently Senior Researcher of that institute. He is also Professor of Environmental Criminology at VU University of Amsterdam (from 2009). He is Past President of the European Society of Criminology. He has published in *Criminology, Crime & Delinquency, Journal of Research in Crime and Delinquency, British Journal of Criminology, Policing,* and *European Journal of Criminology.* With David Weisburd, he edited *The Encyclopedia of Criminology and Criminal Justice.*

Charlotte Gill is an assistant professor at George Mason University and holds degrees in Criminology and Law from the Universities of Pennsylvania and Cambridge. Her primary research interests are community-based crime prevention and place-based approaches, particularly with juveniles and youth; community policing; program evaluation, including randomized controlled trials; and research synthesis. In 2012 she received the Academy of Experimental Criminology's Young Experimental Scholar award. Dr. Gill's current research involves pilot studies of social and community building interventions at hot spots. She is also the coeditor of the Campbell Collaboration Crime and Justice Group.

Elizabeth Groff is an associate professor in the Department of Criminal Justice Temple University, Philadelphia. Her research interests include place-based criminology; modeling geographical influences on human activity; the role of technology in police organizations; and the development of innovative methodologies using geographic information systems, agent-based simulation models, and randomized experiments. She is a fellow of the Academy of Experimental Criminology and a former director of the National Institute of Justice's Crime Mapping Research Center.

Julie Hibdon is an assistant professor in the Department of Criminology and Criminal Justice at Southern Illinois University Carbondale. She received her Ph.D. in Criminology, Law, and Society from George Mason University in 2011. Her research interests include crime and place, environmental criminology, cognitions of crime places, fear of crime, and policing.

Joshua C. Hinkle is an assistant professor in the Department of Criminal Justice and Criminology at Georgia State University. He received his doctoral degree in Criminology and Criminal Justice from the University of Maryland in the summer of 2009 after completing his master's degree in the department in May 2005. His research interests include evidence-based policing, the disorder–crime nexus, fear of crime, and experimental methods. His research has been funded by the National Institute of Justice and the National Science Foundation. His work appears in journals such as *Criminology*, *Criminology & Public Policy*, and the *Journal of Experimental Criminology*.

Shane D. Johnson, a professor at the University College London Department of Security and Crime Science, has worked within the fields of criminology and forensic psychology for over fifteen years. He has particular interests in exploring how methods from other disciplines (e.g. complexity science) can inform understanding of crime and security issues, and the extent to which theories developed to explain everyday crimes can explain more extreme events such as riots, maritime piracy, and insurgency. He has published over 100 peer-reviewed papers and book chapters and his work has been covered in *The Economist* and *New Scientist*, and by the UK media.

Brian Lawton is an assistant professor in the Department of Criminal Justice at John Jay College. His research interests include spatial patterns of crime, police use of force, and the intersection of public health and crime. His research has been published in such journals as the *Journal of Quantitative Criminology*, *Journal of Research in Crime and Delinquency*, and *Police Quarterly*.

Cynthia Lum is Director of the Center for Evidence-Based Crime Policy (CEBCP) and Associate Professor in the Department of Criminology, Law, and Society at George Mason University. She researches primarily in the area of evidence-based policing and security. Her works in this area have included evaluations of policing interventions and police technology, understanding the translation and receptivity of research in policing, examining place-based determinants of street-level police decision-making, and assessing security efforts of federal agencies. She is a former police officer and detective, and a Fulbright Specialist.

Jerry Ratcliffe is a professor in the Department of Criminal Justice, Temple University, Philadelphia, where he also directs the Center for Security and Crime Science. He is a former police officer with London's Metropolitan Police where he served for several years on patrol duties, in an intelligence and information unit, and as a member of the Diplomatic Protection Group. He has a B. Sc. with honors in Geography and GIS and a Ph.D. from the Faculty of Science at the University of Nottingham. He has published over sixty research articles and four books in the areas of crime science and intelligence-led policing.

George F. Rengert is Professor Emeritus of Criminal Justice at Temple University. A geographer by training, he is one of the early contributors to the modern field of spatial analysis in criminology. Dr. Rengert is the recipient of the Ronald V. Clarke Award for Excellence in Environmental Crime Analysis and is the author or editor of nine books and more than 100 scientific articles and papers dealing with such diverse topics as the location of illegal drug markets, spatial justice, and barriers to the spatial movement of criminals. His current research interests center on the application of Geographic information Systems to the analysis of urban crime patterns.

Travis Taniguchi is a research criminologist at RTI International. He received a BS in Criminology and Criminal Justice from Chaminade University of Honolulu, and an MA and Ph.D. in Criminal Justice from Temple University. Dr. Taniguchi's research interests include program and policy evaluation, technology evaluations, crime and place, street gang dynamics, and the spatial distribution of drug markets.

Sue-Ming Yang is an assistant professor in the Department of Criminology, Law, and Society at George Mason University. She received her Ph.D. from the Department of Criminology and Criminal Justice at the University of Maryland. Her research interests include place-based criminology, urban disorder, criminological theory testing, experimental research methods, and international terrorism. In her most recent study, she found strong associations between social and physical attributes of environments and individual perception of disorder, using a laboratory experiment. Her recent works appear in *Journal of Research in Crime and Delinquency, Prevention Science, Journal of Experimental Criminology,* and *Criminology and Public Policy.*

Preface

We have titled this book *Place Matters: Criminology for the Twenty-First Century*. Our choice of this title was not coincidental. It reflects a view of all of the authors regarding what should be important in criminology and crime prevention. As we note in Chapter 1, the approach we offer is not a dominant one in traditional criminology. Indeed, it represents in many ways a radical departure from the mainstream of criminological thinking. But our purpose in developing this work was not to divorce ourselves from the mainstream of criminology, but rather to argue that our interests should become a central part of criminological interests. We make that case throughout the book in terms of what the empirical evidence says about basic and applied research in this area.

In his presidential address to the American Society of Criminology in 2003, John Laub (2004) observed that criminology as a discipline could be viewed as having a developmental life course. Laub and Sampson (2003) offered a radical critique of traditional criminological understandings of criminal careers when they argued that the life courses of criminals were affected not just in the early formative stages of their lives, but also by the experiences they would have as adults. The life-course perspective recognized that people would change many times in their lives, and an immutable idea of inevitable criminal behavior based on experiences in youth was just wrong. Laub (2004) argued that, much like the offenders that he and Robert Sampson studied in identifying life-course criminology (Laub and Sampson 2003), criminology also could be seen as having a life course that had important turning points that fundamentally influenced the directions that the field would take.

In contrast to continuity in the intellectual trajectory of the discipline, a turning point refers to a radical new way of viewing criminology, which allows us to stake out new territory and to make significant new discoveries about crime and criminality. A turning point in a discipline can be seen as a recognition that new ideas develop that are pursued, and often lead to important insights. The successful development of criminology is dependent on being open to new ways of understanding crime. Laub (2004) identifies a number of turning points that have enriched criminological understandings.

Our argument in this book is that it is time for criminology to take another turn in direction. The change is embedded not in a particular theory, but in the units of analysis that criminologists focus upon. The first major turning point that Laub (2004) identified in American criminology was also concerned with units of analysis. The fundamental changes in our understanding of the crime problem that came from the Chicago School of Sociology were linked strongly to its insights about the importance of communities in understanding crime (e.g., see Shaw and McKay 1942). This geographic criminology, as we describe in Chapter 1, had an important influence on criminology. But it is very different from the "places" that we focus upon in this book. Our interest is in "microgeographic" units, specific places where crime is concentrated. We spend a good deal of time in the chapters of our book defining these units and why they are so important to understanding and controlling crime. We think that a turning point in criminology that would focus in on such places is important for criminology in the twenty-first century.

As we note later, study of crime at microgeographic units of analysis began to interest criminologists in the late 1980s (Evans and Herbert 1989; Felson 1987; Pierce et al. 1988; Sherman et al. 1989; Weisburd and Green 1994; Weisburd et al. 1992). The roots of such approaches can be found in the efforts of scholars to identify the relationship between specific aspects of urban design (Jeffery 1971) or urban architecture (Newman 1972) and crime, but broadened to take into account a much larger set of characteristics of physical space and criminal opportunity (e.g., Brantingham and Brantingham 1975; 1977; 1981; Duffala 1976; Hunter 1988; LeBeau 1987; Mayhew et al. 1976; Rengert 1980; 1981; Stoks 1981). These studies drew important distinctions between the site in question and the larger geographical area (such as the neighborhood, community, police beat, or city) that surrounds it. In a 1989 article in *Criminology*, Lawrence Sherman, Patrick Gartin, and Michael Buerger (1989) coined the term "criminology of place" to describe this new area of study. The criminology of place (see also Weisburd et al. 2012) or "crime and place" (see Eck and Weisburd 1995) pushes us to examine very small geographic areas within cities, often as small as addresses or street segments (both sides of a street from intersection to intersection), for their contribution to the crime problem. It pushes us to examine and understand why crime occurs at specific places, rather than focusing our interests on the more traditional criminological concern of why specific types of people commit crime.

In our book we will argue that the study of crime at place offers important new insights about the crime problem and what we can do about it. Indeed, our thesis will be that the potential to understand and control crime that this approach offers represents an important opportunity for criminology and crime prevention. Put simply, a turning point is warranted because of the strong evidence we already have at this early stage of research in this area. But another reason for a turning point in the developmental career of criminology is drawn from the present state of criminological knowledge. Continuing with business as usual will likely not add dramatically to our generation of important insights for theory or policy. This point was made strongly by Frank Cullen in his 2010 Sutherland Address to the American Society of Criminology. He argued there:

> For over a half century, criminology has been dominated by a paradigm – adolescence-limited criminology (ALC) – that has privileged the use of self-report surveys of adolescents to test sociological theories of criminal behavior and has embraced the view that "nothing works" to control crime. Although ALC has created knowledge, opposed injustice, and advanced scholars' careers, it has outlived its utility. The time has come for criminologists to choose a different future. Cullen 2011, 287

Cullen (2011) suggested areas that provided promise for advancing criminology and crime prevention. These included life-course criminology (e.g., see Laub and Sampson 2003), biological social theory (Moffitt 1993), criminal decision making (e.g., see Nagin and Pogarsky 2001), and the study of crime events (e.g., see Clarke 1980). The criminology of place suggests a radical departure from current interests, and that is why we argue for a turning point in the life course of criminology. Its concern is with the units of analysis of criminological study rather than with the measurement of crime or the theory used to understand crime. In this sense, each of the innovations that Cullen describes can be examined or applied in the context of micro-crime places. In this context, the criminology of place offers a promising new direction for criminology, which has tremendous possibilities for advancing criminology as a basic and policy science.

In Chapter 1 we provide evidence suggesting that the criminology of place has received little focus in criminology. This fact presents a particular opportunity for young scholars looking to advance criminology and their careers. In contrast to the traditional concerns that Cullen (2011) critiques, which have been the focus of thousands of papers and studies, crime and place has occupied a marginal location in empirical research in criminology. There is much room to make new discoveries and to examine new problems. This is a field about which we know little and the landscape of knowledge is wide open to young scholars for exploration.

And these questions are not only about understanding crime, they are also about doing something about crime. One of Cullen's main objections to continuity in the life course of criminology is that it has little promise for helping us to do something about crime problems. He argues that "[w]e have contributed valuable work to knowledge destruction – showing what does not work – but have not done much to show what does work through knowledge construction" (Cullen 2011, 318). In contrast, the criminology of place from the start has focused on what we can do about the crime problem. In Chapter 6 we provide strong evidence of effectiveness for place-based interventions. This evidence has been developed when the focus of criminologists and crime prevention experts has ordinarily been on other concerns. If the turning point we are suggesting were to develop, it would seem that a host of new and effective interventions could be developed.

It is time for another turning point in the life course of criminology. That is the underlying lesson of our work, which summarizes what is known about the study of crime at place. It is time for criminologists to focus their attention on place. This will enrich criminology and crime prevention. Place matters! And indeed it should be a key focus of criminology in the twenty-first century.

It is important in introducing the book, that I note something about the processes that led to its development. This book evolved out of the activities of the Crime and Place Working Group (CPWG), which is housed in the Center for Evidence-Based Crime Policy (CEBCP) at George Mason University. Cynthia Lum and I formed the Working Group when the CEBCP was founded in 2008 to advance study of crime at microunits of geography. We thought at the time that there was no organized locus for scholars in this area, and that the conduct of this work and its advancement would benefit much if we could bring key scholars together on a regular basis. So began the group and its meetings, which have led not only to greater interaction among scholars working in this area but also the production of specific products and activities.

The initial activities of the group were supported by a start-up fund granted to me by the former Dean of Humanities and Social Sciences at George Mason, Professor Jack Censer. Initially the CPWG was seen as a vehicle for creating a sense of shared identity among a diverse group of scholars who were writing about crime at place. The initial meetings at GMU helped to reinforce the sense among participants that there was a community of crime and place scholars, in part because the group included a range of scholars at different points in their careers, from graduate students to senior scholars.

From the first meeting it was decided that the CPWG would focus on activities that helped raise the visibility of crime and place studies among criminologists, and that offered opportunities for younger scholars to do work in this area. The CPWG members also agreed that bringing the criminology of place into the mainstream of criminology was a key goal of the group's activities. With that in mind the group sponsored (and continues to sponsor) sessions at the American Society of Criminology's annual meetings and developed special issues in elite criminology journals, including the *Journal of Research in Crime and Delinquency* and the *Journal of Quantitative Criminology*. These special issues not only increased the visibility of crime and place research, but they also provided opportunities for young crime and place scholars to publish in high-prestige journals in the field.

Preface

The idea for a book that summarized knowledge about crime at microunits of geography developed out of discussions of the importance of having a text that would place the study of crime at place in the context of broader criminological questions. Our model for developing the work was the National Academy of Sciences (NAS)/National Research Council (NRC) reviews of evidence that were developed by the NRC Committee on Law and Justice. As a member of the committee, I suggested that NAS do a summary of knowledge in this area, but there was not sufficient interest to develop a panel. That led me to look to the CPWG to carry out a similar effort. The CPWG acted as the panel, and indeed it represented a broad array of interests and experience in this area, as well as including many of the most important crime and place scholars. We set out to review the field, dividing up the work on individual chapters among members of the CPWG. Importantly, the overall outline of the book was developed in meetings of the group.

We began by outlining what needed to be included, and then divided up into small working groups that would draft the initial chapters. We then reviewed those drafts in a meeting at GMU, and the small working groups revised the drafts. We had four meetings overall, including one in San Diego, California, sponsored in part through efforts by Jim Bueermann (now President of the Police Foundation), who was very supportive of our work and gave us important advice at the outset. We had a final meeting to discuss the revised drafts, and at that point John Eck, Anthony Braga, and I worked on drafting introductory and concluding chapters, as well as redrafting chapters so the manuscript would have a single overall voice. We decided not to develop the volume as an edited book, because all of the CPWG members who participated in writing (a few were not able to devote time to this project) participated in the overall organization and review of the manuscript. We wanted this to be a book about crime at place, not a collection of essays on the topic.

With that in mind, all of the writers are listed as authors on the volume. Weisburd, Eck, and Braga are listed first because of their job as editors. Cody Telep also played a key role in consolidating the manuscript, and is listed next. Finally, Breanne Cave, who was a graduate student when we were completing the manuscript, played a key role in developing the final draft and creating consistency across the chapters. Breanne is listed for this reason as the next author. The rest of the CPWG writers follow in the listing in alphabetical order. At the outset of each chapter (except the introduction and conclusions) a footnote lists the CPWG members who led writing of that chapter. I want to thank at the outset Matt Nelson and Alese Wooditch, who helped us with editing of the chapters when the drafts were completed by authors. Their careful work helped a good deal in finishing the work.

When we began this effort it was not clear that we could be successful. But the result follows closely what we set out to do at the outset. This volume provides the most comprehensive synthesis of knowledge about crime at place that is presently available. It is a collective effort in the best sense in that a work this comprehensive could not have been put together by just a few authors. The work represents the broad array of skills, knowledge, and experience of the CPWG. We think that when you are finished reading this work you will agree that a turning point in the developmental career of criminology is warranted.

David Weisburd
Fairfax and Jerusalem, 2015

1

Crime Places within Criminological Thought

A new perspective in criminology has emerged over the last three decades, a perspective with considerable potential to add to our understanding and control of crime. In the same way the invention of the microscope opened up a biological world scientists had not previously seen, this new perspective opens the world of small geographic features we had overlooked. Research has demonstrated that actions at these microplaces have strong connections to crime. Just as the microscope paved the way to new treatments and advances in public health, this new perspective in criminology is yielding improved ways of reducing crime. This new perspective shifts our attention from large geographic units, such as neighborhoods, to small units, such as street segments and addresses. This shift in the "units of analysis" transforms our understanding of the crime problem and what we can do about it.

There are two aspects to this shift in units. The first shifts our attention from large geographic units to small ones. This we have just mentioned. The second shifts our attention from people to events, from those who commit crimes to the crimes themselves. Criminology has been primarily focused on people (Brantingham and Brantingham 1990; Weisburd 2002). Frank Cullen (2011) noted in his Sutherland Address to the American Society of Criminology in 2010 that the focus of criminology has been even more specific. He argued that criminology was dominated by a paradigm, which he termed "adolescence-limited criminology," that had focused primarily on adolescents.

To what extent have person-based studies dominated criminology? Weisburd (2015a) examined units of analysis in all empirical articles published in *Criminology* between 1990 and 2014. *Criminology* is the highest-impact journal in the field and the main scientific publication of the largest criminological society in the world, the American Society of Criminology. He identified 719 research articles. Of the 719 articles, two-thirds focused on people as units of analysis. The next main units of study were situations (15 percent) and macrogeographic areas such as cities and states (11 percent). Eck and Eck (2012) examined the 148 research papers published in *Criminology and Public Policy* from its first issue in 2001 until the end of 2010, and the 230 articles published in *Criminal Justice Policy Review* during the same time period. Fifty to 60 percent of the articles described policies toward offenders (providing assistance or coercion), and 30–40 percent dealt with an assortment of topics describing policy administration, technology, descriptions of criminal behavior, or criminological perspectives. Less than 10 percent dealt with preventing crime events by blocking crime opportunities. Catching criminals, convicting them, sometimes imprisoning them, and sometimes rehabilitating them naturally leads us to the individual as the primary focus of criminal justice interventions (Weisburd 2008).

Understanding why people commit crime is important, and so is understanding the processing of individuals through the criminal justice system. However, the dominance of the person-unit perspective has left the impression that the study of criminality has always been the main focus of criminology. It obscures the fact that from the first studies of crime, researchers have gained insights into crime and its prevention by examining the distribution of events over geographic areas. In the early development of criminology, geographic units of analysis were particularly critical. European scholars such as Guerry (1833) and Quetelet (1831) looked to see how crime varied across large administrative geographic units. These studies in the first half of the nineteenth century helped to encourage a positivist criminology focused on empirical data about crime (Beirne 1987). The founding generation of criminologists in the twentieth century also looked to large geographic areas to understand and do something about the crime problem. Led by Robert Park, William Thomas, Louis Wirth, Ernest Burgess, Clifford Shaw, and Henry McKay, members of the Chicago School of Sociology saw communities as central to our understanding of crime (e.g., see Burgess 1925; Shaw 1929; Shaw and McKay 1942).

This community perspective on crime had strong impacts on theories about the etiology of crime (Reiss 1986; Sampson and Wilson 1995). In particular the social disorganization perspective is directly drawn from community studies of crime in Chicago (Bursik 1988; Sampson 2008; Sampson and Groves 1989; Sampson et al. 1997). Weisburd (2015a) found that only 7 percent of the articles in *Criminology* focused on communities or neighborhoods. Nonetheless, the impact of this perspective on crime prevention has been substantial. Many crime prevention programs are geared toward communities (Corsaro and McGarrell 2009; Corsaro et al. 2013; Dalton 2002; Tita et al. 2006). The broken windows theory (Kelling and Coles 1996; Wilson and Kelling 1982), for example, looks to developmental processes in communities as a key factor in understanding and controlling crime. And the importance of community in crime control can be seen in the large impact that community policing has had on policing in the United States (Hickman and Reaves 2003; Maguire and Mastrofski 2000).

Although people and large areas have been the most commonly examined units of analysis for criminological researchers, there is another perspective with possibly greater potential, a unit of analysis that has been virtually ignored until recent years. This unit is focused on microgeographies, or what we term "place." In studies to date it has been defined in different ways. As we detail later, some scholars define place simply as individual facilities, such as schools or community centers (Clarke and Eck 2007; Eck et al. 2007; Kautt and Roncek 2007), others look to street addresses (Pierce et al. 1988; Sherman et al. 1989), others to street segments (Andresen and Malleson 2011; Weisburd et al. 2004; Weisburd et al. 2006; Weisburd et al. 2012), and still others to clusters of street segments with similar crime problems (Weisburd and Mazerolle 2000; Weisburd et al. 2006). What these perspectives have in common is their recognition of the importance of microgeographic units for our understanding of the crime problem and our efforts to control crime. The "criminology of place" (Sherman et al. 1989; Weisburd et al. 2012) or study of "crime and place" (Eck and Weisburd 1995) suggests a new unit of analysis for criminology.

Beginning with the Minneapolis Hot Spots Patrol Experiment (Sherman and Weisburd 1995) a series of studies has shown that crime prevention focused on microgeographic units of analysis can have strong crime prevention gains. Indeed, the National Academy of Sciences concluded in a report on police practices and policies in 2004 that "studies that focused police resources on crime hot spots provided the strongest collective evidence of police effectiveness that is now available" (National Research Council 2004, 250). A Campbell systematic review by Braga et al. (2014) comes to a similar conclusion. And situational crime prevention studies focused on microgeographic units show similar promise (Eck and Guerette 2012).

The emergence of a large and sound body of empirical evidence about crime places contrasts with the fact that this body of knowledge has been largely overlooked by criminologists. In the review of articles in *Criminology* by Weisburd (2015a) we noted earlier, only 4 percent were focused on microgeographic units of analysis. There is some suggestion of a developing interest in this area of work. Figure 1.1 shows the percentage of articles examining microgeographic units in *Criminology* in five-year intervals. What is clear is that there is a growing trend of interest. Indeed, the percentage of articles in the journal focused on microgeographic units more than doubled comparing the first to last periods. Nonetheless, the absolute number of studies is still very small. Eck and Eck (2012) found an even more startling lack of interest in places in their review. Not a single study published in the two journals they examined focused on microgeographic units. This is particularly surprising, given the strong research evidence for place-based prevention described in Chapter 6. Much of this evidence was developed during the period that Eck and Eck reviewed.

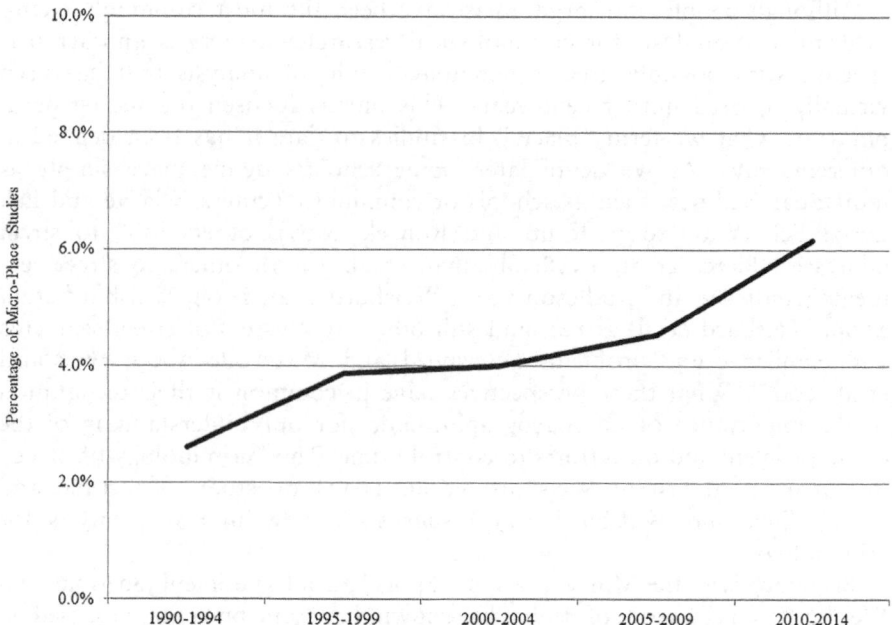

FIGURE 1.1. Changes in rates of microplace studies published in *Criminology* over time. Original source: Weisburd, D. (2015). "The law of crime concentration and the criminology of place." *Criminology*, 53(2), 133–157. Courtesy of Wiley.

Similarly, courses that teach criminological theory rarely use books that discuss microgeographic units of analysis. When examining the textbooks used in courses that teach criminological theory to undergraduates at the top ten criminology programs, we found that only six of the twenty-three different textbooks discuss issues related to microgeographic units of analysis, such as hot spots policing or diffusion of crime control benefits.[1]

Recognizing this dearth of attention to the criminology of place, we thought it was time to compile what is known about this important new area of study, and to describe fruitful directions for further research and improved practice. In this chapter we want to introduce our work by first addressing some key definitional problems. We begin by discussing the relevance of crime and place to criminology. Does the relative paucity of work in the main journals in the field mean that this area of work should not be seen as a key concern of criminologists? We then turn to the unit of analysis problem. Do the multiple microgeographic units that studies in this area focus on mean that we really do not have a systematic focus of study? Do such problems plague criminology focused on communities and people as well? We then examine what is new in the study of the criminology of place, and how it offers opportunities to gain new insights. In concluding we describe the chapters that follow.

IS THE STUDY OF CRIME AND PLACE "CRIMINOLOGICAL"?

We have already noted that crime and place studies have been peripheral in criminology, at least following the reviews that have been carried out. Is that because crime and place studies are not really within the domain of criminology?

Merriam-Webster's dictionary (2015) defines criminology as the "study of crime, criminals, and the punishment of criminals." Clearly the study of crime places falls within this definition of criminology. It relates to the study of crime (e.g., Andresen and Malleson 2011; Block and Block 1995; Sherman 1995; Sherman et al. 1989; Weisburd et al. 2004), how places interact with crime (Brantingham and Brantingham 1993b; 1995; Weisburd et al. 2004), and the reaction of society to crime – perhaps not simply in the punishment of criminals at places, but certainly in the ways in which places can be used as a focus for controlling crime (Braga and Weisburd 2010; 2012; Mastrofski et al. 2010; Weisburd 2008).

The most influential criminologist of the last century, Edwin Sutherland, defined criminology in 1924 as "the body of knowledge regarding crime as a social phenomenon that includes within its scope the process of making laws, of breaking laws, and of reacting toward the breaking of laws" (1). Again the making of laws, the breaking of laws, and the reaction of society to crime are part of the study of crime and place. Some place-based interventions are focused on how law can be used to prevent or control crime (Mazerolle and Roehl 1998; Mazerolle et al. 2000; Weisburd 2008), others on where laws are broken (Andresen and Malleson 2011; Sherman et al. 1989; Weisburd et al. 2004; 2012), and still others, as we already noted, on societal responses to crime, for example through hot spots policing (Braga and Bond 2008; Braga et al. 1999; Sherman and Weisburd 1995; Weisburd 2008; Weisburd et al. 2006).

Part of the definitional problem of crime and place studies comes from the fact that criminology has often focused on particular disciplinary perspectives. For example, some criminologists think of criminology as simply a specialty of sociology (Akers 1992). We do not agree, since economists, psychologists, lawyers, political scientists, and geographers, for example, have all contributed to our understanding of the crime problem and how we can respond to it (Becker 1968; Bushway and Reuter 2008; Feeley and Simon 1992; Fyfe 1991). Indeed, advances in criminological theory are often the result of interdisciplinary conflict or collaboration.

It is true, however, that most criminologists see criminology as centrally focused on why people commit crime, and this is reflected in the reviews of empirical studies described earlier. It is interesting to note in this regard that Edwin Sutherland (1947, 5), in early versions of his well-known textbook in criminology, discussed at the outset the importance of crime places: "a thief may steal from a fruit stand when the owner is not in sight but refrain when the owner is in sight; a burglar may attack a bank which is poorly protected but refrain from attacking a bank protected by watchmen and burglar alarms." But in Sutherland's view, as that of other criminologists at the time, the "provision of an opportunity for a criminal act" provided by places should not be an important concern for criminologists. Crime opportunities provided by places were assumed to be so numerous as to make focus on places of little utility. There were too many potential crime sites to guard them all, all of the time. So Sutherland crafted a theory of differential association that would allow us, at least in theory, to prevent crime by getting at the source of criminal acts, criminal motivation.

Most theories of crime have focused on this problem. Criminology in most places became the study of why people commit crime. This focus on motivation in turn was to dominate criminology at least until Cohen and Felson published their groundbreaking article on routine activities and crime in 1979. That article was perhaps the first to argue that the offender was only one part of the crime equation. It laid out a crime equation we will discuss in more detail in later chapters, in which crime could be affected by influencing the routine activities of victims, guardians, and offenders in their geographic context without influencing the motivations of offenders.

Another reason that crime and place studies failed to become a central feature of our study of crime develops from the complexity of identifying crime at microgeographic units of analysis. A natural setting for the development of interest in microgeographic units of analysis was the Chicago School of sociologists. Their interest in the social ecology of communities naturally led to an examination of crime at microunits of geography. Shaw and Myers (1929) were to come closest to a study of the criminology of place in their examination of juvenile delinquency for the Illinois Crime Survey. They mapped by hand the home addresses of over 9,000 delinquents. In a figure that looks as if it had been generated through modern computer applications (Figure 1.2), they showed that delinquents are clustered in areas marked by "physical deterioration, poverty and social disorganization" (Shaw and Myers 1929, 652). After completing this exercise Shaw (1929, 5) argued that the "study of such a problem as juvenile delinquency necessarily begins with a study of its geographical location."

We think that one simple explanation for the failure of others to take up Shaw and Myers' call was that mapping crime in the 1920s at the level of addresses was a monumental task. Mapping addresses of juveniles was arduous; mapping crime in a major city would have been perhaps an impossible exercise. And indeed data on the exact location of crime were not easily available to researchers at the time. The police in this regard did not keep accurate and easily analyzed records on where crime occurred. Such information was not to be available until the late 1960s in part as a response to the emergence of management information systems linked to emergency police responses. Even by the late 1980s data was poorly geocoded, often having

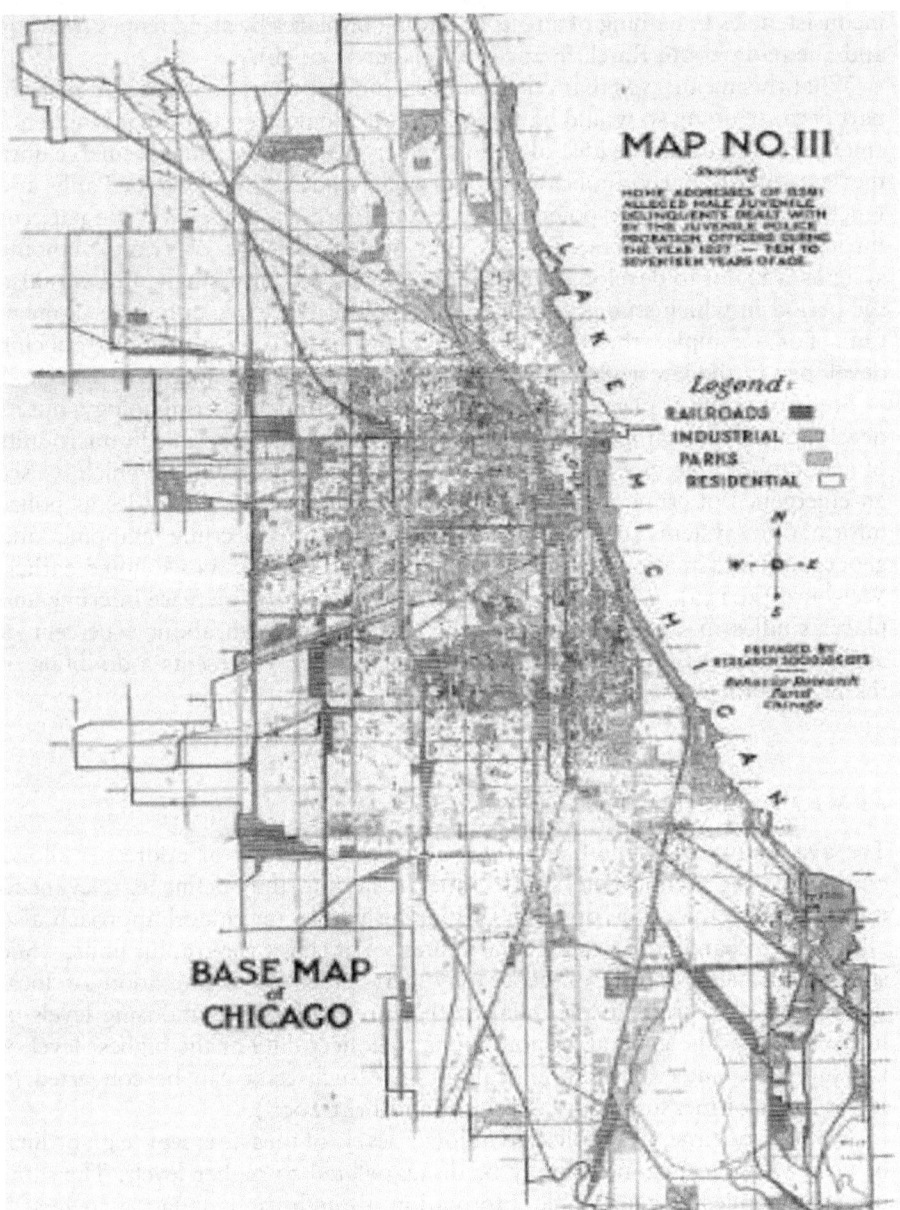

FIGURE 1.2. Map of the home addresses of juvenile offenders.
Original source: Shaw, C.R., Zorbaugh, F.M., McKay, H.D., and Cottrell, L.S. (1929). Delinquency areas. A study of the geographical distribution of school truants, juvenile delinquents, and adult offenders in Chicago. Chicago, IL: University of Chicago Press. Copyright 1929 by the University of Chicago.

inconsistencies in naming of streets or coding of places by slang names (Harada and Shemada 2006; Ratcliffe 2004a; Weisburd 2015b).

What this meant was that criminologists did not focus on crime and place in part because doing so would have required information systems that would not emerge for decades. The idea of automated crime mapping did not emerge until the late 1960s. Early applications (Carnaghi and McEwen 1970; Pauly and Finch 1967) showed the potential for visual representations of crime patterns through computer-generated maps, but wide scale use of crime mapping systems was not to develop until the late 1980s. Not surprisingly, this was also the period in which studies of the criminology of place began to gain momentum. For example, the first large-scale evaluation of hot spots policing developed in the late 1980s in Minneapolis (Sherman and Weisburd 1995).

Study of crime at place clearly falls within the domain of criminology, but its development was hampered by the difficulty of examining crime at microunits of geography. One question to ask in this regard is the extent to which we see an emergence of crime and place studies over the last three decades as police information systems became more sophisticated and crime mapping and geographic information systems became more accessible. As we noted earlier, Weisburd (2015a) reports that there has been a gradual increase in crime and places studies in *Criminology* since the early 1980s with about 6 percent of articles in 2010–2014 focused on these units, which represents a doubling of the proportion in 1990–1994.

AT WHAT SPECIFIC UNIT OF GEOGRAPHY?

The availability of crime data at X and Y coordinates[2] or addresses allows crime and place scholars to study crime at the unit they define as relevant to understanding the crime problem. Beginning with a microlevel approach also allows the researcher to examine the influences of larger geographic units, while starting at higher levels of geography may preclude examination of local variability. This problem is similar to that presented when choosing levels of measurement. The general admonition is to collect data at the highest level of measurement (interval or ratio scales), since such data can be converted to lower levels of measurement (Weisburd and Britt 2007).

At the same time, data collected at lower levels of measurement (e.g., ordinal or nominal scales) cannot simply be disaggregated to higher levels. The same principle applies to geographic information, though the language is reversed. Collecting data at the lowest geographic level, or smallest units of analysis, allows aggregation up to higher levels, but data collection at higher units may not allow conversion to more micro units of analysis. For this reason, Brantingham et al. (2009; see also Brantingham et al. 1976) argue that environmental criminology must begin with small spatial units and build larger units that reflect the reality of crime patterns.

While crime data are now readily available at the most microgeographic levels, it is still the case that a good deal of social data are only available at larger units, such as those examined by the U.S. Census. This means that criminologists often aggregate up when they try to draw conclusions about the causes of crime (e.g., Hipp 2007; Morenoff et al. 2001; Sampson et al. 1997), though the growing availability of data at all levels has begun to change this limitation of place-based studies (Groff et al. 2009; Sherman et al. 1989; Weisburd and Mazerolle 2000; Weisburd et al. 2012). So-called "big data" is changing what criminologists can learn at microgeographic levels on a daily basis (Crampton et al. 2013; Hardey 2007).

But even if other data become available at the X, Y coordinate level, as Michael Maltz (2009) notes, there just may not be enough data at a very micro level from which to draw inferences. Especially if one is interested in specific types of crime, they may be too rare in any single microplace unit to allow the identification of patterns or trends. Accordingly, there may be realities of the data that limit our ability to analyze crime at the most microgeographic levels.

But this belies the point of whether there is a specific unit of analysis that defines this area of study. Study of crime at the individual level seems to begin with a clearly defined unit of analysis – individuals. Is there a similar unit for study of crime at place? The simple answer to this question is that there is. The X and Y coordinates for a place represent a unique identifier for crime and place studies. This is the unique and smallest unit available for study. And a number of studies have used the address or X and Y coordinates for studying crime (e.g., see Pierce et al. 1988; Sherman et al. 1989; Thompson and Fisher 1996). In turn, many place-based criminologists have defined "facilities" as the key factor in understanding crime at place (Clarke and Eck 2007; Eck et al. 2007; Madensen and Eck 2008). In this perspective, we are interested in specific places such as schools, bars, community centers, or malls as places that attract or generate crime (Bowers 2014; Franquez et al. 2013; Groff 2011; Zhu et al. 2004).

There are both practical and theoretical reasons for selecting addresses. Practically, many police agencies in the United States give the address where the crime occurred, thus making the data easily available. And modern geographic information systems (GIS) used by many police can identify and correct invalid addresses, thus making these data relatively clean. Theoretically, addresses are directly connected to property parcels and property owners. The theory of place management (Madensen and Eck 2013), which we describe in Chapter 3, describes how the actions of owners influence crime.

But other scholars who study crime at place have examined aggregated units. Crime may be linked across addresses or streets that are located near to each other. For example, a drug market may operate across a series of blocks (Weisburd and Green 1995b; Worden et al. 1994), and a large housing project and problems associated with it may include many addresses and traverse street segments in multiple directions (see Skogan and Annan 1994). Accordingly, the unit of analysis in crime and place studies may be assigned empirically based on the reality of the crime problem across places.

Does the fact that addresses or streets may be linked in crime challenge the basic idea of the criminology of place as a focus for criminological study? We think that the complexities of units of analysis in this area reflect the complexities of units of analysis more generally in criminology. In the 1980s, scholars began to challenge the traditional focus of criminology on individual offenders, noting that much crime was committed in cooffending groups, and the study of distinct individuals often missed key organizational and social components of the crime problem (Hindelang 1976; Reiss 1988; Reiss and Farrington 1991). While criminologists often study individuals as a unique unit of analysis, the reality of crime often involves aggregates of individuals who join together to commit crimes, from small groups of teenagers to major organized crime families.

In turn, in the study of communities and crime, the unit of analysis has varied not only in regard to the specific data available, but also the theoretical units that scholars have identified. There is no single accepted definition of the geographic boundaries of community (Bursik and Grasmick 1993a; Hipp and Boessen 2013). And indeed, community may be defined differently depending on the nature of the problem that scholars examine (Kwan 2012; Lynch and Addington 2007; Sampson et al. 1997; Sampson et al. 2002; Shaw and McKay 1942). While the ambiguity of community has led to criticism of the communities and crime perspective (e.g., Eck and Weisburd 1995; Groff et al. 2010), it often reflects the changing realities of communities in different settings (Grannis 1998; Guo and Bhat 2007).

Weisburd et al. (2012) have argued that community is also relevant for crime at place scholars, though at a much more microgeographic level than had previously been examined. They examine street segments, defined as both sides of the street between two intersections. They argue that scholars have long recognized the relevance of street blocks in organizing life in the city (Appleyard 1981; Brower 1980; Jacobs 1961; Taylor et al. 1984; Unger and Wandersman 1983). Following Taylor (1997; 1998), they note that street segments function as behavior settings (Barker 1968; Wicker 1987):

First, people who frequent a street segment get to know one another and become familiar with each other's routines. This awareness of the standing patterns of behavior of neighbors provides a basis from which action can be taken. For example, activity at the corner store is normal during business hours but abnormal after closing. Second, residents develop certain roles they play in the life of the street segment (e.g., the busybody, the organizer). Consistency of roles increases the stability of activities at places. On many streets, for example, there is at least one neighbor who will accept packages for other residents when they are not at home. Third, norms about acceptable behavior develop and are generally shared. Shared norms develop from interactions with other residents and observations of behaviors that take place on the block without being challenged. Fourth, blocks have standing patterns of behavior that are temporally specific. The mail carrier delivers at a certain time of day, the corner resident is always home by 5 PM, another neighbor always mows the lawn on Saturday..... Fifth, a street block has boundaries that contain its setting. It is bounded by the cross streets on each end. Interaction is focused inward toward the street. Sixth, street segments, like other behavior settings, are dynamic. Residents move out and new ones move in. Land use could shift as residences become stores at street level and remain residential on the upper floors. These types of changes to the social and physical environment of the street segment can alter the standing patterns of behavior. Weisburd et al. 2012, 23–24

The criminology of place, like study of individuals or communities, can be defined at different units of analysis, depending on the context of crime and the theoretical focus of researchers. At the same time, the focus remains on microgeographies. While scholars have not established a clear geographic maximum for crime and place studies it is generally accepted that geographies should not extend beyond clusters of a few streets that share common crime characteristics (e.g., see Oberwittler and Wikström 2009; Rengert and Lockwood 2009).

WHAT IS NEW IN THE STUDY OF CRIME AT PLACE?

In many ways the criminology of place as we define it is simply part of a larger area of study that might be termed "geographic criminology" (Weisburd et al. 2009). As we noted earlier, criminologists have been studying the geographic distribution of crime at least since the early 1800s. The first geographical map of crime was published by André-Michel Guerry and the Venetian cartographer Adriano Balbi (1829). Quetelet (1831) also explored the distribution of crime at macrounits of geography. Nineteenth-century criminologists concerned with place were constrained by the data they had available and forced to examine very large administrative areas.

John Glyde (1856) from England was the first scholar to question the validity of research findings when large areas were chosen as units of analysis in geographic criminology. In his paper "Localities of crime in Suffolk," he showed very clearly that larger units of analysis hide underlying variations in crime. When smaller units than districts were taken into account, significant differences in crime rates across smaller areas appeared. Similarly, Henry Mayhew (1851) tried to uncover patterns in the distribution of crime in the city of London by combining ethnographic methods with statistical data. He interviewed prostitutes, criminals, and other citizens about alcoholism, poverty, housing conditions, and economic uncertainty. He was the first scholar who focused on small areas such as squares, streets, and buildings as units of analysis in criminological research, predating modern interests in the criminology of place by over a century.

After the turn of the twentieth century, the locus of geographic research on crime moved to the United States, and especially to the city of Chicago. At the University of Chicago, a group of sociologists undertook new research on urban problems, which centered, in part, on delinquency (Beirne and

Messerschmidt 1991; Bulmer 1984; Faris 1967; Harvey 1987). They also moved the action of geographic criminology from broad comparisons across large geographic areas to more careful comparisons within cities. At this point, a group of American sociologists, among them Robert Park, William Thomas, Louis Wirth, Ernest Burgess, Clifford Shaw, and Henry McKay, took a leadership role in the development of geographic criminology, in contrast to the statisticians, criminal lawyers, or psychiatrists who dominated criminology more generally in Europe (Vold et al. 2002).

Clifford Shaw was one of the first Chicago sociologists to carry out extensive empirical research on the geographical distribution of crime on the basis of Burgess's zone model (Shaw 1929). Shaw applied new techniques of examining spatial patterns. First, he introduced *spot maps*, such as the one we show in Figure 1.2, by plotting the home address of thousands of juvenile offenders on a map of Chicago. These were in many ways a precursor of the crime maps produced by recent scholars concerned with the criminology of place. While Shaw focused his theoretical interests on neighborhoods, the visual presentation of data allows the reader to consider crime at a very microgeographic level.

But despite Shaw's recognition of the importance of microgeographic units in understanding crime, later reviewers of the Chicago School criticized their findings in good part because of their focus on large-area communities. Robinson (1950) argued that large-area studies were prone to what he termed an "ecological fallacy." According to Robinson (1950), the object of an ecological correlation is a group of persons, not a person: "the individual correlation depends upon the internal frequencies of the within-areas individual correlations, while the ecological correlation depends upon the marginal frequencies of the within-areas individual correlations" (Robinson 1950, 354). Large areas may reflect similar average concentrations of data but have very different underlying structures. For example, an area classified as "middle income" may be composed of mostly middle-income residents, or it may be composed of very few middle-income residents, but have many very rich residents and very poor residents.

Robinson presented the example of the relationship between immigration and literacy using U.S. state-level data. The correlation at the state level was strong and positive. But the actual correlation between immigration and literacy at the individual level was small and negative. The positive correlation at the state level came from the fact that immigrants tended to settle in states where the native population was overall better educated. He concluded more generally that ecological correlations drawn from large areas can be misleading in drawing conclusions about individual behavior, as was the case in the Chicago studies. This criticism can also be brought to microgeographic studies if scholars try to draw conclusions about individual behavior (as contrasted with the behavior at places). It suggests the importance of recognizing what study of specific units of analysis can tell us.

While we do not discount the relevance of studying varying geographic units, as Weisburd et al. (2009) argue, the trend of geographic criminology has been moving over the last two centuries to the study of microgeographic units. Groff et al. (2009), for example, show that biases in our understanding of crime are likely to result even when the units of geography used for study are measured at such levels as census tracts or census block groups. They examine street-to-street variability in juvenile crime patterns in the city of Seattle over a fourteen-year period. While they find that there is greater clustering of street segments with similar patterns or trajectories than would be expected by chance, their analyses show that there is also very strong street-to-street variability, suggesting "independence" of street blocks in terms of crime patterns over time (see also Weisburd et al. 2012).

Such results imply (as had Glyde's observations more than 150 years earlier; see also Zorbaugh 1929) that when examining crime patterns at larger geographic levels, even such commonly used "smaller" units such as census tracts or census block groups will mask significant lower-order geographic variability (see also Andresen and Malleson 2011). If, for example, a census tract included both increasing and decreasing crime trajectories as identified by Groff and colleagues (2009), the portrait gained when aggregating segments to the census tract would likely lead a researcher to conclude that there is overall a stable trend of crime over time (masking the contrasting trends at the street block level). More generally, when there is a good deal of variability at a very local level of geography (e.g., a street segment or group of street segments), we might in measuring higher order geographic units miss local area effects. This can be referred to as "averaging" and presents today, as in earlier decades, an important challenge to crime and place research.

Such averaging can manifest itself in a number of ways that would lead to a misleading interpretation of geographic data. A number of very active crime areas within a larger geographic unit might, for example, give the impression of an overall crime-prone area, when in fact most places in the larger geographic unit have low levels of crime. Similarly, when the vast majority of places have very little crime, but a few very active places have very high crime counts, there can be a "washing out" effect. In some sense, a conclusion in such a case that the area overall has little crime is correct. However, such a conclusion would miss the very important fact that some places within the larger unit are "hot spots of crime."

The study of crime and place moves the primary attention of scholars to the places where crime occurs. It pushes the focus of geographic criminology to a much lower level of aggregation than has traditionally been its focus. In the study of crime and place, scholars put place at the center of the crime equation and then ask what we can learn about crimes and criminals. Our interest, as the title of our volume implies, is in why place matters for crime. It is drawn, as we describe in more detail in Chapter 2, from the startling geographic concentration of crime at microgeographic units in urban areas. Sherman, Gartin, and

Buerger (1989), observing this concentration, coined the term the "criminology of place" to draw attention to its potential importance to criminologists. We do not think that it is important to stake out territory for one term or another. Whether one places this work in the area of environmental criminology (Brantingham and Brantingham 1981), geographic criminology (Bruinsma 2014), or some other broader framework, study of crime at microgeographic units of analysis – what has been termed the criminology of place (Sherman et al. 1989; Weisburd et al. 2012) or the study of crime at place (Eck and Weisburd 1995) – adds much to understanding of the crime problem. That is the focus of our book.

WHAT FOLLOWS?

The six chapters that follow this introductory chapter take you on an excursion. We begin by describing the concentration of crime at very small geographic locations. If crime were not concentrated at addresses, street segments, and other microplaces, then the study of such locations would not be worthwhile. The fact that it is so concentrated, and the fact that numerous studies, in many cities, in several countries, over twenty-five years have documented this concentration, suggests that this is far more than a quirk. This evidence calls out for an explanation just as much as other criminological empirical regularities, such as the age–crime relationship.

In Chapter 3 we delve into the types of explanations that could explain crime concentration at the place level. We look at two generic explanations – population heterogeneity and state dependence – and describe how these probably work together at places. We then turn to two general substantive explanations: opportunities for crime and social disorganization. Opportunity theories, including place management, have been most widely used to explain crime-place concentration. More recently, Weisburd et al. (2012) and Weisburd et al. (2014) have suggested that social disorganization theory can be revitalized by applying it to crime places.

The concept of place has a larger role in criminological thought than one might realize. Further, it is a concept that is embedded in the theories of other disciplines. In Chapter 4 we show how the concept of place can be used to bring together disparate theoretical and disciplinary perspectives. We also examine how insights from other disciplines can help us advance work in the study of the criminology of place.

Any theoretical perspective is accompanied by a set of research methods. Though these methods are shared across perspectives, each perspective has its own cluster of techniques and practices. This is no less true of the study of crime places. So in Chapter 5 we describe the most prominent methods that may not be familiar to most researchers who study other units of analysis.

Though the concentration of crime and its explanations may be inherently interesting to researchers, one of the strong motivations for studying places is that it can lead to improved crime reduction practices. Chapter 6 describes the considerable research on the effectiveness of intervening at places to reduce crime and disorder. This is an area that is not just interesting for criminological theory; it has concrete and valuable insights for how we can prevent crime. The chapter also touches on several new ideas on the frontiers of crime-place policy. Though these new ideas need more examination, their grounding in the facts of crime and place make them plausible and promising.

In the conclusions we try to draw the themes of the volume together and provide a more general set of discussions of what we have learned so far about the criminology of place and what we think should be the focus of the next generation of studies. We think that the reader will be convinced by our volume that it is time for criminologists to devote greater attention to microgeographic places in the study of crime. We know a great deal, and there is much promise in continuing our explorations in both basic research and evaluation research in this area. Our book focuses on why place is important for understanding and controlling crime. The body of research that we describe in this volume shows that it is possible to understand why crime is concentrated at places, and why it is practical to develop effective crime prevention policies at places. The action of crime in the next generation of criminological study lies at places, in part because it is a new area of study with significant opportunities for young scholars to make contributions.

2

The Concentration of Crime at Place[1]

Take a moment to imagine a crime occurring – perhaps a street robbery or a bag snatch. When you do this, it is difficult not to visualize the crime occurring in a particular setting or place. So, you might imagine a dark street corner with dim street lighting or seating in the outside area of a public bar. It seems intuitively sensible to analyze and understand crime at this unit of analysis – in other words, to investigate how criminals behave and crime concentrates at small microplaces. However, engaging in such microlevel analysis has tended to be a more recent criminological undertaking, and there are still many fruitful avenues to explore in terms of advancing both our knowledge and the sophistication of the methods that we use in this research area.

In this chapter, we raise and endeavor to answer a number of questions concerning the appropriate scale of analysis of criminological enquiry. To do this, we will start by defining what we mean by place and how this differs from other geographic concepts. Next, we highlight what has become the key catalyst for the criminology of place – the tremendous concentration of crime at microgeographic units of analysis. The strong and consistent concentration of crime at addresses, street segments, and other microgeographic units across cities is key to understanding why it is important to study the criminology of place and why it has such strong policy implications. We then turn to some additional statistical benefits of studying crime at microgeographic units that have to do with what is often termed "spatial interaction effects." Finally, we examine problems that crime and place researchers will need to consider, and recommend some future directions for research exploring crime concentration at places.

PLACE AND SPACE

Geographic concepts are sometimes used in criminological research without a clear understanding of their meaning. Place and space are two such concepts.

The subtle difference between them is important to keep in mind, as they can be a guide to establishing a carefully constructed study and influence the interpretation of findings. Furthermore, as will become apparent later in this chapter, a confusion of these concepts can mislead the reader in the interpretation of an argument. For example, it is important to keep in mind that place does not necessarily mean small units of analysis, nor does space necessarily refer to large areas. A careful definition of these two concepts avoids misunderstandings.

A good starting point is to note the dictionary definitions of these two concepts. Webster's dictionary (1936, 1583) defines space as: "Extension considered independently of anything which it may contain: extension in all directions ... the interval between any two objects." Note that it is considered independent of anything it may contain – the distance between two places is a spatial feature. So is direction. We are not interested in what the distance and direction contain, just their values.

Place, on the other hand, is defined as: "A particular portion of space, considered as separate and distinct from the rest of space" (Webster 1936, 1251). A place is defined by its internal characteristics that differentiate it from other places. Although a place must always be smaller than the space that contains it, places do not have to be small. For example, California is a place in the United States of America, Los Angeles is a place in California, and South Central is a place in Los Angeles. This can be continued down to smaller and smaller places within larger spaces until we end up with a specific address on a specific street (e.g., 4808 Florence Avenue). The key point is that places, large or small, are defined by their internal characteristics, while space is not. Space is the interval between two places in terms of distance and/or direction. Our concern in this book is with places. Place studies are concerned with the nature of the places within and around which crime occurs. The particular emphasis here is on microplaces. By a microplace, we mean a setting that is no larger than a small group of street blocks. As noted in Chapter 1, we have termed study at this geographic level as study of the criminology of place (Sherman et al. 1989; Weisburd et al. 2012) or study of crime and place (Eck and Weisburd 1995). We will see that focusing on such small units of analysis can be a particularly fruitful line of inquiry in developing our understanding of crime problems. We are concerned with not only the concentration of crime at these microplaces in space, but also what it is about them that makes them conducive to criminal activity.

CRIME CONCENTRATIONS AT PLACES

In the nineteenth century, Emile Durkheim suggested that crime was not indicative of pathology or illness in society, but at certain levels was simply evidence of the normal functioning of communities (Durkheim 1895). For Durkheim, the idea of a normal level of crime reinforced his theoretical position that crime helped to define and solidify norms in society. While Durkheim's proposition regarding a normal level of crime in society does not seem to fit recent experience and is seldom discussed by criminologists today, Weisburd et al. (2012) argue that there is indeed a normal level of crime in cities, but one that relates to the concentration of crime at place and not to the overall rate of crime. While the absolute levels of crime in cities vary year to year, the extent of crime concentrations remains similar (Pierce et al. 1988; Sherman et al. 1989; Weisburd 2015a; Weisburd et al. 2004). Empirical findings about the extent of crime concentrations at places have become key to the development of this area of study in criminology and its importance for crime prevention.

A number of studies, beginning in the late 1980s, suggest that significant clustering of crime at place exists, regardless of the specific unit of analysis defined (see Brantingham and Brantingham 1999; Crow and Bull 1975; Pierce et al. 1988; Roncek 1999; Sherman et al. 1989; Weisburd and Green 1995a; Weisburd et al. 1992; Weisburd et al. 2004; Weisburd et al. 2009). Perhaps the most influential of these was Sherman, Gartin, and Buerger's (1989) analysis of emergency calls to street addresses over a single year in Minneapolis, Minnesota. Sherman et al. (1989) were not the only scholars to identify strong crime concentrations at a microgeographic level at that time (see Pierce et al. 1988), but they were the first to recognize the criminological importance of such findings, and called in their seminal article for the creation of a new area of criminology – the criminology of place. They divided Minneapolis into 115,000 places (intersections and street addresses) and examined the distribution of crime across these places using one year of police calls for service data. Their analyses showed remarkable amounts of concentration of crime. Just over half of all the crime calls for service during the study year were generated by a mere 3.3 percent of places in the city (see Table 2.1). Approximately 40 percent of places in the city had no crime calls over this year.

There was remarkable similarity in the concentrations of crime at place observed by Pierce et al. (1988) in a study in Boston (see Table 2.2) conducted around the same time. Looking again at emergency calls for crime to the police, they found that 3.6 percent of addresses produced 50 percent of crime calls to the police. Other studies produced similar evidence of the concentration of crime in what began to be called crime hot spots (Sherman and Weisburd 1995; Sherman et al. 1989). Weisburd and Mazerolle (2000), for example, found that approximately 20 percent of all disorder crimes and 14 percent of crimes against persons were concentrated in just 56 drug crime hot spots in Jersey City, New Jersey, an area that comprised only 4.4 percent of street segments and intersections in the city. Similarly, Eck et al. (1999) found that the most active 10 percent of places (in terms of crime) in the Bronx and Baltimore accounted for approximately 32 percent of a combination of robberies, assaults, burglaries, grand larcenies, and auto thefts.

TABLE 2.1 *Distribution of All Dispatched Calls for Police Service in Minneapolis, MN, by Frequency at Each*

No. of Calls	Observed No. of Places	Expected No. of Places	Cumulative % of Places	Cumulative % of Calls
0	45,561	6,854	100.0	-
1	35,858	19,328	60.4	100.0
2	11,318	27,253	29.2	88.9
3	5,683	25,618	19.4	81.9
4	3,508	18,060	14.4	76.7
5	2,299	10,186	11.4	72.4
6	1,678	4,787	9.4	68.8
7	1,250	1,929	7.9	65.7
8	963	680	6.8	63.0
9	814	213	6.0	60.6
10	652	60	5.3	58.4
11	506	15	4.7	56.3
12	415	4	4.3	54.6
13	357	1	3.9	53.1
14	297	0	3.6	51.7
15 ≥	3,841	0	3.3	50.4

Source: Sherman, L.W., Gartin, P., and Buerger, M.E. (1989). "Hot spots of predatory crime: Routine activities and the criminology of place." *Criminology*, 27(1), 27–55.

TABLE 2.2 *The Distribution of Total Demand for Police Services among Street Addresses Experiencing a Given Annual Rate of Demand in Boston, MA, for the Period 1977–1982*

Annual Rate of Demand for Services per Street Address	Percent of All Street Addresses	Percent of Total Demand for Police Services
1 or more	80.8	100.0
2 or more	43.6	91.0
3 or more	30.1	84.4
4 or more	22.9	79.2
5 or more	18.3	74.8
10 or more	8.7	59.6
20 or more	3.6	50.1
30 or more	2.0	34.0
40 or more	1.3	27.9
50 or more	0.9	23.6
75 or more	0.4	16.8
100 or more	0.2	13.1
150 or more	0.1	9.4
Total Number of Cases	703,830[2]	2,905,440[3]

Original source: Pierce, G., Spaar, S., and Briggs, L. (1988). *The character of police work: Strategic and tactical implications*. Boston, MA: Center for Applied Social Research, Northeastern University.

In Sherman et al. (1989) original work, they also documented crime concentrations by specific crime types. All robbery calls came from only 2.2 percent of places in the city, all motor vehicle thefts came from 2.7 percent of places, and all rape calls came from 1.2 percent of places. Even some crimes that would perhaps seem less likely to concentrate so dramatically, such as burglaries, assaults, and domestic disturbances, were also found to show high levels of concentration at the place level. All burglaries came from 11 percent of places, all assaults from 7 percent of places, and all domestic disturbances came from 9 percent of places. While study of crime concentrations for specific crimes has often been hindered because of low base rates in specific microgeographic areas, more recent study of specific crime types also shows strong evidence of high levels of concentrations (Braga et al. 2010; Townsley et al. 2003). For example, in Boston et al. (2010) examined incidents of gun violence between 1980 and 2008. They found incidents of gun violence were concentrated at less than 5 percent of street segments and intersections. In studying juvenile crime hot spots, Weisburd et al. (2009) also found similar crime concentrations and stability across time.

A series of studies conducted over the last fifteen years looking at crime incidents at street segments has provided important evidence of consistent crime concentrations across time and across cities. Weisburd et al. (2012, 2014) termed this phenomenon the *law of crime concentrations at places* because of the remarkable consistency observed. Weisburd et al. (2012) found that about 5 percent of street segments produced 50 percent of crime incidents each year over a fourteen-year period in Seattle (Figure 2.1). About 1 percent of street segments in the city accounted for 23 percent of crime incidents in that period. Using crime incidents and street segments as units, Weisburd et al. (2014) find that 5 percent of street segments in New York City produced about 52 percent of crime at street segments over a two year period (see Table 2.3). One percent of streets produced about 25 percent of crime.

Weisburd and Amram (2014) find a very similar distribution of crime in Tel Aviv, Israel (see Figure 2.2). A total of 4.5 percent of street segments produced 50 percent of crime, and 0.9 percent of street segments produced 25 percent of crime on Tel Aviv streets. A number of studies in the United Kingdom and the Netherlands examining repeat victimization and near repeat victimization – respectively, the degree to which the same places and nearby places suffer elevated crime risk over time – also show similar patterns of crime concentrations (e.g., Bernasco 2008; Johnson and Bowers 2004a; Johnson et al. 1997; Johnson et al. 2007; Pease 1998; Ratcliffe and Rengert 2008; Townsley et al. 2003).

Wilcox and Eck (2011) identify a similar law of crime concentrations regarding specific facilities. They call it the "iron law of troublesome places." Building on a study of crime at facilities by Eck et al. (2007) they argue that

TABLE 2.3 *Summary of Crime Incident Data in New York City, 2009–2010*

Street Incidents	2009 n	2009 %	2010 n	2010 %
Crime Incidents				
Total Number of Crime Incidents on Street Segments	332,819	77.4	333,574	77.5
Street Segments with Crime Incidents	48,927	44.7	48,546	44.3
Incidents in the Top 10% of the Street Segments	229,236	68.9	232,192	69.6
Incidents in the Top 5% of the Street Segments	173,591	52.2	175,571	52.6
Incidents in the Top 1% of the Street Segments	51,454	24.5	82,005	24.6

Original source: Weisburd, D., Telep, C.W., and Lawton, B.A. (2014). "Could innovations in policing have contributed to the New York city crime drop even in a period of declining police strength?: The case of stop, question and frisk as a hot spots policing strategy." *Justice Quarterly*, 31(1), 129–153. Reprinted with permission of Taylor & Francis Ltd.

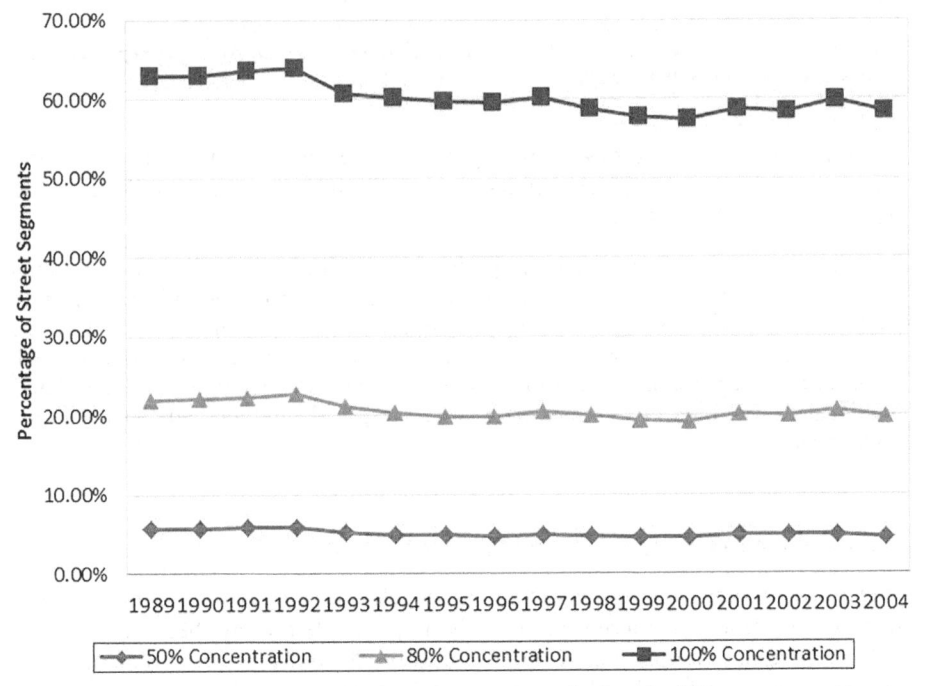

FIGURE 2.1. Crime concentrations by street segments in Seattle, WA.
Original source: Weisburd, D., Groff, E.R., and Yang, S.-M. (2012). *The criminology of place: Street segments and our understanding of the crime problem*. New York: Oxford University Press. Used by permission of Oxford University Press.

```
40% ┐                                                    ┌──────┐
                                                         │36.8% │
35% ┤                                                    │      │
                                                         │      │
30% ┤                                                    │      │
                                                         │      │
25% ┤                                                    │      │
                                                         │      │
20% ┤                                                    │      │
                                                         │      │
15% ┤                                   ┌──────┐         │      │
                                        │12.1% │         │      │
10% ┤                                   │      │         │      │
                        ┌──────┐        │      │         │      │
 5% ┤                   │ 4.5% │        │      │         │      │
       ┌──────┐         │      │        │      │         │      │
       │ 0.9% │         │      │        │      │         │      │
 0% ┴───┴──────┴─────────┴──────┴────────┴──────┴─────────┴──────┴──
         25%               50%              75%              100%
```

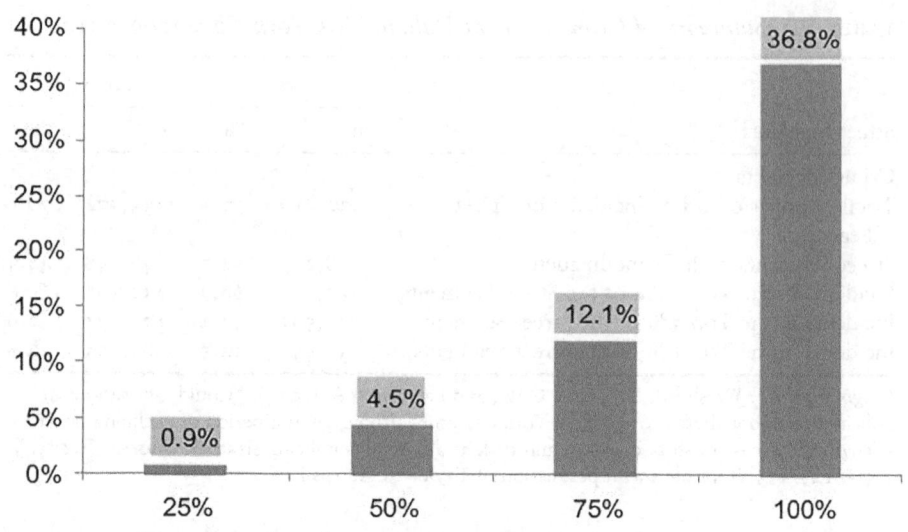

FIGURE 2.2. The proportion of street segments that account for 25 percent, 50 percent, 75 percent, and 100 percent of crime in Tel Aviv-Jaffa, 2010.
Original source: Weisburd, D., and Amram, S. (2014). "The law of concentrations of crime at place: The case of Tel Aviv-Jaffa." *Police Practice and Research*, 15(2), 101–114. Reprinted with permission of Taylor & Francis Ltd.

a small number of facilities of any type produce most of the crime. Drawing from 37 studies of 16 different types of facilities in four countries, Wilcox and Eck (2011, 476) conclude:

All studies showed the following crime distribution: a small proportion of facilities produce a much larger proportion of the crimes, and most facilities had little crime. In studies that included places that never reported crime, zero crime facilities were the modal category. This finding was true regardless of the crime type examined, the size of the facilities, or even subcategories of facilities (e.g., dividing motels into national chains and locally owned). No exceptions were noted, despite the authors' attempts to locate such studies.

A LAW OF CRIME CONCENTRATION AT PLACES

Weisburd (2015a) has gone further in developing the law of crime concentrations, arguing that there is an underlying principle that applies with remarkable consistency across places. One limitation in many prior studies of crime concentrations is that they have focused on single jurisdictions, and often have used differing units of analysis, types of data, and types of crime. Weisburd (2015a) asked whether there is a tight bandwidth of concentration of crime, suggesting a specific scientific principle that holds in similar magnitudes across a variety of circumstances. The generally established criterion of a *physical law* as defined by the Oxford English Dictionary (2010) is as follows: "A physical law is a principle deduced from particular facts, applicable to a defined group or class of phenomena, and expressible by the statement that a particular phenomenon always occurs if certain conditions be present." In this context, he presents data to suggest that there is a *"law of crime concentration. This law states that for a defined measure of crime at a specific microgeographic unit, the concentration of crime will fall within a narrow bandwidth of percentages for a defined cumulative proportion of crime"* (Weisburd 2015a, 138, emphasis in original).

A defined measure of crime is necessary because crime concentration may vary depending on the types of crimes and nature of the crime data examined. For example, as illustrated previously, earlier studies have looked at broad general measures of crime as well as at specific types of crime, and they have examined emergency calls to the police, crime victimization, and crime incidents. In turn, crime concentration may fluctuate according to the specific microgeographic unit of analysis examined, from addresses or facilities to clusters of street segments or defined geographic buffers. Scholars have argued generally that crime concentrates at microgeographic units (Weisburd et al. 2012; Wilcox and Eck 2011). A specific law of crime concentration predicts that the range in percentage of microgeographic units – what Weisburd (2015a) terms a "bandwidth" of percentages – that is associated with a specific *cumulative proportion of crime* (e.g., 25 percent or 50 percent of crime in the city) would be very narrow for a standard unit of crime and geography.

Weisburd (2015a) was able to gather crime data on eight cities coded at the same geographic units (the street segment), using the same type of data (crime incidents) and the same measure of crime (a broad general measure, see the following). Five of the cities are what we would ordinarily term large cities, with populations ranging from about 300,000 people (Cincinnati, Ohio) to over 8,000,000 (New York City). Three of the cities are small cities, less urbanized than the larger cities, including populations ranging from about 70,000 (Redlands, California) to 108,000 (Ventura, California) people. The time range of the data available in the cities ranged from a single year to twenty-one years. While the cities examined were not representative of a specific population of cities, they had a broad array of characteristics, including being spread geographically across the United States and including one non-U.S. city, Tel Aviv-Yafo.[4]

For each city a broad crime measure was used, drawing from incident reports at street segments. Looking at the larger cities, Weisburd (2015a) found that crime concentration occurs within a very tight bandwidth despite the variability in characteristics of the cities studied (see Figure 2.3). Fifty percent of crime at street segments is found to concentrate in just 4.2 (Sacramento, California) to 6 (Cincinnati) percent of the streets. Twenty-five percent of the crime is found at between 0.8 and 1.6 percent of the street segments.

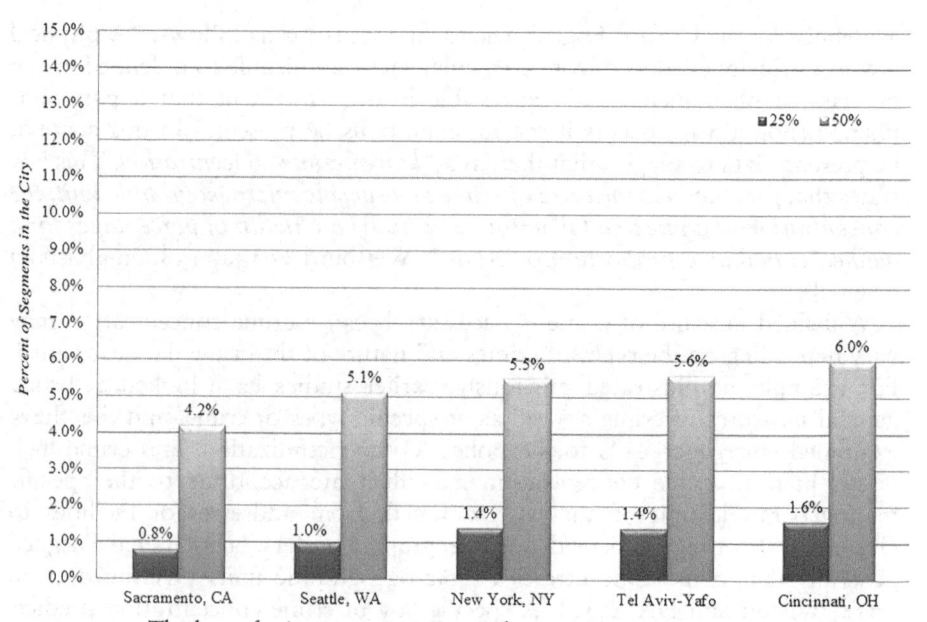

FIGURE 2.3. The law of crime concentration in large cities.
Original source: Weisburd, D. (2015). "The law of crime concentrations and the criminology of place." *Criminology*, 53(2), 133–157. Courtesy of Wiley.

Accordingly, there appears to be a law of crime concentration operating in these cities that follows a very consistent pattern.

Smaller cities followed a similar pattern with even higher levels of crime concentration (see Figure 2.4). Between 2.1 percent (Brooklyn Park, Minnesota; Redlands) and 3.5 (Ventura) of street segments produce 50 percent of crime at street segments. The percentage of street segments responsible for 25 percent of crime is just 0.4 percent in Brooklyn Park and Redlands and 0.7 percent in Ventura. While caution is warranted in trying to explain small absolute differences between the larger urban areas and more suburban cities examined here, these data suggest that the law of crime concentration may operate differently in small suburban cities than in large metropolises. Crime concentration in smaller cities is just beginning to be studied (e.g., see Dario et al. 2015; Hibdon 2013), which should shed more light on this question in the future.

But whatever the variability Weisburd (2015a) observes across smaller and larger cities, the overall conclusion is that there is a tight bandwidth of crime concentration at places suggesting a law of crime concentration across cities. For 50 percent concentration that bandwidth is about 4 percent (from 2.1 to 6 percent), and for 25 percent concentration the bandwidth is less than 1.5 percent (from 0.4 to 1.6 percent).

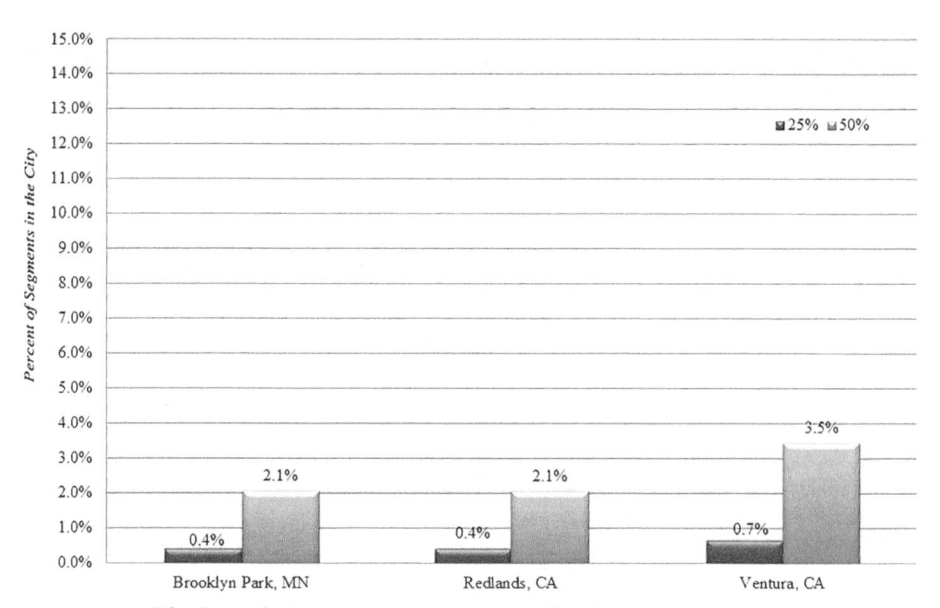

FIGURE 2.4. The law of crime concentration in small cities.
Source: Weisburd, D. (2015). "The law of crime concentrations and the criminology of place." Criminology, 53(2), 133–157. Courtesy of Wiley.

DOES THE LAW OF CRIME CONCENTRATION APPLY ACROSS TIME?

Weisburd (2015a) also asks whether there is a tight bandwidth of crime concentration across time. Does that consistency hold even if there are strong trends or fluctuations in crime over time? For four of the cities he studied (Tel Aviv-Yafo, Seattle, Brooklyn Park, New York), longitudinal data were available that allowed examination of these questions. In Figure 2.5, the crime concentration trends at 25 and 50 percent of crime are presented, as well as trends in crime incidents over the time period examined for each of the four cities.

As in the examination of crime concentration across cities, a relatively small bandwidth of crime concentration within cities across time is identified. In Seattle over sixteen years, the bandwidth for a cumulative proportion of 50 percent of crime varied between 4.6 and 5.8 percent, and that for 25 percent of crime between 0.9 and 1.2 percent of street segments (see more on longitudinal trends in Seattle below). Similarly, in New York, the bandwidth varies between 4.7 and 6 percent for 50 percent of crime and 1.1 and 1.5 percent for 25 percent of crime over a nine-year period. In Brooklyn Park, the concentration is greater, as noted earlier, but the bandwidth is again small, varying between 1.5 and 2.6 percent for 50 percent of crime and 0.3 and 0.5 percent for

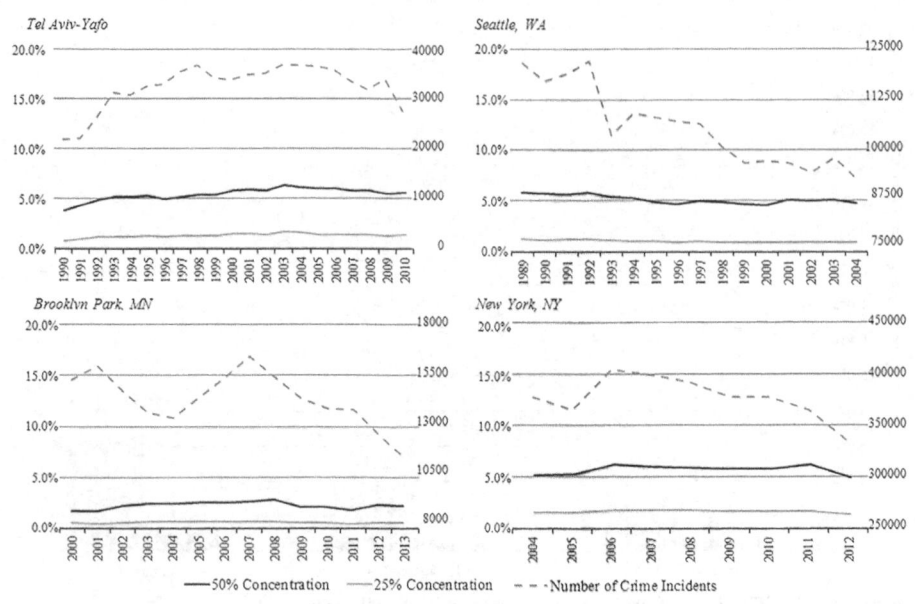

FIGURE 2.5. Changes in crime concentration and number of crime incidents over time.
Source: Weisburd, D. (2015). "The law of crime concentrations and the criminology of place." *Criminology*, 53(2), 133–157. Courtesy of Wiley.

25 percent of crime over a fourteen-year period. Tel Aviv-Yafo follows the general pattern of stability, but the variation across time is somewhat greater. The bandwidth for the 50 percent cumulative proportion of crime varies between 3.9 (1990) and 6.5 percent (2003), and the 25 percent cumulative proportion between 0.8 and 1.8 percent.

The number of crime incidents each year appears much more volatile both within and between cities (see Figure 2.5). For example, in Tel Aviv-Yafo, there was a large crime wave between 1991 and 1998 (in contrast to American cities during this period, see Blumstein and Wallman 2000), and a smaller but still meaningful crime drop between 2004 and 2010. In contrast, Brooklyn Park saw a crime drop between 2001 and 2004 of more than 2,500 incidents, then a crime wave increase of over 3,000 crime incidents, and finally a larger crime drop between 2007 and 2013 of almost 5,000 crime incidents. Seattle shows a fairly consistent overall crime drop of 28,545 incidents between 1989 and 2004. Finally, New York evidences a mixed trend between 2004 and 2006 and then a decline of almost 70,000 crimes between 2006 and 2012. Clearly, the crime patterns differ considerably between the cities. There is also a very significant degree of fluctuation of crime incidents across time within cities.

Weisburd (2015a) argues from these data that crime concentration stays within a relatively tight bandwidth across time within the cities studied. This strengthens the evidence for a law of crime concentration at place as a specific scientific principle. It also speaks to the general law in criminology proposed by Émile Durkheim more than 100 years ago that we noted earlier. Durkheim suggested that crime was not indicative of pathology or illness in society, but, at certain levels, was simply evidence of the normal functioning of communities (Durkheim 1895). For Durkheim, the idea of a normal level of crime reinforced his theoretical position that crime helped to define and solidify norms in society.

Crime rates over the last few decades would seem to strongly contradict Durkheim's conception of normal levels of crime in society. Between 1973 and 1990, violent crime doubled in the United States (National Research Council 1993), and in the 1990s, the United States experienced a well-documented crime drop (Blumstein and Wallman 2000). In the 1970s, Alfred Blumstein and colleagues (Blumstein and Cohen 1973; Blumstein and Moitra 1979; Blumstein et al. 1976) hypothesized that Durkheim's proposition could be applied to punishment in America, where imprisonment rates had remained static for a long period of time (see also Tremblay 1986). But recent dramatic increases in U.S. incarcerations in the 1980s and 1990s would seem inconsistent with the normal crime or normal punishment hypothesis – unless, of course, we were to postulate that these are periods of dramatic social change where the normal crime hypothesis would not apply (Durkheim 1895). The cities studied by Weisburd (2015a) suggest as well that levels of crime vary widely across time. But despite the fluctuations in crime over time in the cities, crime concentration stays within a relatively narrow range. In this sense, Durkheim's proposition of a normal level of crime in society can be reinterpreted. There does not appear to be a normal level of crime in urban areas. But there does appear to be a normal level of concentration of crime at place (see also Weisburd and Amram 2014; Weisburd et al. 2012).

THE IMPLICATIONS OF CRIME CONCENTRATIONS

Overall, these findings have provided a strong catalyst for the development of interest in the criminology of place. The crime concentrations produced consistently in studies raise key criminological questions that we will examine in subsequent chapters. Why does crime concentrate in specific places in the city? What are the specific risk and protective factors for crime at place? Why do we find such similar concentrations across cities?

In turn, these findings provide strong policy implications that have become a key focus of crime prevention over the last two decades – especially in the application of hot spots policing programs (Braga et al. 2014; Braga and Weisburd 2010; Sherman and Weisburd 1995) that we will examine in Chapter 6. The concentration of crime at place in a city provides a strong basis for concentration of crime prevention at such places. Moreover, the levels of crime concentration at places suggest that at least in terms of identifying targets for intervention, focusing crime prevention at places makes more sense than focusing crime prevention on individuals. Sherman et al. (1989) found that the concentration of crime at microplaces (50 percent of crime from 3 percent of these places) was twice that found among repeat offenders, given that Wolfgang and colleagues (1972) found that 6 percent of offenders accounted for 50 percent of the crime in their seminal birth cohort study (see Sherman 1995). Weisburd et al. (2012) came to a similar conclusion looking at the idea of the number of targets presented to crime prevention agents. They found that on average fewer than 1,500 street segments in Seattle accounted for 50 percent of the crime each year. During the same period, about 6,000 offenders were responsible for 50 percent of the crime each year. Simply stated, the police or other crime prevention practitioners would have to approach four times as many targets to identify the same level of overall crime when they focus on people as opposed to places.

Importantly, as well, places are not moving targets. The American Housing Survey from the United States Census Bureau shows that on average Americans move once every seven years (U.S. Census Bureau 2006). It is reasonable to assume that offenders move even more often than this. Studies have often noted the difficulty of tracking offenders for survey research (Sampson and Laub 2003; Wolfgang et al. 1987), and it is a common experience of the police to look for an offender and find that he or she no longer lives at the last known address. Place-based crime prevention provides a target that stays in the same place. This is not an insignificant issue when considering the investment of crime prevention resources.

But a showing that crime is concentrated at place leaves key questions in the development of a criminology of place unanswered. For example, showing that crime is concentrated at specific microgeographies leaves open the possibility that crime concentrations are unstable. There could be a law of crime concentrations across time, but it might be the case that the specific places where crime is concentrated shift from year to year. If this were the case, then it may not make sense to shift criminological or policy interest to small geographic areas. Understanding concentrations in such cases would not provide a key to understanding long-term crime trends or preventing crime in the long term. Is crime at microgeographic places stable over time or does crime shift from place to place, perhaps reflecting a process of "regression to the mean," where places become hot spots and then shift to cool spots naturally over short periods of time?

A second important question is whether the concentrations observed at very microgeographic levels reflect phenomena at that geographic level, or whether it is just a reification of higher-order trends. For example, are most hot spots of crime in so-called bad neighborhoods? Is there important street-by-street variability of crime in cities, or do small hot spots of crime cluster up to larger geographic areas? For the criminology of place to have salience for criminology and crime prevention, we must be able to show that the action of crime is in fact occurring at a microgeographic level.

THE COUPLING OF CRIME TO PLACE

The first large empirical study to examine the stability of crime at places across time was conducted in Seattle by Weisburd and colleagues (2012; see also Weisburd et al. 2004). Using group-based trajectory approaches (see Nagin 1999), they grouped street segments in Seattle into twenty-two patterns of crime changes at street segments (see Figure 2.6). A key finding was that most segments remained relatively stable over a sixteen-year period. These findings have two important implications for understanding the stability of crime concentrations. First, the findings show remarkable stability of crime concentration across time. Segments that started high on crime in 1989 were still generally high on crime in the early 2000s and vice versa. Second, while there is stability within street segments, the twenty-two different trajectory groups identified show that there is a great deal of variability *across* street segments over time in Seattle. This again highlights the importance of examining crime at the microplace level to truly understand crime concentration and crime trends. Finally, while this is only one study, other recent research has found similar evidence that there is strong stability of crime at microgeographic units over time. In a replication of the Weisburd et al. (2012) study in Vancouver, Canada, Curman and colleagues (2015) found that the majority of street segments had relatively stable crime trends over a sixteen-year period. In turn, Braga and his

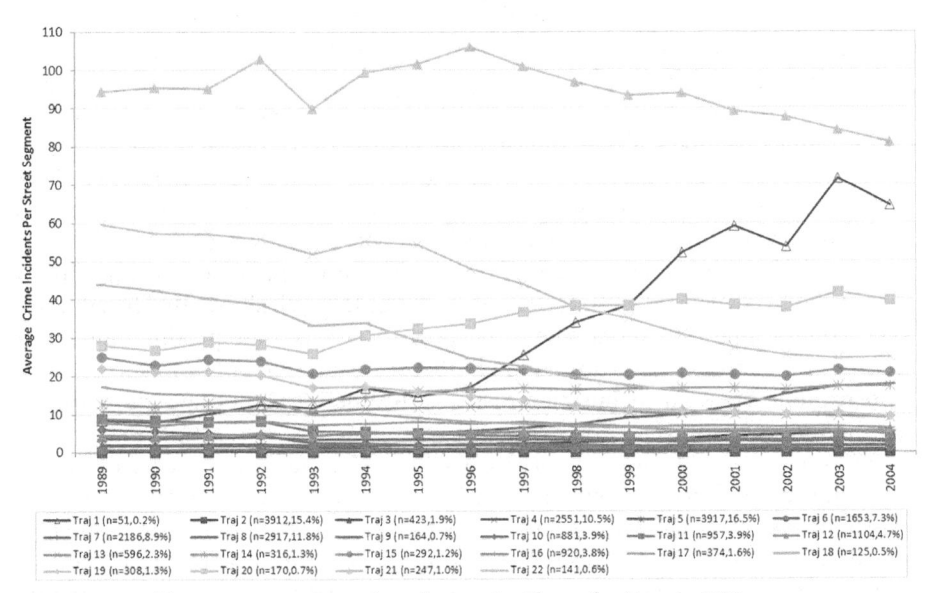

FIGURE 2.6. Twenty-two trajectories of crime incidents for Seattle, WA, street segments. *Original source*: Weisburd, D., Groff, E.R., and Yang, S.-M. (2012). *The criminology of place: Street segments and our understanding of the crime problem.* New York: Oxford University Press. Used by permission of Oxford University Press.

colleagues found evidence of stability in gun violence concentrations and robbery concentrations in Boston from 1980 to 2008 (Braga et al. 2010; 2011a).

These studies suggest that crime does not simply move from place to place. Weisburd et al. (2012) argue that this suggests a strong coupling of crime to place and indicates the importance of identifying the factors that lead to this coupling. But more directly, these findings add weight to the importance of study of the law of crime concentrations at places. What we observe in a city is not simply a process of regression to the mean with places becoming extreme and then moving back to normal through natural stochastic processes, but rather a potential set of underlying processes leading to concentrations of crime in specific microplaces.

Are Hot Spots Concentrated within a City?

A final key issue in research on crime concentration is whether microplace hot spots – such as the consistently high crime street segments in the Seattle study or places that suffer repeat victimization – tend to be concentrated within certain areas. This question has important implications for crime and place. If crime places are located mainly within certain neighborhoods, then it may be better to focus on larger area trends in understanding crime at place.

The first indication of the strong variability of crime hot spots across neighborhoods was found in a study by Weisburd and Green (1995b) of drug market areas in Jersey City, New Jersey. They identified drug markets using a variety of data sources, and then mapped the drug markets across the city (see Figure 2.7). There was a surprising degree of spread of the drug markets, which were found not just in the high-crime areas of the city but across Jersey City neighborhoods. Moreover, even in the highest-activity drug crime areas, there were many streets without drug markets and with little crime located near to the most active drug markets (Weisburd and Mazerollle 2000).

This reality of the presence of high-crime hot spots across the city is reinforced by Weisburd et al. (2014) in Figure 2.8, which shows the distribution of chronic crime hot spots (the 1 percent of streets that produce almost a quarter of crime) in Seattle. Though there are clusters of hot spots, most noticeable in the central business district, chronic crime hot spots are spread throughout the city.

Weisburd and colleagues (2012) went further using sixteen years of Seattle data, and created maps showing street-by-street variability in crime. Figure 2.9 reproduces a map showing what is generally considered the more disadvantaged areas of southern Seattle. The streets shaded darkly with thick lines are the higher-rate crime hot spot street segments, while the streets shaded lightly with thinner lines represent streets with little crime. What is clear from this figure is that hot spots are spread throughout these areas and not clustered in only one neighborhood. Moreover, there is a large degree of street-level

FIGURE 2.7. Drug hot spots in Jersey City, NJ.
Source: Weisburd, D., and Mazerolle, L.G. (2000). "Crime and disorder in drug hot spots: Implications for theory and practice in policing." *Police Quarterly*, 3(3), 331–349. Reprinted by permission of SAGE Publications.

variability observed in this map. Finally, it is clear that even in a so-called bad area of town, most streets have little or no crime. Weisburd et al. (2012) also conduct a series of spatial analyses showing strong spatial heterogeneity of street-level crime patterns within areas. Their work identifies area wide influences; for example, there are more crime hot spots in certain neighborhoods,

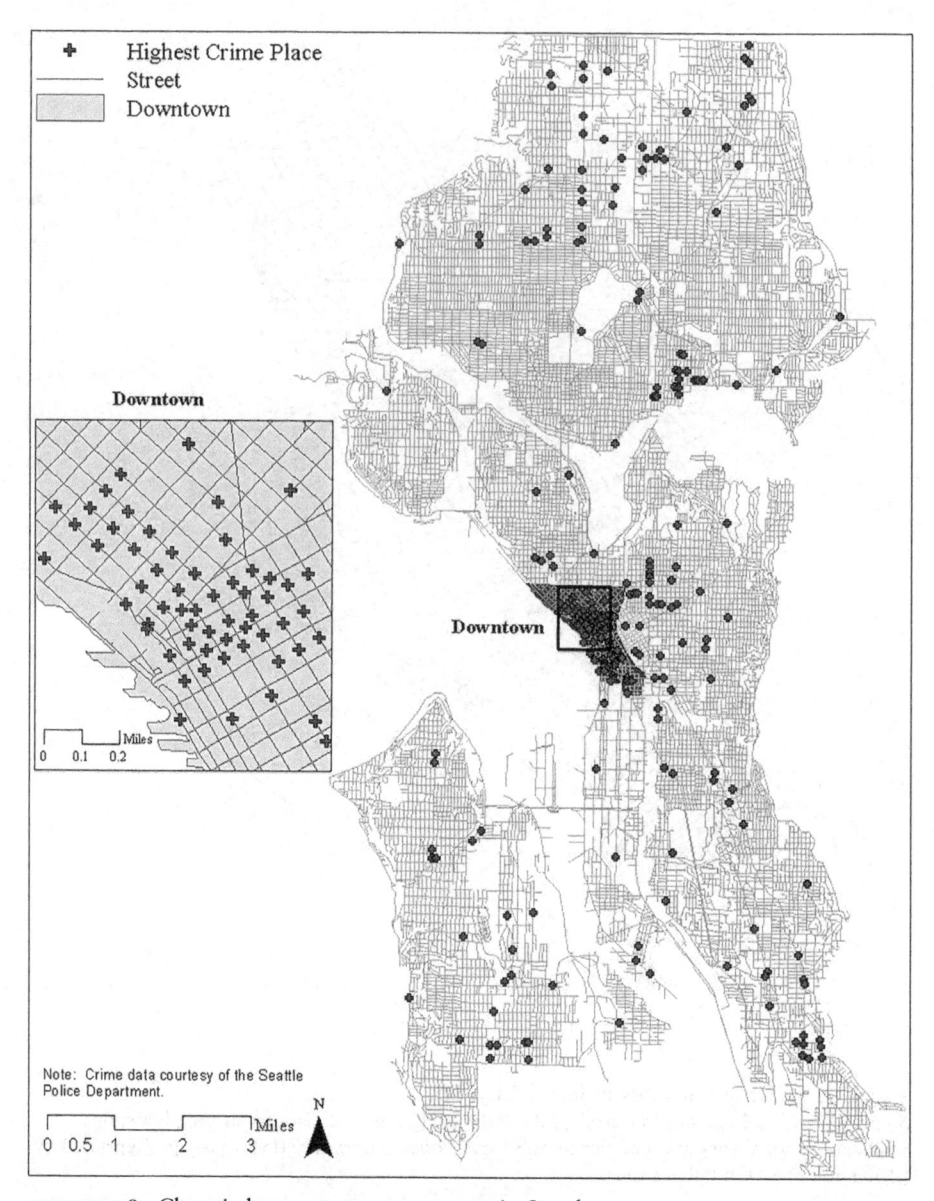

FIGURE 2.8. Chronic hot spot street segments in Seattle.
Original source: Weisburd, D., Groff, E.R., and Yang, S.-M. (2014). "Understanding and controlling hot spots of crime: The importance of formal and informal social controls." *Prevention Science*, 15(1), 31–43, Figure 2. With kind permission from Springer Science and Business Media.

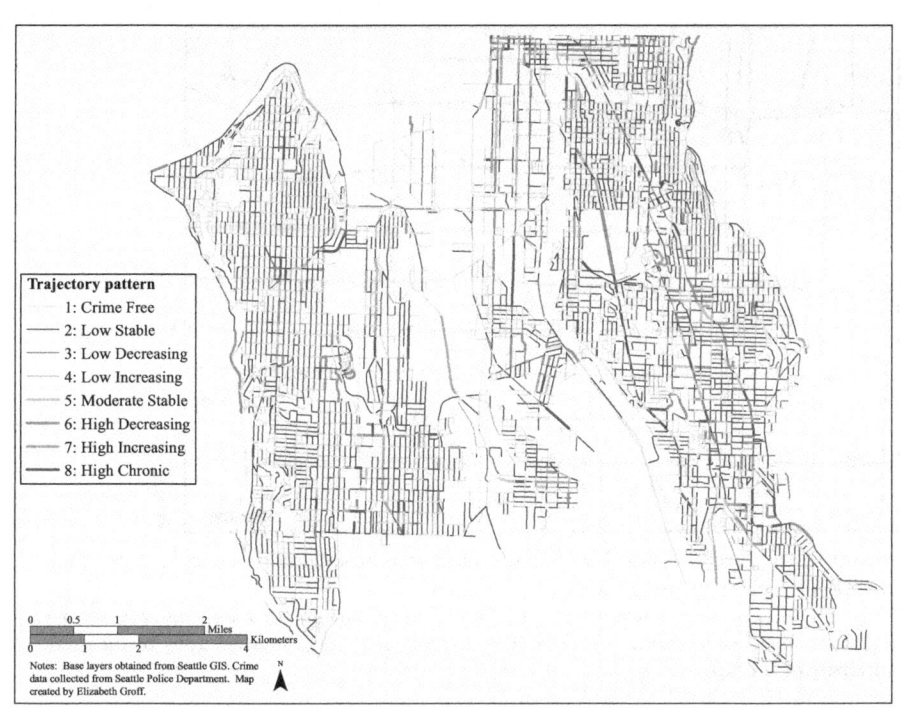

FIGURE 2.9. Spatial distribution of trajectory patterns in southern Seattle, WA. *Original source*: Weisburd, D., Groff, E.R., and Yang, S.-M. (2012). *The criminology of place: Street segments and our understanding of the crime problem.* New York: Oxford University Press. Used by permission of Oxford University Press.

but the strongest statistical outcomes are ones that suggest strong street-by-street variation in crime patterns (see also Andresen and Malleson 2011).

A study by St. Jean (2007), which examined crime concentration within one of Chicago's historically highest-crime police beats using a mixed-methods approach involving crime mapping and qualitative interviews, reinforced these findings. His work also showed tremendous block-to-block variability of crime within this high-crime police beat (see Figure 2.10). While the whole area was generally considered a bad area, many blocks were crime-free and most of the crime was concentrated at a few places he termed "crime pockets."

These findings overall suggest that even within high-crime neighborhoods, there is a lot of variation in crime rates across microplaces. Furthermore, research has demonstrated that areas that generally suffer high crime rates also tend to be areas that have levels of repeat victimization, suggesting that chronic victimization can be one of the driving forces behind area-level risk (e.g., Johnson et al. 1997). These findings, along with the other evidence on crime concentration reviewed earlier, clearly illustrate the importance of studying crime at microunits of geography.

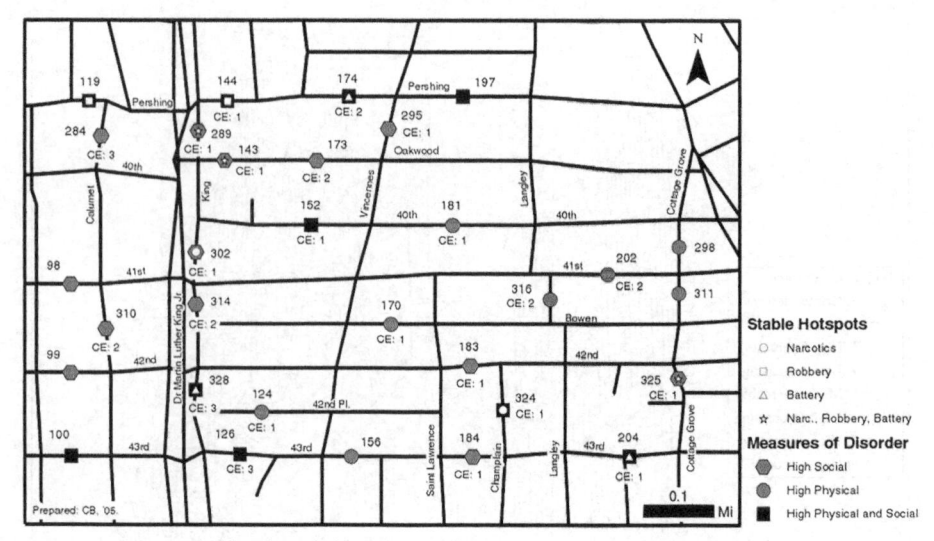

FIGURE 2.10. Neighborhood disorder, collective efficacy, and street crimes per face block, in Chicago, 1999–2000.
Original source: St. Jean, P.K.B. (2007). *Pockets of crime: Broken windows, collective efficacy, and the criminal point of view*. Chicago, IL: University of Chicago Press. © 2007 by the University of Chicago.

We now have a large and growing body of evidence that shows that crime is extremely concentrated in small places, that this concentration is stable across time, and that crime hot spots are not bad neighborhoods, but rather are a few small crime pockets (clusters of street blocks, street segments, street corners, or even single addresses) that are driving the crime rates for larger areas. These findings have major implications for crime theory and crime prevention policy, as will be discussed in detail later in this volume. In short, they suggest that theories of crime places should focus on microlevel factors that can explain why one place has a high crime rate, while other nearby places do not. In terms of policy, the high and stable concentration of crime at microplaces suggests that the most effective tactics will be those that address microplace risk factors for crime (see Weisburd et al. 2012).

MICROGEOGRAPHIC PLACES AND SPATIAL INTERACTION EFFECTS

A major strength of microplace analyses is the ability to investigate spatial interaction effects. As illustrated by Rengert and colleagues (2005), the impact of a place often is not contained within the place itself, but rather spills over into the surrounding area. The same spillover effect was identified in a series of studies concerning crime around schools and bars (Roncek and Bell 1981;

Roncek and Faggiani 1985; Roncek and LoBosco 1983; Roncek and Mair 1991; Roncek and Pravatiner 1989). The degree of spillover generally is associated with the situation of the place in space. In other words, what is near and/or around it? These interaction effects can be examined using geographic information systems to buffer around a place and the surrounding facilities. Census information also can be included within this analysis of the interaction between a place and its surroundings.

With the overlay function of a geographic information system, the researcher can ask "and" questions. For example, the researcher can ask the geographic information system to identify all the areas that are within 400 feet of a tavern and located in block groups that are below the poverty level. Geographic information systems can also address "or" questions. An example of this would be to ask the system to identify all the taverns or liquor stores that are within 400 feet of an exit from a limited access highway. Then, the amount of crime within these areas can be compared with the amount of crime within 400 feet of a tavern or liquor store that is not within 400 feet from an exit from a limited access highway. In other words, we can answer questions of whether a situation is necessary to cause a place to have elevated crime rates.

Caplan et al. (2011) used the "or" function of this spatial interaction technique to construct risk terrain models. Using small cells of 100 square feet, the authors determined whether a particular cell was within a specific distance of a bar, liquor store, fast food restaurant, or subway stop. By placing a value of one if the cell was located within the specified distance of one of these facilities and a zero if not, the author could sum the values for each cell, thus aggregating the risk associated with each cell. The risk terrain surface then can be compared with the density of a particular crime, such as shootings, drug dealing arrests, or muggings. A similar routine was constructed by Kennedy and colleagues (2011). Their approach can be extended by using Rengert et al.'s (2005) technique of testing whether a facility does in fact negatively impact the surrounding area, rather than just assuming that it does from previous studies. As noted below in the case of drug treatment centers, it may in fact be the case that a facility is located in a bad area rather than it causing the area to be bad.

The use of microplaces has been taken a step further by Groff (2007a,b), where she uses them for theory-based simulation and predictive modeling. Agent-based simulation that assigns probabilities to activities in a place-based simulation environment can be used to test whether our assumptions are accurate predictors of real world phenomena. The model's parameters can be tweaked between runs to improve its predictive qualities. Simulation techniques hold much promise for the future of place-based research. They allow us to examine very small places and simulate human interaction with these places. An excellent conceptual background to this genre of investigation is given by Brantingham and Tita (2008).

The Importance of Distinguishing between Site and Situation

If small places are to be used in analysis whenever possible, we need to understand the characteristics of these places. Much confusion can be alleviated if we classify data collected at small places into a couple of basic geographic concepts that focus and clarify our interpretations. These concepts are parallel to the place and space concepts discussed earlier; they are site and situation. Site characteristics are the internal characteristics of the place (Abler et al. 1971). For example, the site characteristics of an address would be the type of building (if one exists), such as residence, store, or factory. If the address is a residence, further site characteristics would include whether it is single family or an apartment complex. Finally, if it is a single-family home, security measures (such as alarm systems or bars on windows) would be further site characteristics.

Situational characteristics are the situation of the place in space. They are what it is near and the characteristics of the features it is near. For example, a home situated near the exit ramp of a limited access highway may be more vulnerable to residential burglary. Ignoring situational characteristics of a place may cause a researcher to misinterpret a site feature of a home. For example, Rengert and Groff (2011) reported that in one suburb, homes with bars on their windows had high burglary rates. This was not because bars were on the windows but because these homes tended to be situated in highly vulnerable areas, such as near an exit ramp of a limited access highway. This indicates clearly that a complete analysis must include both the site and the situational characteristics of a place. Ignoring one or the other can cause misleading interpretations. Also, some clusters of crime are sometimes explained by statistically spurious factors. In this case, some simple statistical controls explain the clusters.

Rengert (1997) provides one example of a spurious finding that was explained by a simple control resulting from a study initially ignoring the site characteristics of a place. In this analysis, the author discovered a hot spot cluster of auto theft on South Street in central Philadelphia. He first attributed the hot spot to a late night theater situated nearby that attracted a youthful clientele. This was attributing the cluster of crime to a situational characteristic, while ignoring the site characteristic of the place. An examination of the data determined that most of the auto theft in the hot spot was associated with a single address. This was a multistory parking garage. In other words, the opportunity for auto theft was stacked in a vertical dimension.

Further analysis questioned what would happen if each deck of the parking garage were laid end-to-end along the street face. When this was done, it was discovered that the concentration of crime per linear foot of the parking garage surface was less than per linear foot along the street face. In other words, there was no spatial clustering of crime when the site characteristic of the vertical height of the parking garage was taken into consideration. The clustering or concentration of crime was caused by the agglomeration of opportunities vertically rather than due to the situation of being near a late night theater or to the physical nature of the parking garage. In other words, crime was projected down onto the building footprint, making it seem that there was a concentration of crime. If police patrols were assigned to the parking garage, they would be less effective than if they patrolled the street face. A simple control for the vertical integration accounts for the apparent clustering of crime on the street segment.

Place studies that analyze the spatial arrangement of crime within buildings can usefully expand understanding of a problem. For example, projecting crime onto the building footprint may determine that crime is concentrated in a specific type of room. Hence, crime may not occur in the same place very often but may occur in the same type of place more often. For example, in high-rise building facilities, places such as restrooms tend to be placed directly above each other for plumbing purposes. There may not be many assaults in a single restroom, but when the crimes occurring in all the restrooms in the building are projected onto the building footprint, a concentration of crime in this type of facility may become apparent (Rengert et al. 2001). The same technique can be used to determine whether crime clusters around elevators, stairwells, or in offices located toward the interior or toward the outside walls of a building.

A final example is one of a spurious relationship between a place and crime in the surrounding community. This example concerns casino gambling. Crime has been found to concentrate within and around certain facilities or certain land uses (e.g., Eck et al. 2007). For this reason, it appears justified to undertake a crime impact assessment (Ekblom 1997) to examine the extent to which a new development, such as a casino, increases risk in the surrounding locale. Rengert (1986) examined the impact of the onset of casino gambling on crime in Atlantic City. It was discovered that the crime rate of the city went up dramatically with the onset of casino gambling, especially theft and larceny. However, when the spatial arrangement of this crime was inspected, it was determined that almost all the increase took place within the casinos. There was negligible impact on the surrounding neighborhoods. Simply controlling for where the crime took place demonstrated that if this had not been done, one would surmise that Atlantic City casino gambling had a negative effect on the crime rate of the surrounding neighborhoods. In fact, the increase was concentrated within the casinos with little impact on residential areas. That is to say, the increase in crime was place-specific.

We also need to proceed with caution when considering crime and place and its potential correlates. In this case, we need to ensure that we are not falsely assuming it is location that is driving the concentration of crime at places. This is exactly the issue on which Pease (2001) focuses in his discussion of the "tyranny of geography and its consequences." His argument rests on the recognition that location is not an independent variable per se because places (or maybe he should have said spaces) themselves do not cause crime.

He suggests that geographic information system (GIS)-based studies can run the risk of poorly handling or assessing the contribution of nonspatial variables, and gives some examples based on repeat domestic violence and burglary of instances where nonspatial methods of analysis prove more fruitful than spatial ones. So, it might not always be the geography that is important (or at least most important) in the explanation of the pattern of crime.

A good example of what Pease (2001) is talking about is repeat burglary victimization in which the best predictor of whether a place will be burglarized in the future is whether or not it has been burglarized in the past. There are two explanations for why certain homes are repeatedly burglarized. One is the geographic explanation of the site and situational characteristics of the home, which have been termed *flag* explanations. This explanation suggests that there are particular site and/or situational characteristics about the particular house that flag it to all offenders as a good potential opportunity for crime. For example, it might be accessible because it is situated on the corner of a street, it might have site characteristics of overgrown shrubs that lower natural surveillance, or it might advertise a good potential yield by having expensive items on display through the windows. These are characteristics of the place. Its vulnerability is thus general and will therefore be the potential target of many different offenders. Hence, the house might be repeatedly burglarized, but not necessarily by the same offender. This is a geographic explanation of repeat victimization of a place.

The other explanation is *boost*. This proposes that risks to properties are boosted by an initial visit from an offender. The initial visit may not have been for criminal purposes and are not related to characteristics of the place. It may be that the prospective burglar attended a party at the house and noticed a lot of good things to steal. If the burglar returns and completes a successful burglary, there will be an incentive to return to repeat the success. Because an offender now has more knowledge of the property, he or she might as well go back to reoffend because he or she knows what to expect. Hence, the concentration of crime is shaped by the offender's choices and psychology, not just by the objective characteristics of the place itself. Research literature illustrates that the nongeographic boost is often a reality (e.g., Johnson 2008). Hence, in this example, it is important to consider factors other than those merely to do with the place itself.

Some may argue that place management is a nongeographic concept associated with the likelihood of crime at a place. As described more in Chapter 3, place management refers to the care with which a person in charge of a facility takes in its upkeep and management (Eck and Wartell 1997). If a place manager allows unsavory patrons to use a facility, criminal elements are more likely to be among this clientele. Likewise, if a place manager allows a facility to deteriorate physically, it will be more attractive to criminals than a well-kept facility. Whether or not this is a geographic factor depends on whether or not

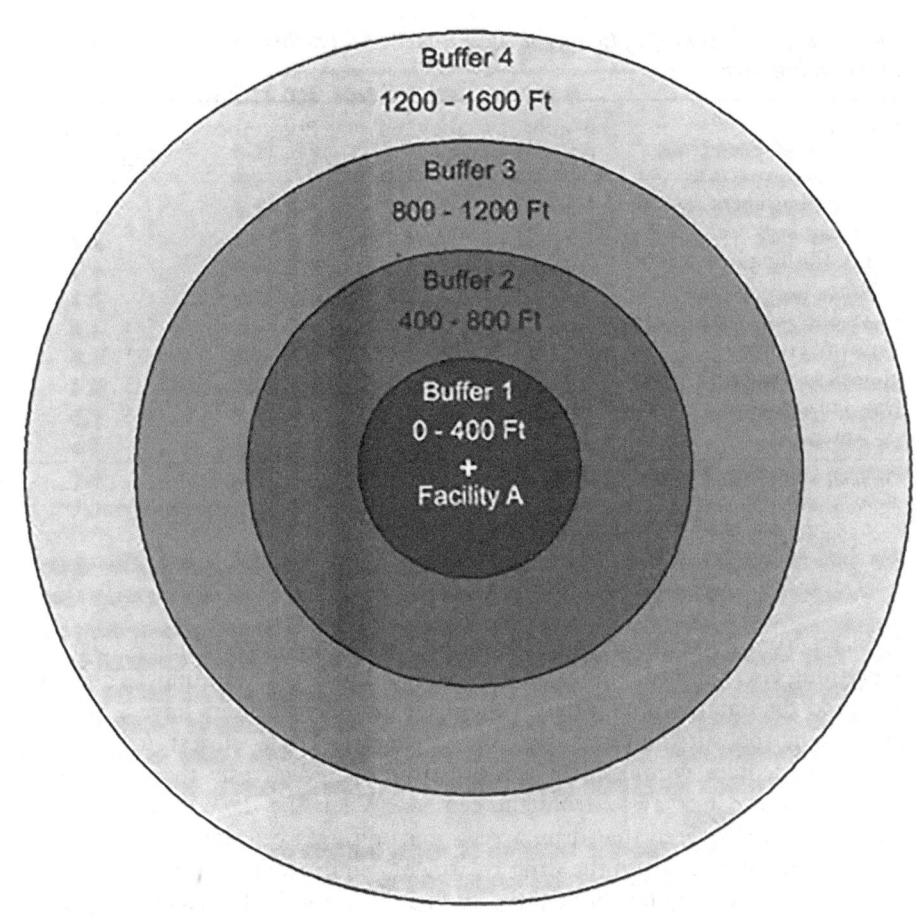

FIGURE 2.11. Example of concentric circles buffers surrounding a facility.
Original source: Taniguchi, T.A., Rengert, G.F., and McCord, E.S. (2009). "Where size matters: Agglomeration economies of illegal drug markets in Philadelphia." *Justice Quarterly*, 26(4), 670–694. Reprinted with permission of Taylor & Francis Ltd.

poor place management is randomly distributed over space or is more likely to be clustered in specific neighborhoods.

Another issue that confounds site and situation characteristics of a place is the question of whether a facility, such as a drug treatment center, makes the surrounding area bad (has a negative impact on the space surrounding it) or whether it was just situated in a bad area because that is where the drug addicts it serves are located (Taniguchi et al. 2009; Wooditch et al. 2013). Taniguchi et al. (2009) illustrate a GIS method of disentangling this issue. The authors constructed four concentric circles of 400-foot-radius intervals around all the drug treatment centers in Philadelphia (see Figure 2.11). Then, they used

TABLE 2.4 *Location Quotients for the Impact of a Facility on the Surrounding Area*

Facility	n	0–400 feet	400–800 feet	800–1200 feet	1200–1600 feet
Beer Establishment	146	6.8	3.4	2.4	1.7
State Liquor Store	53	2.5	1.9	1.8	1.8
Check Cashing Store	96	4.9	3.7	2.8	2.2
Pawn Shop	30	7.2	4.7	3.3	2.3
Halfway House	41	5.2	6.1	4.1	4.1
Homeless Shelter	39	2.5	2.8	2.9	2.3
Day Treatment Center	20	3.6	4.7	4.9	3.2

Original source: Taniguchi, T.A., Rengert, G.F., and McCord, E.S. (2009). "Where size matters: Agglomeration economies of illegal drug markets in Philadelphia." *Justice Quarterly*, 26(4), 670–694. Reprinted with permission of Taylor & Francis Ltd.

Tobler's (1970) first law of geography, which states that everything is related to everything else, but near things are more related than distant things. Thus, they analyzed the data assuming that if the drug treatment centers have a negative impact on the surrounding area, the concentric circle closest to the drug treatment centers would contain more drug-related arrests than the circles 1,200 or 1,600 feet away from the centers. When the data were examined, the authors discovered that drug arrests per unit area did not decrease monotonically as distance from the drug treatment centers increased (see Table 2.4; last row). In fact, the first four types of facility in the table, which are private facilities, seem to have a negative impact on the surrounding area, while the last three public social service agencies (including day treatment centers) did not. The social service agencies that are commonly associated with a negative environment seem to be due to the environment within which they are situated, rather than their making the environment bad.

This implies that the drug treatment centers did not negatively impact the space surrounding them. Rather, the fact that there were a lot of drug-related arrests around the drug treatment centers was due to the fact that they were situated in high-drug-usage spaces. Again, a careful researcher cannot ignore situational characteristics if a true picture of the criminogenic aspects of the site characteristics of a microplace is to be fully understood. Its situation in space can be just as important as the site characteristics of the place. In fact, there may be statistical interaction effects such that a site characteristic only is criminogenic in a specific situation. Eck (1994) demonstrated this interaction effect for illegal drug sales on major street intersections in high and low socioeconomic communities.

CONCLUSIONS

We began this chapter by emphasizing that our book is focused on places, and in particular on microgeographic places where crime is found. We then argued that the law of crime concentrations at places provides a raison d'être for the criminology of place. Our review of the data in this area shows us that crime is concentrated at a small number of places in the city and that this phenomenon is common across cities, and is not restricted to research in the United States. The levels of crime concentrations are stable across time as well, and chronic crime hot spots produce substantial proportions of crime over long periods. These are dramatic findings, and they call for concentrated criminological study of microgeographic places and crime. We also emphasized in the chapter the importance of recognizing spatial interaction effects in understanding the concentration of crime at place, and of distinguishing between place and situation. Crime in a specific microplace may be influenced by areas nearby. And often in understanding the importance of place we must recognize that it is a specific type of situation at places that is key to explaining crime concentrations.

3

Theories of Crime and Place[1]

In the previous chapter, we showed that crime is concentrated at very small geographic units, substantially smaller than neighborhoods, and that these concentrations, on average, are relatively stable. This is true whether examining high- or low-crime neighborhoods. Although high-crime places do cluster, they seldom form a homogeneous block of high-crime places. Rather, interspersed within concentrations of high-crime places are many low- and modest-crime places.

Why is crime concentrated in a relatively small number of places? Standard criminology has not asked this question, largely because standard criminology focuses on criminality and implicitly assumes that the density of offenders explains crime density. Recognition that place characteristics matter is the starting point for this chapter. We look at two perspectives on crime place characteristics. We use the term "perspective" because each type of explanation is comprised of multiple theories linked by a common orientation. The first perspective arises from opportunity theories of crime. The second perspective arises from social disorganization theories of crime.

We begin by contrasting two ways of thinking about how a place becomes a crime hot spot and suggest that the process by which high-crime places evolve must involve place characteristics. In the next sections, we examine opportunity and social disorganization explanations. In the final section of the chapter, we examine possible ways researchers might link these two perspectives.

PROCESSES THAT CREATE CRIME PLACES

Before we look for explanations of why places become hot spots of crime it is important to consider two processes that might lead to such an outcome. Criminologists have generally proposed two generic models to account for the processes that lead to variation in place susceptibility to crime. One model suggests that places may start with reasonably similar risks of an initial criminal attack, but once attacked the risk of a subsequent attack on the place rises. Over time, places diverge in their crime risk, and consequently in their crime counts. This temporal contagion model is also known as a boost model (see Chapter 2) or a state-dependence model. It puts the emphasis on offenders' willingness to return to a previously successful crime site (Johnson et al. 2007; Townsley et al. 2000). It suggests that irrespective of initial crime risk the occurrence of a crime will lead to changes in risk of crime at a place.

An alternative model suggests that places have radically dissimilar initial crime risks. This might be due either to their internal characteristics or to their immediate surroundings. According to this second model, offenders who encounter low-risk sites routinely avoid offending, but when they come across high-risk sites, they are more likely to commit a crime. This is also known as a flag model, or a population heterogeneity model (Pease 1998). There is, of course, no reason these two models must be mutually exclusive. In fact, they could work together.

Consider the following hypothetical example. Assume an area comprised mostly of places unsuitable for crime but with a scattering of high suitability locations. Initially, there are no crimes. Consequently, a researcher could not distinguish among the places based on crime counts. If offenders start operating within the area they will mostly discover places unsuitable for crime and ignore them. Occasionally, they will encounter highly suitable locations where they are likely to commit crimes. Having learned of a suitable crime place, and having been successful at exploiting it, they are more likely to return, or inform other offenders who then attack the place. If some nearby places have similar characteristics to successfully exploited crime places, these too will eventually suffer criminal attacks. In this hypothetical illustration both models operate, though as this suggests, the contagion model operates only on those places with suitable characteristics for crime (just as a contagious disease spreads only among people who have no immunity, and skips those with immunity).

This suggests that an explanation of high-crime places or hot spots of crime (relative to the more numerous low-crime and crime-free places) should address place characteristics, as these characteristics drive initial crime risk or become drivers for heightening crime risk, and because modification of these characteristics is the principal way we address high-crime places.

TWO THEORETICAL PERSPECTIVES

What place characteristics should we be concerned with? The answer depends on one's theoretical perspective: opportunity or social disorganization. What precisely are opportunity and social disorganization perspectives? How do they help explain high-versus low-crime places? In this section, we will answer these questions. These two perspectives derive from different traditions: social disorganization theory from the Chicago School's explanation of why some neighborhoods have more juvenile delinquents than others, and opportunity explanations from more recent theories of the causes of crime events. We will give brief overviews of each as if they were complete alternatives to each other. They may not be, though it helps to assume they are to clarify their differences. In a later section, we will show how they may be compatible.

Opportunity Perspectives on High-Crime Places

Rather than seek to explain why some people become offenders (and others do not), opportunity theorists try to explain why some things are taken (and other things are not), why offenders select some actions (rather than others) to commit crimes, why crime events occur at some times (but less at others), and why crime events occur in some places (and not others). One reason for this approach is that opportunity theories were developed primarily by criminologists who were working in the field of crime prevention (Laycock 2005). They naturally took an especially applied focus, since their interest was in reducing crime at specific places.

The opportunity perspective is comprised of several mutually supporting theories of crime events and crime patterns. Common to all opportunity theories are two basic assumptions. First, most crime is driven by peoples' perceptions that a criminal act is personally useful and that they can get away with it. Second, offender perceptions are highly contingent on specific proximate circumstances (as opposed to distal vague propensities). With these common assumptions, each specific opportunity theory seeks to answer a different question.

How Do Offenders Choose When, Where, and How to Attack a Specific Target? Opportunity theorists contend that people operate within a rational choice framework. Though opportunity theorists eschew the hyperrational decision maker of classical economics, they also reject the antichoice framework that permeates sociologically based theories of criminality (Cornish and Clarke 2003). According to opportunity theorists, offenders make bounded rational decisions: they operate within their cognitive limits and available information, and they rely on heuristics to make reasonable "good enough" decisions. Generally, these decisions are based on offenders' appraisal of rewards, risks, effort, provocations, and excuses (Clarke 1995; Clarke and Felson 1993; Felson and Boba 2009). The rational choice perspective provides a mechanism for crime (choice) in specific contexts (e.g., places).

By itself, a rational choice perspective, even when well informed by recent research in cognition and decision making, is not powerful enough to explain crime. This brings us to the second question: *How do offenders select targets within a large geographic area?* Crime pattern theory seeks to answer this question. The core of crime pattern theory is that offenders follow basic routines that take them to and from destinations (nodes) along streets (paths) (Brantingham and Brantingham 1993b). Places are important within offender search theory[2] in two ways. First, nodes are places – home, school, stores, work, recreation areas, and so forth. Second, places are arrayed along paths – stores and parking lots that line avenues, houses that face streets, and so forth. Thus, offenders look for likely targets at places they routinely encounter (Beavon et al. 1994; Benson et al. 2009; Brantingham and Brantingham 1981; 1984; Eck and Weisburd 1995). In short, offenders do not roam arbitrarily, looking for targets. Instead, offender knowledge and routines structure their hunting.

Opportunity theorists do not just explain the behavior of offenders. They also account for behaviors of others involved in crime processes, most notably potential victims, guardians who protect them, people who try to keep offenders out of trouble (handlers), and people who control places (managers) (Eck 1995; Felson 1995; Felson and Boba 2009; Miethe et al. 1987; Reynald 2010; Tillyer and Eck 2011).

Routine activity theory integrates the behaviors of offenders with these other people to help answer the question: *What makes some targets more vulnerable to attack than others?* The simple answer is that unguarded targets at poorly managed locations are highly vulnerable to criminal attack when confronted by unhandled offenders (Bichler et al. 2014; Eck et al. 2007; Madensen and Eck 2008). Like offenders, targets, guardians, handlers, and place managers follow spatial–temporal routines, thus making targets differentially vulnerable over space and time (Reynald 2011; Wilcox et al. 2007). Because place is an explicit element of routine activity, it is not surprising that routine activity theory specifically, and opportunity theories in general, are invoked to explain high-crime places (Eck and Weisburd 1995; Sherman et al. 1989; Weisburd et al. 2012).

Finally, opportunity theorists ask: *What types of interventions will work to prevent offenders from committing a crime?* Situational crime prevention helps provide the answer (Clarke 1980; 1995; Cornish and Clarke 2003). The most general answer from situational crime prevention is that actions that make possible crime situations less rewarding, less excusable, less provocative, more risky, and requiring more effort will reduce crime (Cornish and Clarke 2003; Wortley 2001). Consistent with the two assumptions of opportunity theories, situational crime prevention states that offenders' perceptions of the utility of a crime depend on the specific characteristics of the context where the offender is making the decision. This context is typically a place.

The particular interventions that work best depend on the specific nature of the crime being considered (theft of vehicles in a parking garage may require different interventions than theft of vehicles parked on streets, though in both cases we are trying to prevent thefts involving vehicles). Many institutions can use situational crime prevention, including product manufacturers (Clarke 2000; Ekblom 1995; Felson 1995), but as we are interested in places, the most important people are often those who own and operate places – place managers and formal guardians such as the police who are assigned to protect high-crime places.

Place Management and Crime Opportunity

Place management is a simple and powerful explanation of why some proprietary places have exceptionally high levels of crime and why others do not. The place management role is to assure the functioning of the place (Eck 1994). This role will vary to some degree depending on the place. Place managers for a school – the principal, teachers, staff, and volunteers – are confronting a different set of circumstances than the place managers of a shoe store – the owner and sales staff. But in both cases, their interests are in assuring that the purposes of their place are achieved – the education of children in the first instance, and the profitable sales of shoes in the second.

Madensen (2007) described the four basic components of place management: organization of space, regulation of conduct, control of access, and acquisition of resources (ORCA). Environmental psychologists have noted that there is a strong connection between the physical arrangements of space and the behaviors that routinely occur in a place (Barker 1968; Canter 1991). For example, places of worship typically have a very different physical environment than bars and pubs. A commercial fitness facility will have a different spatial arrangement than a parking garage, to use another pair of examples. This becomes very obvious when a place changes function. When an orthopedic supply store goes out of business and is purchased by a restauranteur, the new owner has to completely rearrange the interior space, as well as the entrance and public façade. The organization of space is tightly bound to place function. But this same organization can facilitate or impede crime, as well. The placement of expensive scarves on tables at the first department stores increased sales, but this also created an opportunity for massive shoplifting. To counter this, department stores invented and installed the now ubiquitous glass-fronted display case for small, easily taken, expensive items (Abelson 1992).

Conduct regulation is both obvious and subtle in places. Posted rules make this obvious. These typically explain what users should not do – for example, litter, tip, enter with bare feet, or wear a hoodie or hat – and what sorts of behaviors are encouraged – for example, wayfinding signage, signs showing locations of items for sale, credit card icons on doors, and announcements of coming activities. Conduct regulation is most obvious with signage, but there are many ways to promote some activities and discourage others. A bar that encourages dancing will create dance space and have danceable music. A sports bar encourages rooting for teams by posting team regalia and televising games. The sports bar's encouragement of cheering for teams discourages dancing, and the dance bar's format discourages watching sports. Among the many things place managers discourage are crime and some forms of disorder. The bank that asks customers to remove hats and hoods is regulating conduct that is sometimes used by bank robbers.

Place managers try to determine who uses their places. They do this by encouraging some people and discouraging others. The bouncer at the hot nightclub is an obvious example, as are secure facilities that require special identification to enter. Discounts and sales sometimes bring in customers who would not show up in other circumstances – family night at baseball games, for example. The parking garage that is available only for drivers with assigned spaces will get a different mix of users than the nearby garage without assigned spaces. Price is often used to sort those place users who are desired from those who are not. Some landlords screen potential tenants by using extensive background checks, but many landlords do not.

Finally, place managers need resources. Often the purpose of the place is to obtain resources, in the form of profits. We call such places businesses. But even government, nongovernment nonprofit, religious, and educational places need resources. The museum that is free to the public needs to encourage visitors and generate support so that others donate to its continued operations. This is true for a church-run soup kitchen as well. Resource acquisition has important indirect effects on crime. After World War II, many motels opened up on U.S. highways. When interstate highways opened up in the 1960s, customers increasingly sought newer motels at the interstate exits, and the older motels on the older highways lost customers. The financial stress created conditions where managers of these older motels were more willing to cater to people engaged in criminal activity – prostitution and drug sales (Schmerler 2005), for example. Profitability has three links to crime at places. First, prevention often costs money, so less-profitable businesses have fewer resources to spend on prevention. Second, as business declines, increasingly unprofitable businesses may search for revenue from customers they would not have tolerated in the past. Third, lower profitability reduces the wages owners can offer and the training they can provide; thus, they employ less-talented people and provide less guidance on how to manage the place.

Eck's (1994) concept of place management and Madensen's (2007) four components of place management have been described here in terms of their relationship to crime. However, it is important to acknowledge that neither Eck nor Madensen suggested that place managers are concerned primarily about crime. The ORCA components all deal with business and organizational practices that facilitate the overall functioning of a place: whether it involves selling shoes, educating children, entertaining adults, treating drug addicts, providing a spiritual sanctuary, or any of the myriad purposes of places. For many place managers, crime might be a very unimportant concern. Nevertheless, the ORCA functions do have implications for crime vulnerability, whether or not a place manager realizes it.

These place management functions suggest an important reason why some places are more criminogenic than others: poor organization of space; inept

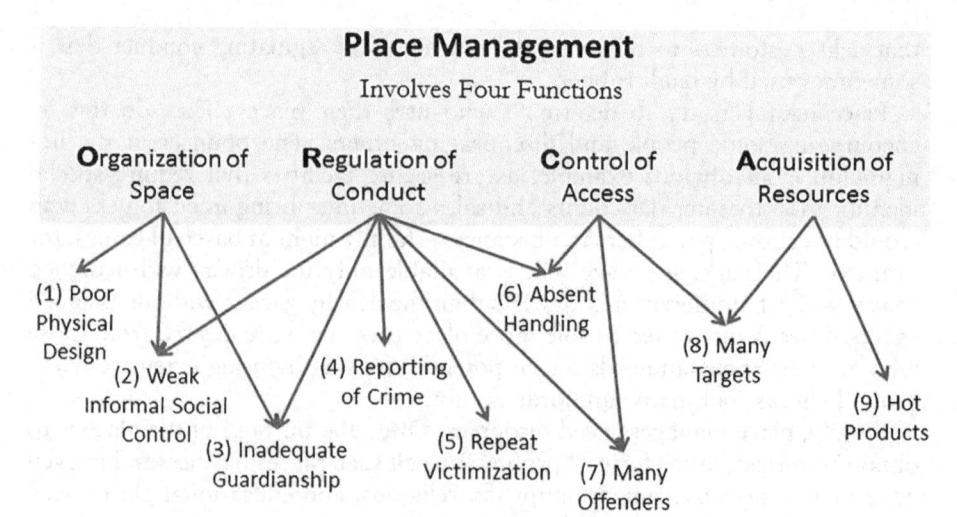

Place Management

Involves Four Functions

Organization of Space — (1) Poor Physical Design; (2) Weak Informal Social Control; (3) Inadequate Guardianship

Regulation of Conduct — (2) Weak Informal Social Control; (3) Inadequate Guardianship; (4) Reporting of Crime; (5) Repeat Victimization

Control of Access — (6) Absent Handling; (7) Many Offenders

Acquisition of Resources — (8) Many Targets; (9) Hot Products

Individually and together the four place management functions affect mechanisms that influence crime at the place

FIGURE 3.1. Place management and other explanations for crime concentration at places.

regulation of conduct; lack of control of access or catering to the wrong clientele; and inability to garner resources. But what of other explanations of concentration of crime at places?

There are ten explanations of why crime is concentrated (if one ignores random variation): (1) poor physical design (Jeffery 1971; Newman 1972); (2) lack of informal social control (Weisburd et al. 2012); (3) inadequate guardianship (Reynald 2010); (4) excessive reporting of crime (Sherman, Gartin, and Buerger 1989); (5) repeat victimization (Farrell, Phillips, and Pease 1995); (6) inadequate handling (Felson 1986); (7) large number of offenders (crime attractors in Brantingham and Brantingham 1995); (8) many targets (crime generators in Brantingham and Brantingham 1995); and (9) hot products (Clarke 1999). Inadequate place management is the tenth explanation. These are not mutually exclusive explanations as, for example, informal social control overlaps with guardianship and handling. Earlier, we showed how the relevant explanation can vary over time. So these explanations are not generally competitive, but their importance may vary from place to place and time to time.

However, we can map Madensen's (2007) ORCA categories to the first nine explanations. Figure 3.1 shows that place management provides an overarching opportunity theory that encompasses the first nine explanations. Organization of space influences explanations 1, 2, and 3 by making it easier to detect offending, thereby increasing the risks of offending. Poor physical design has been linked to crime for more than forty years (Jeffery 1971; Newman 1972) but it is the owner of the place who directs the design and orders redesign. Guardianship and informal social control are two of the important mechanisms by which design is supposed to influence crime and its prevention.

The regulation of conduct affects explanations 2 through 7. Conduct regulation can enhance informal social control, promote guardianship, influence reporting of offenses, curtail repeat victimization, promote handling, and deter offenders from entering the place. Place managers can enhance informal social control by promoting awareness of risky situations. They can promote guardianship through numerous means, from signage to hiring security personnel. Place managers can act to promote or discourage reporting of crime, and to whom it is reported. Providing additional protection to particularly vulnerable patrons can curb repeat victimization. Signage that requests parents to control their children is an attempt to mobilize handling. Place managers also use regulation to discourage offenders from entering the place by signaling that the employees of the location are watching (e.g., requirements that hats and hoods be removed upon entering a bank).

Control of access can be linked to explanations 6 and 7. When place managers only allow juveniles to enter when they are accompanied by parents, they are promoting handling. Keeping a list of patrons who have been caught offending, or who are at high risk of offending, can help exclude offenders from places. When place managers believe that some people are particularly vulnerable to victimization, these people are sometimes excluded. This is particularly true for children and juveniles.

Finally, acquisition of resources can influence the last two explanations. For places that sell goods, the choice of which items to display and sell influences profits as well as crime. Place managers have direct control over the number and type of goods they will sell. Additionally, by clearly signaling to place users that the location is safe, place managers can increase foot traffic, and thus increase resources for place operations.

Place management, therefore, is a broad explanation for concentration of crime or disorder at places. Place management does not fit the formal versus informal social control dichotomy. Like formal controls, place management is intentional, and like informal social control, place management is usually not a government or police function. It draws on the legal powers of owners of property to do things that other place users cannot. Very little prevention can occur at places without the explicit involvement of the people who have the legal control to make changes. Those with legal control will always be the people or organizations who have place property rights, or who have been delegated authority to make decisions by the place owner. When place managers strongly resist changing their practices, police and other government authorities cannot unilaterally take over management. Rather they need to go to court to get the legal authority to force change.

The mapping of place management functions to explanations for crime concentration at places demonstrates that place managers have numerous mechanisms by which they can influence crime and disorder. Not all these mechanisms will work in any particular circumstance. For any particular place, however, it is probably the case that one or more of these mechanisms will work. We revisit the importance of place managers in preventing and blocking opportunities for crime in Chapter 6.

In summary, opportunity theorists have created a set of interlocking explanations for crime event clustering that describe how offenders, targets, and others meet in time and space and why some places will have more crime than most others. Place managers are a critical dimension in opportunity theories because they are the people who often influence routines (e.g., opening and closing times) of places and the guardianship at places (e.g., hiring security, installing lighting or closed circuit television [CCTV], controlling access, or mobilizing police). Place managers' decisions influence both the physical and the social arrangements at places, and this can influence offender contact with targets as well as the willingness of bystanders to intervene. Formal guardians, such as the police, as we will see in Chapter 6, are also key agents in reducing opportunities for crime at places through their influence on offenders' perceived risks of apprehension (Nagin 2013) and changes in the specific environments that offer opportunities for crime.

Social Disorganization Perspectives on High-Crime Places

Social disorganization theories of crime focus on how characteristics of areas, such as neighborhoods or communities, influence their levels of crime. The characteristics of interest in social disorganization theories involve the social structure, principally how residents work together to keep order (Weisburd et al. 2009). Here we provide an overview of these large-area theories.

Durkheim (1893) identified "collective conscience" as essential to the formation and maintenance of an orderly society. Chicago School theorists applied this idea to neighborhoods. They suggested that when members of a neighborhood were similar to one another, and were rooted in a locality, they developed a shared sense of acceptable behavior. Park and Burgess (1924) explained how "natural areas" developed in the form of neighborhoods with similar demographic and built environment characteristics. They identified the competition for land among different uses as the primary mechanism underlying the development of these zones of spatial differentiation within cities.

Reacting against individual theories of crime that prevailed in the early twentieth century – theories that claimed the sources of criminality could be found in the characteristics of people – Shaw and McKay (1942) applied this theory of urban development to crime. They wanted to know whether neighborhood juvenile delinquency was related to neighborhood ethnic make-up or to "structural" characteristics such as low education levels, unemployment rates, residential stability, and poverty – because they form the structure within which individuals interact. They suspected that juvenile delinquency stemmed from the social/structural environment of the neighborhood rather than from the characteristics of individuals who act in a delinquent manner. They discovered that changes in neighborhood ethnicity were not associated with changes in delinquency. Instead, they found that residential mobility (i.e., turnover of residents), population heterogeneity, and poverty were related to changes in crime.

If the types of individuals who resided in a neighborhood were unrelated to crime, and environmental characteristics were related, then criminologists should shift attention from individual explanations to social explanations of crime. Shaw and McKay (1942) posited that organized neighborhoods – those with low turnover in their population, relatively homogeneous populations (regardless of ethnicity), and moderate- to high-income populations – had less crime than disorganized communities, because organized communities had agreed upon definitions of order and processes to maintain order. Disorganization, then, was the cause of crime. Shaw and McKay's emphasis on environmental influences on individuals sparked a fundamental change in criminological thought and formed the basis of social disorganization theories.

In the decades since Shaw and McKay's writing, criminologists have modified social disorganization theory in a number of ways. While acknowledging the role of structural factors in setting the stage, some newer theories emphasize social networks and relationships. Systemic theory is one such social disorganization theory (Berry and Kasarda 1977; Bursik and Grasmick 1993b). It describes neighborhoods as "complex systems of friendship and kinship networks, and formal and informal associational ties rooted in family life and person socialization requirements" (Berry and Kasarda 1977, 56). The focus is on "the degree to which a neighborhood can employ the *interactional networks* that tie together community residents to effectively regulate the nature of the activities within its boundaries" (Bursik 2000, 92). Support for this form of social disorganization theory comes from Sampson and Groves (1989), who found that friendship networks, control of teenagers, and participation in neighborhood organizations influenced criminality.

Sampson and colleagues (1997) extended systemic theory with their concept of "collective efficacy." Like Shaw and McKay, Sampson and colleagues (1997) were primarily interested in how communities supervised children and teenagers to maintain public order. They defined collective efficacy as "social cohesion among neighbors combined with their willingness to intervene on behalf of the common good" (Sampson et al. 1997, 918). Social cohesion stems from high levels of trust among neighbors, which, in turn, develops from shared expectations for behavior. The willingness to intervene is directly related to the level of confidence residents have that they know when intervention is appropriate and will be supported by their neighbors. These versions of social disorganization theory follow Shaw and McKay's (1942) contention that residential stability is the key to establishing the social networks that underpin social organization and enable both informal social control and collective action on the part of the neighborhood (Bursik and Webb 1982; Bursik and Grasmick 1993b; Sampson et al. 1997).

Wilson and Kelling (1982) took social disorganization theory in a different direction to create broken windows theory. They contend that people's willingness to engage in informal social control depends on the cues they receive from their neighborhood context. When residents perceive others to be orderly and the physical space is clean, residents are willing to intervene to prevent disorder. Further, if there is order, offenders will perceive the area to be unattractive for crime. In short, social and physical order send signals to law-abiding residents and potential offenders. If minor disorders go unaddressed this undercuts residents' willingness to engage in informal social control, thus leading to more disorder, and even less informal control. Serious offenders sense that no one will intervene, so criminality increases, which further impairs informal controls. The result is an upward neighborhood crime spiral. Wilson and Kelling (1982) suggested that to restore neighborhoods, police have to step in to control disorder and crime and allow informal social controls to be renewed.

Scholars who study the criminology of place have virtually ignored social disorganization theories in empirical analysis and theoretical discussion. In one sense, this is understandable because the impetus for study of micro crime places came from opportunity theories. Such theories justified examination of small geographic units because of their emphasis on the specific situations and contexts that make crime possible. But we think there may be room for greater "theoretical integration" (Bernard and Snipes 1996) in the study of crime and place (e.g., see Elliott 1985). This is, indeed, not a radical new idea. As Cullen (1988) noted, Cloward (1959) sought to integrate opportunity perspectives with traditional social disorganization ideas more than half a century ago. More recently, several criminologists have sought theoretical integration of opportunity and social disorganization theories at place, although their level of geographic analysis has been much higher than the microgeographic units that are our focus (see Joiner and Mansourian 2009; Wikström et al. 2010; Wilcox et al. 2007).

Of course, theoretical integration of opportunity and social disorganization theories in a model for understanding crime at street segments does not make sense if social disorganization is a concept that is irrelevant to small microgeographic units of analysis. This seems to be the position of many scholars in this area. Sherman, Gartin, and Buerger (1989, 30), for example, argued in introducing the idea of a criminology of place that "(t)raditional collectivity theories [referred to here as social disorganization theories] may be appropriate for explaining community-level variation, but they seem inappropriate for small, publicly visible places with highly transient populations."

Is the concept of social disorganization "inappropriate" for understanding variability of crime at specific places? Scholars concerned with social disorganization have focused their interests on larger geographic areas, often communities, and have linked their theories to the ways in which the characteristics and dynamics of these larger social units influence crime. If indeed the only units of analysis relevant to social disorganization are large geographic units such as communities or neighborhoods, then it is reasonable to say that social disorganization is irrelevant to the study of the criminology of place.

But another approach is possible, and we think relevant, to the study of crime at small units of geography. Microgeographic units, such as street segments or specific facilities, do not simply represent physical entities. They also are social settings (see Chapter 1), or, following Wicker (1987, 614), "behavior settings," which can be considered "small-scale social systems." In this context, Weisburd et al. (2012) argue that micro crime places can be considered examples of small-scale communities (see also Taylor 1997). Accordingly, we may often be able to consider microunits of place as "microcommunities" and as "microplaces." They have many of the traits of communities that have been considered crucial to social disorganization theory, in that these physical units function also as social units with specific routines. For example, such microcommunities might have specific routines that govern activities, such as times of day when drug dealers may be found on the street. If it is a group of streets with businesses, they may open at similar times, and the business owners may work together to deal with specific sorts of problems. In the case of a unit such as a street segment, this idea becomes even stronger. As Taylor (1997; see also Weisburd et al. 2012) has suggested, people who frequent a street segment get to know one another and become familiar with each other's routines. Residents develop certain roles they play in the life of the street segment (e.g., the busybody or the organizer). Norms about acceptable behavior develop and are generally shared. Blocks have standing patterns of behavior, for example, people whose routines are regular such as the mail carrier or the shop owner. The case for seeing microplaces as microcommunities may even be stronger at the level of such places as schools or community centers, where clear routines and rules apply that are often different from those of places nearby.

One key question is whether social disorganization varies at the microgeographic unit of analysis. If communities are uniform in such characteristics, then there would be little reason to explore the importance of social disorganization perspectives for the criminology of place. Weisburd et al. (2012) show that social disorganization varies at microgeographic units. Thus, their research reinforces the importance of considering social features of places in crime prevention. They collected geographic data on structural factors reflecting social disorganization at the street segment level (Sampson and Groves 1989; Shaw and McKay 1942; Wilcox et al. 2004) and what some have termed "intermediate variables of social control" (Sampson and Groves 1989; Sampson et al. 1997). Their findings indicate that there are also microgeographic hot spots of social disorganization and low social control. For example, they collected data on public housing and Section 8 vouchers at street segments in Seattle, finding that there are public housing assistance hot spots. Indeed,

50 percent of housing assistance is consistently found on approximately 0.4 percent of the street segments in Seattle. There is also strong street-by-street variability, emphasizing the importance of hot spot segments rather than larger area concentrations. Within 800 feet of the public assistance hot spots, 84.3 percent of street segments do not have any public housing assistance recipients.

Though social disorganization theories were created to describe neighborhood-level concentrations in criminality and crime, we think that they are likely as well to be applicable to places. Indeed, it is possible that they may be more applicable to places than neighborhoods (Weisburd et al. 2012). To see why, consider the principal fact we have set out to explain – that crime is concentrated at very small geographic units that are far smaller than neighborhoods. Social disorganization theories applied at the neighborhood level cannot explain this internal heterogeneity. Why would a neighborhood with low collective efficacy, low informal social control, or high disorder display high crime on one street segment but low crime on surrounding segments?

"Neighborhood" is a vague term (Taylor 2012). Hunter (1979, 270) stated a neighborhood is "a social/spatial unit of social organization, and that it is larger than a household and smaller than a city." The range he noted supports our contention here that places as small as street blocks (both sides of a street between two intersections) fit within the domain of the social disorganization perspective, and any processes commonly studied in larger areas probably apply as well, or perhaps even better, when studied at places.

Summary

In this section, we have examined two different ways of explaining crime at places – opportunity theories and social disorganization theories. Opportunity theories have been used to explain place crime concentration since these concentrations have been documented (Sherman et al. 1989), but only recently have researchers considered applying social disorganization theories at this level (Weisburd et al. 2004; Weisburd et al. 2012). Both ways of explaining high-crime places make use of the close physical proximity of the people involved in creating and preventing crime. Both invoke control mechanisms operating in small behavior settings. In the next two sections, we will look at each perspective in greater detail, examine the mechanisms that each invokes to explain crime concentration at places, and briefly summarize the available evidence to suggest that these perspectives are useful.

OPPORTUNITY MECHANISMS

To understand how opportunity theories can explain crime concentration at places, we begin with a plausible hypothetical example. We will follow the rise and fall of thefts from vehicles parked at a regional suburban shopping mall. We begin this example (summarized in Figure 3.2) when the place is a

Theories of Crime and Place

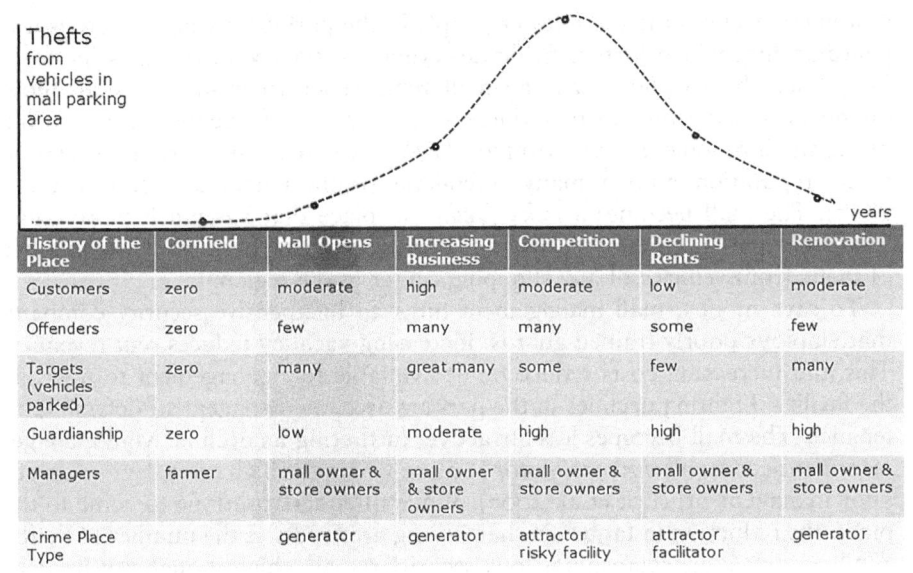

History of the Place	Cornfield	Mall Opens	Increasing Business	Competition	Declining Rents	Renovation
Customers	zero	moderate	high	moderate	low	moderate
Offenders	zero	few	many	many	some	few
Targets (vehicles parked)	zero	many	great many	some	few	many
Guardianship	zero	low	moderate	high	high	high
Managers	farmer	mall owner & store owners	mall owner & store owners	mall owner & store owners	mall owner & store owners	mall owner & store owners
Crime Place Type		generator	generator	attractor risky facility	attractor facilitator	generator

Because elements of routine activity theory interact, there may be a low correlation between individual elements and crime.

FIGURE 3.2. A hypothetical history of opportunity and crime at a place: a shopping mall.

cornfield on the edge of a metropolitan area. The place manager is a local farmer. There are no offenders, targets, or guardians, relative to our crime of interest, though there is a place manager (the farmer). There are no thefts from vehicles at this stage.

The farmer sells the land to a developer who builds a shopping mall with a very large parking area. Within the first year that it is open most of the retail space within the mall is leased. Though the mall is doing well, it is not operating at capacity. Nevertheless, many vehicles are in the parking area. The mall owner does not have security cameras in the parking area, nor security patrols, though at night the parking areas are well lit. Few offenders have discovered the place, so thefts from vehicles are very low.

Some of the customers are willing to steal from vehicles, and they discover this opportunity. Mall management hires a security company to patrol the parking lot during the evening operating hours. Compared to other places in the area, the mall is a hot spot of crime, primarily due to the high number of targets. Thus, the place has become a *crime generator* (a place where high crime levels are due to target concentration) (Brantingham and Brantingham 1995).

Several other shopping malls open in the region and draw off customers. In addition, our mall gains a reputation of being unsafe relative to other malls, driving off more customers. This has two consequences. First, as the number of customers declines there are fewer people in the parking areas, so there is less guardianship, which further facilitates crime. Second, vacancy rates increase. To reduce the vacancy rate, the mall rents space to businesses that allow offenders to hang out. In time, increasing numbers of offenders come to the place, and it becomes a *crime attractor* (a place where the high crime level is due to its reputation among many offenders) (Brantingham and Brantingham 1995). The mall becomes a *risky facility* (a place that has much more crime than other similar types of places) (Eck et al. 2007), as it has the highest number of thefts from vehicles of any shopping center in the region.

To save money, mall management hires an inexpensive security company that employs poorly trained guards. Increasing vacancy reduces rent revenues. This and increasing costs reduce funds available for management to upgrade the facility. Lighting declines in the parking area, as management defers maintenance. The mall becomes less attractive, furthering its decline. Mall management has become a *crime facilitator* (a place where the high crime level is due to poor management) (Eck et al. 2007). While offenders continue to come to the place, the reduction in targets in the parking area reduces the number of thefts. While informal guardianship is low, security remains high though not particularly effective.

Finally, the original owner sells the mall. The new owner temporarily closes it, guts the interior spaces, adds new space, and reopens it as a new mall under a different name with new stores and higher rents. Mindful of the previous mall's reputation, the new owner maintains a high level of guardianship by employing a much more professional security service, modern CCTV, and much better lighting. Customers return to the place. Offenders find the new environment hard to operate within, though there are plenty of targets. The place is no longer a crime generator, crime attractor, crime facilitator, or risky facility.

In this example, we see how various elements of opportunity theory interact to create or suppress crime. Critical to this hypothetical but realistic story is the role of place management. Management created the mall, thus producing the density of targets and attracting initial offenders. Management decisions also influenced guardianship – both directly through hiring security and providing lighting, and indirectly by influencing informal security by customers. Though many management decisions were based on noncrime events (e.g., increasing competition), they nevertheless have consequences for crime.

Opportunity theories of crime are inherently nonlinear. This is particularly true of routine activity theory (Eck 1995), though it is also true of crime pattern theory. A linear theory of guardianship, for example, would predict that as guardianship increases, crime would decline, and as guardianship declines, crime would increase. But adding guardianship to places without offenders will not drive crime below zero, and subtracting guardianship from offender-free places will not result in crime increases. Further, as much guardianship is costly, guardianship may remain low until crime events make it clear to the place manager that investing in guardianship is worthwhile. This makes it difficult to

Theories of Crime and Place

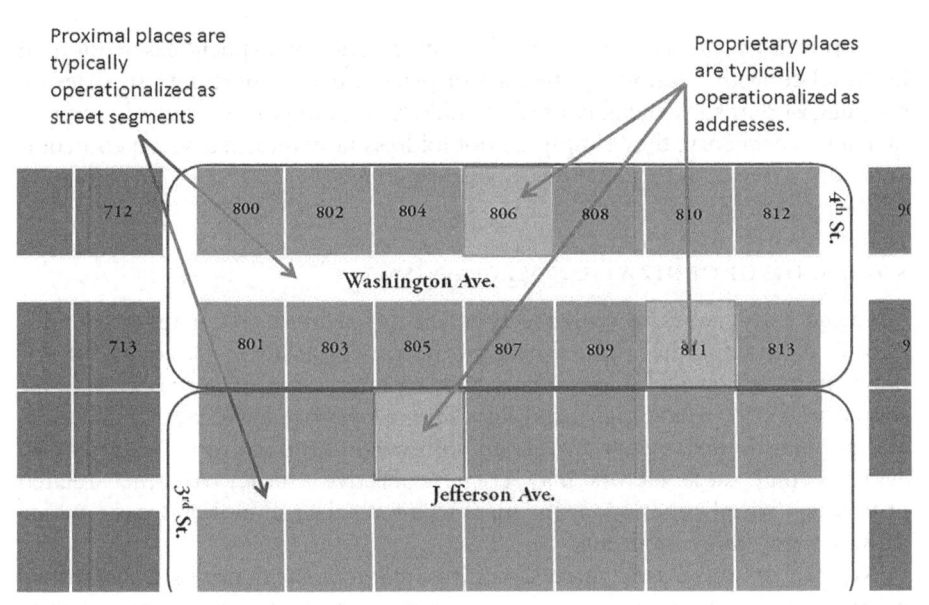

FIGURE 3.3. Proprietary and proximal places.

test elements of opportunity theories using cross-sectional data. Further complicating matters is the fact that the concepts of opportunity theories are complex. Guardianship, for example, has three parts according to Reynald (2010): the willingness to watch, the capacity to identify possible offenders, and the disposition to act, if necessary. Management is even more difficult to measure (Madensen and Eck 2008).

Opportunity theories are easiest to imagine working at the address level, what Eck and Madensen (2012) call *proprietary places*. Proprietary places are locations with unitary ownership, such as stores, apartment buildings, single-family homes, and bars. Ownership carries with it the legal authority to manipulate the place: without that specific authority from the owner, no one but the owner has permission to make physical changes to sites. Further, civil laws hold place owners accountable for events at their sites – from accidents to food poisoning to violent attacks. Legal authority and accountability are often absent on most street segments.

Proprietary places are usually smaller than units such as street segments – what Eck and Madensen (2012) call *proximal places*. The smaller the place, the more likely the place users will interact. This means that an offender can control others within the space when committing a crime (e.g., it is easier to hold up a liquor store than to hold up an entire street of stores). Though opportunity matters within proximal places, we may need to consider other influences on crime at street segments. The distinction between proprietary and proximal places is illustrated in Figure 3.3.

Opportunity theories of crime do not include an explicit description of informal collective action on the part of place users. Opportunity theories do not suggest that such social control is unlikely or unimportant; outside of place management theory, they simply do not address how informal social control is created. So, we turn to social disorganization next.

SOCIAL DISORGANIZATION MECHANISMS

Since the early 1980s, there have been on the order of 100 papers per year published studying the topic of neighborhoods (Sampson et al. 2002). At this point, there is considerable evidence that structural factors such as economic status (poverty), residential instability, ethnic heterogeneity, family structure, and population density are correlated with neighborhood crime. There is also evidence that these factors may create collective efficacy or other related processes – social cohesion, willingness to intervene, and mutual trust – which then, in turn, influence crime.

Researchers have used three structural characteristics, originally identified by Shaw and McKay (1942), when examining social disorganization theory: low economic status, residential instability, and ethnic heterogeneity. Recently, researchers have added collective efficacy and disorder levels in neighborhoods as important structural characteristics. Each characteristic has a relationship with neighborhood crime.

More Poverty, More Crime. Poverty/low economic status has been a frequently used structural characteristic (Byrne and Sampson 1986). Even in recent social disorganization theory, economic status is often used to represent the available resources and capabilities of residents to invest in the community where they live (e.g., see Bellair 1997; Bursik and Grasmick 1993a; Sampson and Groves 1989; Veysey and Messner 1999). Other tests have uncovered a consistent relationship between the poverty rate and crime (Bellair 1997; Bursik and Grasmick 1993b; Kornhauser 1978; Sampson and Groves 1989; Veysey and Messner 1999).

More Residential Instability, More Crime. Residential instability is one of the keys to the inability to foster informal social control in neighborhoods. Informal social control allows the self-regulation of behavior (both of residents and of visitors) by a local community to achieve a commonly held goal (usually a safe neighborhood). When there is residential turnover, there is no time for informal networks to form and for residents to learn the standards for behavior within the neighborhood. As a result, residents are less likely to intervene in situations. Research has consistently found a strong relationship between residential instability and crime (Berry and Kasarda 1977; Bursik and Grasmick 1993b; Lewis and Salem 1986).

More Ethnic Heterogeneity, More Crime. Since Shaw and McKay (1942), ethnic heterogeneity has consistently been associated with higher rates of crime and delinquency. More heterogeneous neighborhoods have lower levels of informal social control because it is harder for residents to identify with one another and find common ground for forming relationships (Bursik and Grasmick 1993b; Kornhauser 1978; Sampson and Groves 1989). If residents fail to form social ties they may be more likely to move, which contributes to the lack of social cohesion. Subsequent research has questioned the direct link between heterogeneity and crime. Sampson (1995) found that once he controlled for mobility and poverty, heterogeneity had little impact on neighborhood crime. It may be that neighborhood collective efficacy determines the degree to which heterogeneity influences crime, however (Sampson and Groves 1989; Sampson et al. 1997).

More Informal Social Control or Collective Efficacy, Less Crime. With the recognition that structural characteristics may not be directly related to crime but rather are conditioned on the level of social control in neighborhoods, as we discussed earlier, researchers began to include measures of social control (Bursik 1988; Sampson and Groves 1989; Sampson and Wilson 1995). Measures representing social control include residents' level of social cohesion and mutual trust and their willingness to intervene, especially as it relates to the behavior of children and teenagers.

Studies have shown that the lack of informal social control is associated with higher crime rates (Bellair 1997; Morenoff et al. 2001; Sampson et al. 1997). Researchers have used a number of indicators of informal social control to explain neighborhood crime: participation in local organizations (Taylor et al. 1984; Sampson and Groves 1989), willingness (or perception of responsibility) to intervene in public affairs (Taylor et al. 1984; Sampson et al. 1997), local friendship networks (Sampson and Groves 1989), mutual trust (Sampson et al. 1997), and unsupervised teens (Sampson and Groves 1989). A community with strong collective efficacy is characterized by "high capacities for collective action for the public good" (St. Jean 2007, 3). Voting behavior has been used to quantify residents' conformity to social norms and engagement with civic life (Coleman 2002; Dreier 1996; Friedrichs and Blasius 2003). These variables are believed to condition the effects of structural disadvantage on local crime problems.

More Disorder, More Crime. As we have described, broken windows theory also claims that informal social controls by local residents are responsible for keeping crime low, and when this fails, crime goes up. Instead of mobility, heterogeneity, or poverty undermining informal social controls, broken windows theory claims that disorder does that. At the neighborhood level, however, the available research evidence on the connections between disorder and more serious crime is mixed. Skogan's (1990) survey research found disorder to be significantly correlated with perceived crime problems in a neighborhood even after controlling for the population's poverty, stability, and racial composition. Further, Skogan's (1990) analysis of robbery victimization data from thirty neighborhoods found that economic and social factors' links to crime were indirect and mediated through disorder. In his reanalysis of the Skogan data, Harcourt (2001) removed several neighborhoods with very strong disorder–crime connections from Newark, New Jersey, and reported no significant relationship between disorder and more serious crime in the remaining neighborhoods. Eck and Maguire (2000) suggested that Harcourt's analyses do not disprove Skogan's results; rather, his analyses simply document that the data are sensitive to outliers.

In his longitudinal analysis of Baltimore neighborhoods, Taylor (2001) found some support for the idea that disorderly conditions lead to more serious crime. However, these results varied according to types of disorder and types of crime. Taylor (2001) suggested that other indicators, such as initial neighborhood status, are more consistent predictors of later serious crimes. Using systematic social observation data to capture social and physical incivilities on the streets of Chicago, Sampson and Raudenbush (1999) found that, with the exception of robbery, public disorder was not significantly related to most forms of serious crime when neighborhood characteristics such as poverty, stability, race, and collective efficacy were considered.

APPLYING SOCIAL DISORGANIZATION TO PLACES

Findings from Weisburd and colleagues' (2012) longitudinal study of street segments in Seattle, Washington, provide important evidence of the variability of social disorganization at a microgeographic level. They collected geographic data on structural factors reflecting social disorganization at the street segment level (Shaw and McKay 1942; Sampson and Groves 1989; Wilcox et al. 2004) and intermediate variables of social control (Sampson and Groves 1989; Sampson et al. 1997). Their findings indicate that there are also microgeographic hot spots of social disorganization and low social control.

We noted earlier that Weisburd et al. (2012) found evidence of hot spots of public housing assistance and that such hot spots were generally surrounded by street segments without housing assistance recipients. Weisburd et al. also found similar evidence of spatial heterogeneity within areas in collective efficacy at street segments. They represented collective efficacy using the percent of active voters on each street segment (see also Coleman 2002; Putnam 2001). On average, there are around seven active voters per street and a little less than 40 percent of the voters on each street are considered active voters. When they examine the street segments within 800 feet of the "hot spots" of active voters (the top 10 percent), only 25 percent of neighboring street segments also evidenced such high levels of active voting.[3]

Visual representations of the spread of measures of social disorganization across the city, and their street to street variability, reinforce the salience of a microplace interest in this perspective. Figure 3.4 shows the concentration of 50 percent of public housing assistance in Seattle. It is clear that the hot spots of public housing assistance are spread throughout the city. Spatial heterogeneity is also illustrated in Figure 3.5, which shows the streets in Seattle where 75 percent of registered voters are active voters – a measure of collective efficacy in the Weisburd et al. study.

SYNTHESIS

Although we have intentionally contrasted opportunity and social disorganization theories, there is no logical reason to conclude that they are in direct opposition. As we noted earlier, we think that theoretical integration rather than competition is a more appropriate approach in this area of study. Nothing in either theory rules out the existence of mechanisms invoked by the other.

Weisburd et al. (2014) include both opportunity and social disorganization in models for understanding crime hot spots in their retrospective longitudinal study of crime at street segments in Seattle, Washington. What they find is that both sets of variables contribute to explanation of crime at place. Though the largest impacts are found in the opportunities created by the availability of larger numbers of potential targets and accessibility provided by such characteristics as bus stops or arterial roads, economic deprivation, physical disorder, and collective efficacy were also important contributors to the understanding of chronic crime hot spots. While this is just one study, it suggests that we will develop better models for understanding crime at place if we consider both opportunity and social disorganization perspectives.

If we begin with the reasonable assumption that opportunity matters, but social disorganization also plays a nontrivial role, then we have two possible mixed-perspective explanations for high-crime places. First, it may be that opportunity theories and social disorganization theories are both important, but they are important in different contexts. That is, at some places mechanisms from one perspective are responsible for the creation of high-crime places, and at other types of places another set of mechanisms is at work. Second, it may be that elements of both theories work together in most circumstances. Let's briefly consider these two possibilities.

Context-Specific Explanations

Let's begin by assuming that social disorganization theories, first and foremost, are explanations for the absence of effective guardianship. If this is true, then it is possible that the factors that mobilize guardianship vary by place type. In some places, social organization does this. In other places, place management carries the water. Place management is most obviously applicable when

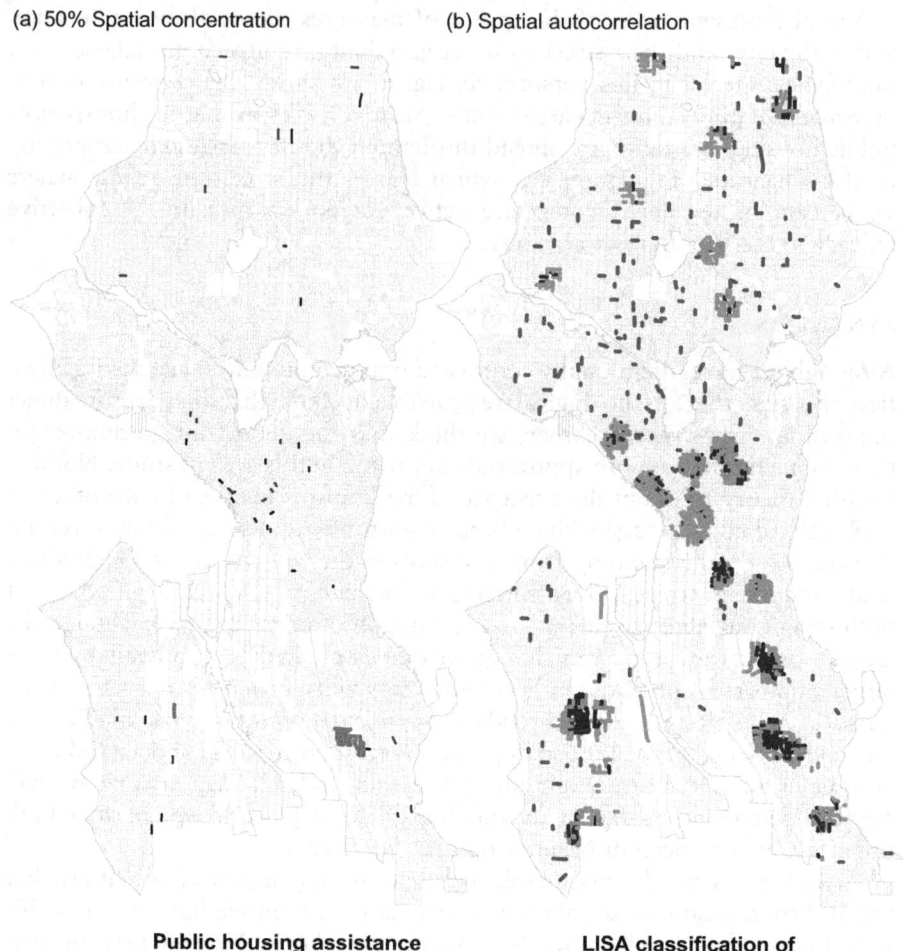

(a) 50% Spatial concentration   (b) Spatial autocorrelation

Public housing assistance per street segment in 1998

—— 90–299

—— 17–89

—— 16

      Street

LISA classification of public housing assistance per street segment in 1998

—— High-High

—— High-Low

—— Low-High

      Street

Note: All base geographic base files were obtained from Seattle GIS. Public housing assistance data were obtained from Seattle Housing Authority. Map (a) depicts only the 0.37 percent of street segments that account for 50 percent of all public housing assistance. Significant low-low autocorrelations are not displayed on map (b) to improve legibility. Map designed by Elizabeth Groff and produced by Julie Hibdon.

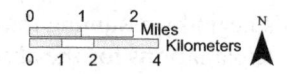

FIGURE 3.4. Spatial concentration and spatial autocorrelation for public housing assistance.
Source: Weisburd, D., Groff, E.R., and Yang, S.-M. (2012). *The criminology of place: Street segments and our understanding of the crime problem.* New York: Oxford University Press. Used by permission of Oxford University Press.

Theories of Crime and Place

Streets where 75% of registered voters are active voters

— 98%–100%
— 82%–97%
— 75%–81%
    Street

Note: All base geographic base files were obtained from Seattle GIS. Active voter data were obtained from Labels & Lists, Inc. Map designed by Elizabeth Groff and produced by Julie Hibdon.

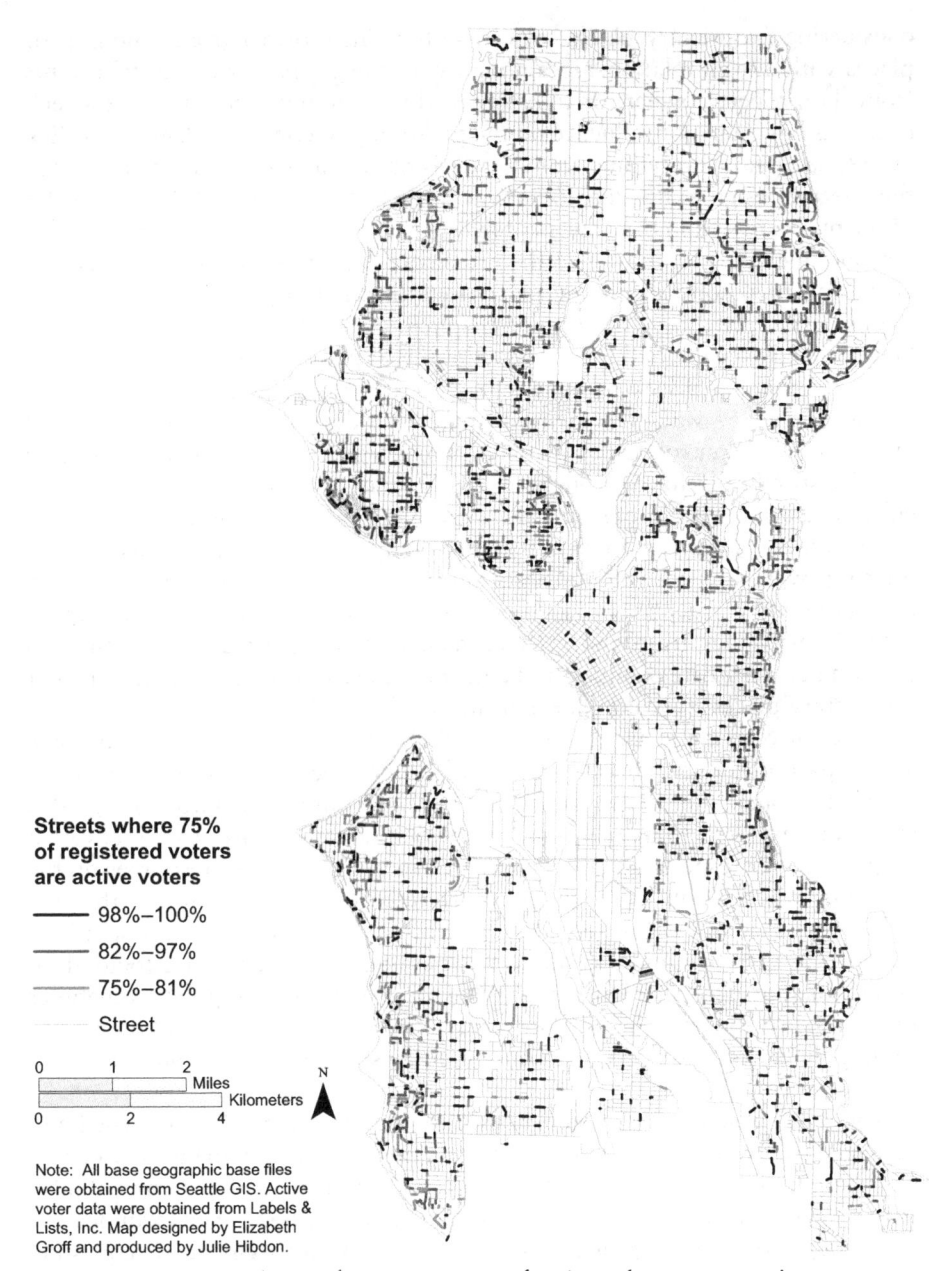

FIGURE 3.5. Streets where at least 75 percent of registered voters are active voters. *Source*: Weisburd, D., Groff, E.R., and Yang, S.-M. (2012). *The criminology of place: Street segments and our understanding of the crime problem*. New York: Oxford University Press. Used by permission of Oxford University Press.

considering proprietary places, places with a single owner (e.g., a house), or places with a legal relationship among owners (e.g., the bar owner who rents from the property owner, or the store within a shopping mall). The owner's decisions have a major influence on the possibility of crime. Madensen and Eck (2008) detail how everything from the decision of where to locate the facility to the interior design to the decision about who to attract to the place to the rules of the place are within the powers of the owner. The owner has the authority to create crime opportunities or to thwart them. The owner can also do much to create informal controls among place users through displaying and enforcing "house" rules, and by setting an atmosphere conducive to peaceful behavior. Since crime is usually bad for the functioning of places, most owners and their employed managers seek to limit crime. So at proprietary places, place management is a key way that guardianship is produced – through formal and informal social control. One way place managers create guardianship is to hire security specifically for this purpose. Hired guardians may be employees specifically tasked with protecting the place and its users, or they might be contractors – a firm specializing in providing guardianship. By its nature, formal private security will not occur unless a place manager creates it. However, even in the absence of formal private security, place managers can induce it by the way they train and manage their employees, organize the physical environment, regulate conduct, and control access. When place management at proprietary places is weak, guardianship will be weak.[4]

Police also create guardianship at publicly owned places. This has become a key part of police efforts to control crime (see Chapter 6). Hot spots policing (Braga and Weisburd 2010; Sherman and Weisburd 1995), also sometimes referred to as place-based policing (see Weisburd 2008), covers a range of police responses that all share in common a focus of resources on the locations where crime is highly concentrated. Nagin (2013) argues that the police role as sentinel (or guardian) is central to a deterrence regime and is likely to be effective under conditions where police resources are focused on crime hot spots (see also Durlauf and Nagin 2011). Though police sometimes focus on proprietary places, they generally focus crime prevention in hot spots policing on proximal locations, such as street segments and clusters of street segments.

The police role is rather complex. Where the place is publically owned and managed by government, the police can function as a place manager as well as a guardian. In this capacity, they can mobilize other agencies of government (also part of place management) to aid in opportunity blocking. For example, the police might respond to prostitution activity on a street segment by requesting the public works department erect barriers and signage to make the through street a cul-de-sac (see Matthews 1993 for an example). This makes the street segment less suitable for prostitutes and their customers. In a number of problem-oriented police programs the police work to reduce opportunities for crime at specific places (see Chapter 6).

Theories of Crime and Place

When dealing with privately owned places, the police must either enlist the cooperation of the private place manager or compel the owner to make alterations that influence crime opportunities, including enhancing guardianship. In this capacity the police are acting as supercontrollers, entities that regulate the behaviors of place managers, target guardians, and offender handlers (Sampson et al. 2009). Mazerolle and Ransley (2006) refer to this as "third party" policing. Cooperative methods include landlord training (Campbell 2006), where methods of compellence (Gilboy 1997; Peterson 1986) might entail the use of code enforcement or civil suits.

Street segments, and other proximal places, typically do not have a single owner or a strong legal connection among owners dictating management responsibilities. A street segment may have multiple properties, each owned by someone different, lined up on both sides of a public space (the street and sidewalk) owned by the local government. Here it is easier to envision that social organization plays the larger role in mobilizing guardianship, perhaps exclusively through various forms of informal social control. Obviously, other opportunity related constructs would also be involved – targets, for example. But if social disorganization is responsible for high crime levels in proximal places, then it would seem to operate primarily through the absence of guardianship.

Interaction Explanations

We can also imagine opportunity and social disorganization theories working in partnership, rather than at different types of places. Here are at least five forms of interaction, though there may be more. If any or all of these mechanisms is at work, then parceling out explanations for crime to only one of these two perspectives will be impossible: they share responsibility.

Informal Social Control Influences Opportunities. We have already mentioned that Reynald (2010) shows that guardianship has three components. Each of these elements of guardianship may be influenced by social organization in the place (proprietary or proximal). We can also imagine social organization influences target availability, offender handling, place management, or offending. If true, then social organization influences aspects of opportunity, which in turn influence crime at places.

Management-Created Informal Social Control. We have already suggested this possibility – place managers set rules and organize the environments or their places to create informal social controls that augment management-imposed controls. Here, opportunity mechanisms create social organization, which in turn influences crime.

Proprietary to Proximal Place Interactions. A street segment with well-managed proprietary places may have far less disorder and crime outside on sidewalks, streets, and other public spaces than a street segment with one or more poorly managed places. That is because disorder might spill out from disorderly facilities and overwhelm informal social controls on the street segment. The strong evidence for the diffusion of crime-control benefits (Clarke and Weisburd 1994) implies such a result (e.g., see Guerrette and Bowers 2009; Weisburd et al. 2006). If cleaning up a proprietary place reduces crime in its surroundings, then prior to the cleanup, the place was probably exporting crimes to its environment. There are numerous studies showing that particular facilities on street blocks increase block-level crime. Though the reasons for this are unclear (Wilcox and Eck 2011), one possibility is that some facilities export crime to street segments. If true, then proximal street crime or disorder is largely determined by constituent proprietary places. This may not be a linear relationship. A street segment could be relatively crime-free due to informal social controls until the number of poorly run places on the block exceeds some threshold. At the extreme, a single badly run place is all it takes for the informal social controls to break down.

Looked at from the opposite angle, well-run places may foster informal social control along a street segment. The way owners run their businesses might enhance informal controls that would not exist otherwise along the street. Or informal social control evidenced by residents and businesses might reinforce one another, making the street segment less vulnerable to changes in the level of informal controls exerted by either residents or businesses.

Proximal-to-Proprietary Interactions. Some street segments may be so disorderly it is difficult to run an orderly proprietary place on that segment. Characteristics of the proximal place may create disorder, which in turn inhibits proprietary place order. Put another way, the cost of running a crime-free proprietary place on the street is prohibitively expensive. This might also affect the types of proprietary places that locate on a street segment. In these circumstances, proximal places provide an important context for proprietary places.

Business-to-Business Networks. In her dissertation on the Cincinnati business improvement district (BID), Khadija Monk (2012) shows how business owners network to solve crime problems. Here the BID formalized and expanded a network of relationships among place managers that obligated place managers to behave in certain ways. The BID also provided central business district owners ways of pressuring other owners to improve management. Further, the formal association of business and property owners hired place managers for downtown streets and influenced police guardianship of the area. All of this was designed to drive down crime and disorder. Although the BID operates in a "neighborhood," the same process can be envisioned on a street segment or other proximal place.

These possible ways opportunity and social disorganization theories might combine are probably not exhaustive. We raise them as examples of why we should not simply portray the two theoretical perspectives as necessarily conflicting. At the same time, we have to be mindful that these are two very different perspectives, and though they may interact, they invoke different mechanisms.

CONCLUSIONS

In this chapter, we have considered two different theoretical perspectives on why we have a few high-crime places among many low-crime places. Opportunity theories suggest that high-crime places are the result of repeated interactions at places. Repeatedly, offenders have to come into contact with targets at these places, and repeatedly, when offenders are present there can be little or no guardianship, handling, or place management. This combination of circumstances is relatively rare, so we have relatively few high-crime places. More common is the lack of offender–target interaction, or its occurrence only in the presence of a handler, guardian, or manager. Consequently, we have many low- or no-crime places.

Social disorganization theories have a long, rich tradition in criminology, but have only been applied to microplaces very recently. We have argued here that they also have relevance to understanding the concentrations of crime at place. Social conditions of places, collective efficacy, and their impacts on informal social controls can be seen as potential theoretical explanations for crime at place, just as opportunity theories. Social disorganization at the level of microgeographic places with its result of weakened informal social controls provides a theoretical context for understanding crime at place.

There is no a priori reason to believe that we must choose between one perspective and another. It may be that these two theoretical perspectives are part of a larger explanation where opportunity elements interact with social organization elements. Clearly, we have much to learn from more in-depth empirical examination of places.

4

The Importance of Place in Mainstream Criminology and Related Fields[1]

Influences and Lessons to be Learned

This chapter explores the importance of place in theory and research in both mainstream criminology and other disciplines. As we noted in earlier chapters, traditional criminology has focused primarily on understanding why people commit crime. This focus on criminality has generally inhibited study of microgeographies and their role in producing crime. However, more recently there has been a trend toward integrating microgeographic places into traditional theorizing about criminality. In the first part of the chapter we discuss this trend, focusing on some recent innovations in understanding criminality that have incorporated place-based perspectives. In the second part of the chapter we focus on how other disciplines have influenced thinking in this area, focusing in particular on contributions in psychology, economics, and public health. Finally, we explore how trends in other disciplines might influence future directions of study in the criminology of place.

THE GROWING ROLE OF MICROGEOGRAPHIC PLACES IN TRADITIONAL THEORIZING OF CRIMINALITY

As we noted in Chapter 1, places, at least at a macro level, played a key part in the development of criminology in the nineteenth and early twentieth centuries. But despite the role of place in crime in empirical study in Europe and theoretical development in the Chicago School through social disorganization theory, microgeographic places were mostly ignored. This was not because early criminologists failed to recognize the role of place in crime. Crime occurs in specific environments, and this was apparent to observers of the crime problem. Nonetheless, as we noted in Chapter 1, early criminologists did not see "crime places" – small discrete areas within communities – as a relevant focus of criminological study. This was the case, in part, because crime opportunities provided by places were assumed to be so numerous as to make concentration on specific places of little utility for theory or policy. What is the point of focusing theory or research on the opportunities offered by specific places if such opportunities can be found throughout the urban context?

Moreover, criminologists did not see the utility in focusing in on situational opportunities when criminal motivation was the key to understanding crime rates. Criminologists traditionally assumed that situational factors played a relatively minor role in explaining crime as compared with the "driving force of criminal dispositions" (Clarke and Felson 1993, 4; Trasler 1993). Combining an assumption of a wide array of criminal opportunities and a view of offenders as highly motivated to commit crime, it is understandable that criminologists paid little attention to the problem of the development of crime at place.

For this reason, while both individuals and places have long been important in criminology, the majority of theoretical and empirical inquiry focuses on individual criminal involvement (Kempf 1993; Reiss 1986; Sampson 1986; Weisburd et al. 1992). Well-known examples are strain theory (Agnew 2006), differential association theory (Sutherland 1947), and self-control theory (Gottfredson and Hirschi 1990). These major criminological theories often consider places to play a relatively minor role in explaining crime compared to an individual's criminal propensity (Clarke and Felson 1993; Trasler 1993; Weisburd et al. 2006). We think that this overemphasis on individuals has resulted in a flawed understanding of crime. Sampson (1993) pointed out that criminology had been dominated by methodological individualism; as such, the understanding of crime had been decontextualized. Putting crime back in its place has thus become salient for a more holistic understanding of crime not only for community-based criminology, as noted by Sampson, but also for the criminology of place as described in this volume (see also Weisburd et al. 2009).

Perhaps the key general theoretical contribution for the emerging study of crime and place in the 1980s came from Cohen and Felson's important article "Social Change and Crime Rates: A Routine Activity Approach" published in 1979 in the influential journal the *American Sociological Review*. It is interesting but not surprising that the article was initially not well received by Cohen and Felson's peers.[2] The article offered a perspective that was a radical departure from traditional theorizing about the crime problem. It suggested that crime rates were determined not only by the number of motivated offenders, but also by the presence of suitable targets and the absence of capable guardians. In this theoretical perspective, criminologists were asked to recognize that the situational context, and thus the place where crime occurs, would influence the production of crime. The idea that criminal motivation was not the only or necessarily the key factor in the crime equation altered not only the trajectory of crime and place study, but also the willingness of traditional criminologists to consider the role of place in crime.

This is not to say that place quickly became a key concern in criminology. As we noted in Chapter 1, place is still regularly ignored in empirical studies and criminological theory. Nonetheless, it has begun to be recognized as an important part of the story of crime. What is interesting from our perspective is that even in studies of why people commit crime (studies of "criminality") there is growing interest in microgeographic places.

Perhaps the earliest recognition of the importance of place in general explanations for crime comes with Michael Gottfredson and Travis Hirschi's book *A General Theory of Crime*, published in 1990. Gottfredson and Hirschi's main thesis is that low self-control is the key to understanding why some people become involved in crime and deviance and others do not. But Gottfredson and Hirschi also recognized the importance of places and crime opportunities in the development of crime. They gave considerable attention to the role of crime opportunities in the direction and intensity of criminal behavior. Such opportunities obviously occur in very specific environments. Nonetheless, it is fair to say that Gottfredson and Hirschi's position is that the key criminological concern should lie with the question of self-control. Inevitably there will be opportunities for crime, and criminality cannot be constrained without focusing on its key cause in their approach – low self-control.

A more recent theoretical innovation in trying to understand criminality places the situation and offender motivation on equal ground. Situational action theory, proposed by Per-Olof Wikström (2010), also incorporates both the individual's propensity and his or her exposure to criminogenic settings. But in this case, it is clear that the spread and degree of criminal opportunities are as important a focus as the offenders themselves. According to Wikström (2010), a person's propensity to commit crime consists of his or her self-control, his or her morality, and the interaction between the two. Self-control is described as the extent to which an individual is capable to resist impulsivity, insensitivity, risk taking, and short-term orientation. Although this concept is based on Gottfredson and Hirschi's (1990) theory of self-control, Wikström (2010) assumes that the level of self-control can vary, rather than being stable throughout the life course. Morality is the extent to which individuals allow themselves to engage in rule-breaking behavior. Morality contains not only the cognitive component of moral rules, but also the emotional components of shame and guilt. When individuals have a high level of morality, their level of self-control is irrelevant as a causal factor.

However, the (criminogenic) setting within which individuals make their decisions is just as important for criminal involvement as their propensity for crime in Wikström's model. In this case, places are viewed as behavior settings for individuals, which are defined as "the part(s) of the environment (the configuration of objects, persons and events) that, at any given moment in time, is (are) accessible to a person through his or her senses (including any media present)" (Wikström et al. 2012, 15). Thus, if places offer more opportunities for illicit behaviors, individuals are then more likely to commit crime in the given places. Recent studies that have made use of Wikström's space-time-budget method to assess the situational factors of offending (Bernasco, Block, and Ruiter 2013; Bernasco, Ruiter, Bruinsma, Pauwels, and Weerman 2013) demonstrate that characteristics of street segments play an important role in offending – given the propensity of the offender.

Agnew (2013) has also acknowledged the importance of places and incorporated features of environment into general strain theory, though he only considers larger geographic areas such as neighborhoods. He argues that the extent of strain could vary by the type of neighborhood, leading to different levels of criminal activity when individuals are unable to cope with strain. As for life-course theories, historical times and places are seen to determine individuals' experiences and how they perceive opportunities for crime (Elder 1998). Additionally, the availability of crime places in one's life may contribute to onset, continuation, and desistance in a criminal career (Blokland and Nieuwbeerta 2010; Blumstein et al. 1988; Laub and Sampson 2003; Piquero and Mazerolle 2001; Piquero et al. 2007; Sampson and Laub 1993; Stokols 1983). Individuals' experiences with places vary across different stages of life, so a life-course approach is important to understand the complex relationships between individual and environment (Stokols 1987). Relocations to new places can also have an impact on criminal careers (Maltz 1995). Connecting the behavior settings (crime places) and the propensities of offenders expands the scope and explanatory power of criminological theories.

Clearly, the role of place in traditional theorizing about why people commit crime has increased over the last few decades. While the dominant focus of criminology remains on individuals and why they commit crime, there is growing recognition of the need to recognize the influence of places on individual behavior. In the next section we consider how place has been conceptualized in other disciplines and how criminology has drawn lessons from such perspectives.

CONTRIBUTIONS OF PLACE PERSPECTIVES FROM OTHER DISCIPLINES INTO MAINSTREAM CRIMINOLOGICAL THEORY AND RESEARCH

In addition to the theories and research cited earlier, valuable insights drawn from other disciplines have also been integrated into criminology research. Below we identify some important examples from psychology, public health, and economics to illustrate how these disciplines have contributed to enrich modern criminological research.

Psychology and Place

Though psychology is generally viewed as a discipline that focuses on individuals, more than a hundred years ago a groundbreaking theoretical perspective introduced by William James incorporated ecological factors into the theorization of psychology. In his work, James made attempts to reconcile the two seemingly conflicting perspectives of psychology and ecology, to identify the common grounds between the two, and to provide an integrated perspective to understand human behavior (see Heft 2001). However, the importance of contextualizing individual behaviors was not fully recognized until several decades later.

Around the 1940s, pioneers including Kurt Lewin, Egon Brunswik, and Roger Barker pointed out that people act differently within different social and physical settings. They argued that we cannot gain a full understanding of human behavior without taking into account peoples' surroundings. Nonetheless, understanding of the influence of place was still very limited within psychological research until the 1960s (Gifford 2007). The new emphasis on community research in the social sciences sparked interest among psychologists in bridging research across multiple units of analysis. Specifically, psychologists realized that individual-level characteristics alone were not sufficient in explaining variations among people and their behaviors. As such, the importance of places was further recognized and a more contextualized approach was called for to achieve a more holistic understanding of human behavior within many subdivisions of psychology (Stokols 1987). Psychologists who focus on place believe it is not just a physical location; rather, it also carries spatial, temporal and sociocultural meanings to individuals.

The emphasis of the interactions between people and their socio-physical-cultural environment led to the emergence of a new field called "environmental psychology" (Stokols and Altman 1987). Bell et al. (2001, 4) outlined two main perspectives that guide the study of places in environmental psychology. First, places often serve as the *context* of individual behaviors. We can only understand people's mood and behavior fully within their original context. Second, places could also affect individuals in a more active way. For example, Rapoport (1982) and Altman and Chemers (1980) suggested that characteristics of the physical environment, such as graffiti, litter, and lighting, convey nonverbal messages to local residents and even outsiders about the nature of the place, leading them to adjust their behaviors and actions accordingly (Innes 2004; Taylor 1987).

Taylor (1987) drew heavily from environmental psychology to explain the variety of human behaviors under different circumstances (see also Bell et al. 2001; Stokols and Altman 1987). Thus, knowledge from environmental or ecological psychology is useful to understand the mentality and behavior of law-abiding individuals as well as potential offenders (Taylor 1987). The understanding of the transactions between people and environment helps the advancement of individual-oriented criminology research.

Behavior Settings. Early ecological psychologists noticed the importance of the environment to human behavior and began systematic inquiry on the topic.

Barker and his colleague Herbert Wright (1955) founded a lab to study the interactions between the environment and human behaviors. They argued that the environment is a broad concept that includes the physical environment as well as the social interactions embedded in the settings (Barker 1968). As such, places function as a "behavior setting" in which human behaviors are contextualized. Wicker went further and defined behavior settings as "small-scale social systems whose components include people and inanimate objects. Within the temporal and spatial boundaries of the system, the various components interact in an orderly, established fashion to carry out the setting's essential functions" (Wicker 1987, 614).

As we described in Chapter 3, the concept of behavior settings has been adopted by criminologists. Weisburd et al. (2012), following Taylor (1997), integrated this concept into the study of crime at microgeographic units (street blocks in Taylor's case). Taylor argued that a street block provides a natural setting to study human activities such as crime for several reasons. First, people who frequent a street tend to develop an understanding of people's routines on the street. Second, long-term residents tend to play stable roles in the life of the street. For example, some people are willing to accept packages for neighbors, while other people might look after neighbors' kids. Third, through the life experiences of residents, commonly acceptable norms are gradually developed in the street segments. For example, people are careful to avoid making excessive noise after a certain time. The influx and outflux of residents also change the dynamics of the street over time. All of these characteristics make each street a unique environment for residents' life experiences.

Furthermore, the norms and routines in a behavior setting are not just determined by residents of the street. Nonresidents who pass through the street also alter the dynamic of the street. For example, streets with better accessibility tend to be more diverse and unpredictable, with more traffic from nonresidents. As such, Taylor (1997, 1998) believes that street segments serve as a reasonable unit of analysis for the study of crime patterns. Many forms of informal social control and crime opportunities occur within the microgeographic unit.

Weisburd et al. (2012; Weisburd et al. 2014) take this perspective further, arguing that street segments can be seen as microcommunities. This allows them to integrate traditional theorizing about crime at the community level to a microgeographic unit of analysis. Weisburd et al. (2012), as we noted in Chapter 3, integrate concepts of social disorganization and collective efficacy to the criminology of place. Though this approach has generated controversy (see Braga and Clarke 2014; Weisburd et al. 2014), it illustrates how the conceptualization of places in other disciplines has enriched study of the criminology of place.

Cognitive Mapping. Another important line of psychological research that focuses on perception of places is the study of cognitive mapping – the organized mental representation of one's environment that aids wayfinding in daily life (Bell et al. 2001). Following the concepts of "imaginary maps" coined by Trowbridge (1913), Kevin Lynch (1960) published his seminal piece, *The Image of the City*, in which he thoroughly discussed both the data collection for studying cognitive maps and the creation of new vocabulary describing cognitive maps. Lynch proposed five important components of places that affect our cognitive mapping ability: places with clear paths, distinct edges, recognizable districts, nodes, and landmarks are more legible for users.

Nonetheless, cognitive maps are inaccurate compared to the objective environment. Cognitive maps are mental analogies of spatial relations of objects in the real world. Thus, they tend to be incomplete, distorted, biased, and simplified based on an individual's life experiences. Yet even though cognitive maps do not fully represent the real world, they highlight important places, the spatial relationship between places, and travel preferences from one place to another place within each person's living environment. In other words, cognitive maps include both objective information about physical places and subjective interpretation reflecting individual preferences and perceptions.

Lynch's first comprehensive study was done at the city level; however, he also applied the concepts to small geographic units, such as the area surrounding Quincy Market in Boston, Massachusetts. The ideas associated with cognitive mapping are widely used in everyday life to create a user-friendly environment to assist "wayfinding." The "you-are-here" maps that appear in shopping malls, around street corners, and inside theme parks are the best illustrations of efforts to connect individual psychological processes to places in order to improve our quality of life.

The concepts related to cognitive mapping have been applied to the study of crime and delinquency. Specifically, scholars have paid attention to factors including emotions, demographic factors, and fears and how those affect the accuracy of perceptions of the environment. For instance, Newman (1972) noticed that the layout of public housing projects affected how police officers responded to calls for service in New York City. When an officer perceived the environment to be more dangerous, she or he held a more authoritative attitude when handling conflicts; as a result, the police–citizen relationship got worse. Mattson and Rengert (1995) also found that people tend to overestimate physical distance in dangerous places compared with places that are perceived to be safer. Thus, this type of life experience affects how individuals perceive their physical environment. They concluded that the process of individuals' cognitive mapping involves social actors, the surrounding environment, experiences, knowledge gained from experiencing the environment, and behaviors in response to environmental stimuli (Rengert and Pelfrey 1997, 195).

Rengert and Pelfrey (1997) further tested the impacts of cognitive mapping on community service recruits in Philadelphia. They found that the service recruits did not judge the levels of safety based on objective information such as crime rates. Rather, it was their preconceived concepts that heavily influenced their judgments of the levels of safety of the places. Particularly, places with higher percentages of black population were more likely to be rated as dangerous places compared with places with high percentages of white population.

Though the discussion so far has focused on the effects of places and their characteristics on individuals' psychological outcomes, cultural research also focuses on how subculture and values fostered in specific regions affect the attitudes and behaviors of people who live in those places. The "culture of honor" arguments raised by Nisbett and Cohen (1996) and the "code of the street" theory proposed by Anderson (1999) are two good examples.

Public Health and Place

While mainstream public health research typically focuses on larger geographic areas, such as nations, regions, and cities, interest in small and micro place effects on health is not new. Florence Nightingale, in the mid-nineteenth century, was thinking about immediate environmental and geographic contexts of health, such as the association between disease and standard of living and the physical and interpersonal elements of care settings. This was the first time that the characteristics of places and the relationship between human behavior and place features were recognized as crucial elements of health care. As such, health professionals, especially nurses, have long understood the importance of the environment at the microlevel (Crooks and Andrews 2009).

A famous early example of the relationship between place and public health is John Snow's work on cholera, specifically his effort to understand the cholera epidemic that broke out in London in 1854. As part of his inquiry, he used mapping at the address level to support his theory that cholera was a disease of the gut that could be transmitted through a contaminated water supply – a hypothesis that contradicted the miasma ("bad air") explanations of disease that prevailed at the time. While it is less often discussed in popular retellings of Snow's story, his work also recognized the intersection between a place (the contaminated Broad Street water pump) and the routine activities of people. Mapping out the locations and number of fatalities (see Figure 4.1) at each house allowed him to identify differential use of the pump by household residents, which helped Snow to conclude that disease was a product of the intersection between individual behavior and places (Brody et al. 2000).

Public health scholars with an interest in small geographic places, like their counterparts in criminology, have recognized that studying health at larger scales tends to hide local variations in risk, exposure, and incidence of disease, as well as the organization and distribution of care (e.g., Hayward et al. 2000; Krieger et al. 2002; Weisburd et al. 2012). Furthermore, like offenders, health service users are not necessarily constrained by administrative boundaries in seeking care. Focusing on the natural distribution of outcomes at the microlevel allows researchers to better identify the "true" numerators and denominators

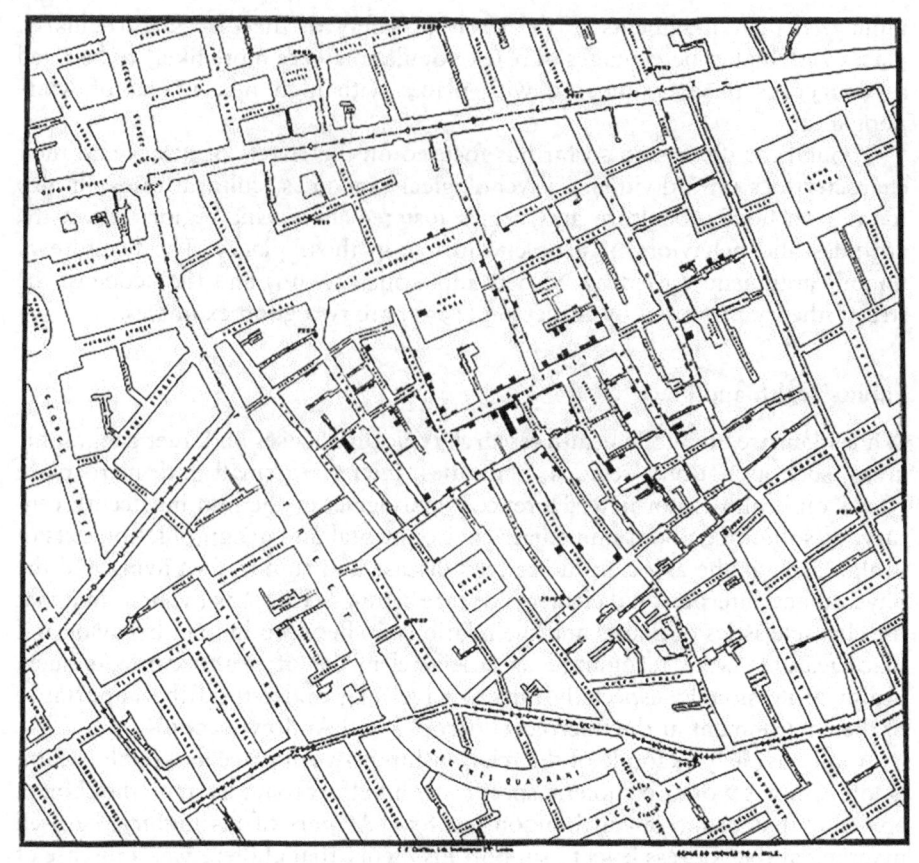

FIGURE 4.1. Map of cholera fatalities in London.
Original source: Map by Dr. John Snow, 1854.

when assessing disease incidence or planning health services (Pong and Pitblado 2001). One systematic review of community health promotion interventions even suggests that a lack of attention to scale (or the use of inappropriate scales or boundaries) may partially explain the limited success of these programs (Merzel and D'Afflitti 2003).

Kearns and Joseph (1993) note the role of small place effects in shaping the social geography of a wider area. Just as hot spots of crime concentrate at a small number of street segments and can drive the overall crime rate of a city (e.g., Weisburd et al. 2012), the characteristics of specific locations can attract certain health or health care activities that mirror macrolevel concepts such as social stratification. Disadvantaged places are less likely to resist the building of, for example, treatment facilities that cater to violent or drug-dependent individuals and thus create "negative externalities." These clusterings shape the overall "social geography" of the city. Kearns and Joseph (1993, 714) suggest that places therefore "record the constant ebb and flow of social policy and its local outcomes."

Microplace approaches to crime prevention reflect what has been known for some time in public health: that changing the situation is much easier than changing individual behavior. "Technological manipulations of the environment" (Moore 1995, 252) have, therefore, been a key public health approach to prevention at the microlevel (e.g., the removal of the Broad Street pump handle during London's cholera epidemic), and this is reflected in place-based policing and situational crime prevention strategies, such as street closures and barriers. In an example of research that spans the fields of place-based criminology and public health, Branas et al. (2011) recognized the challenges of targeting large numbers of individuals and changing individual behavior and shifted their focus to environmental change intended to precipitate eventual behavior modifications. They found that "greening" vacant lots in U.S. cities has benefits for crime and health outcomes: reductions in violence and stress, improved collective efficacy among residents living around the lots, and increased participation in outdoor exercise.

Pong and Pitblado (2001) also highlight the importance of using geographic areas that make sense. Their observations from public health research provide a useful framework for crime and place researchers thinking about which geographic scales and boundaries to incorporate in their analyses. The geographic areas used in health and place research are often artificial (i.e., based on administrative boundaries, such as census tracts) and do not reflect the natural spatial patterns of health service delivery and use. The challenge for health and crime researchers alike is that spatial data is usually available at these administrative levels. However, the use of artificial boundaries can create the erroneous assumption that all health service use by a certain population takes place within a set area that may be completely arbitrary in relation to the outcome. Criminologists should also consider that offending behavior, victimization, and use of justice system services (e.g., probation) are distributed across as well as within these artificial boundaries, and the implications of this for the organization of law enforcement and other criminal justice interventions, which tend to be organized along administrative lines. Furthermore, in the same way that access to online health data and services is changing the way public health researchers conceptualize space and place, crime and place researchers will increasingly need to consider the implications of technology and the Internet for the spatial distribution of certain offenders, offenses, and victims.

It is important to note that public health and crime and place research have not necessarily developed in line with each other. In many cases it is difficult to say with certainty that public health perspectives have informed crime and place research. Though the mapping of spatial patterns of disease is very similar to the mapping of crime hot spots in police practices, tracing the historical development of these two strategies does not reveal much evidence that one field directly influenced the other (e.g., Weisburd et al. 2012). But in health geography and the discipline of public health more broadly, as in criminology, there is an increased awareness that place matters, and a growing awareness of place as a complex, dynamic construct that reflects individual experience rather than a "passive container" or black box (Kearns and Moon 2002; see also Tunstall et al. 2004). In turn, there are a number of themes in crime and place research that are analogous to public health research, and some current developments in the latter field that crime and place scholars might consider.

Prevention Perspective from Public Health. The classic definition of public health is

the science and art of preventing disease, prolonging life, and promoting physical health and efficiency through organized community efforts for the sanitation of the environment, the control of community infections, the education of the individual in principles of personal hygiene, the organization of medical and nursing services for the early diagnosis and preventive treatment of disease, and the development of the social machinery which will ensure to every individual in the community a standard of living adequate for the maintenance of health. Winslow 1920, 30

Thus, the concept of prevention is key to the discipline. The public health approach to prevention is threefold, reflecting different opportunities for intervention. *Primary* prevention seeks to prevent disease or injury before it occurs and promote good health. *Secondary* prevention focuses on identifying and addressing early risk factors that indicate a potential for more serious problems later on. *Tertiary* prevention is concerned with the treatment or management of outcomes once disease is already present (Akers and Lanier 2009; Brantingham and Faust 1976; Moore 1995; Welsh and Farrington 2010). Moore (1995) emphasizes primary prevention as the most important concern of public health in general.

Criminologists are already familiar with the public health approach to prevention, and have used the framework broadly to classify crime prevention programs and strategies (e.g., Brantingham and Faust 1976; Welsh and Farrington 2010; Welsh et al. 2014). The primary prevention concept is particularly appropriate for place-based crime prevention strategies, such as situational crime prevention efforts. Thus, a key contribution of public health to the criminology of place is the shift in focus from individuals to broad risk factors. Of course, risk factors of crime are not exclusively place-based: there is a substantial body of literature on individual risk and protective factors for crime (e.g., Farrington et al. 1998, Hawkins et al. 1998). However, crime and place research uniquely examines the times, places, and other microlevel circumstances surrounding the environments of high-risk people (e.g., see Weisburd et al. 2012; Weisburd et al. 2014). The public health approach highlights the possibility that apparently minor, situational risk factors for crime problems exist within narrowly defined spatial boundaries that can be easily targeted for intervention. This stands in contrast to individual-level risk factors, such as biological and psychological processes, socioeconomic status, and poor parenting, which can be addressed but often present a narrow window for intervention (e.g., in early childhood) and may require efforts to reach a more widely dispersed segment of the population.

Akers and Lanier (2009), for example, suggest that broken windows (Wilson and Kelling 1982) and other indicators of disorder are analogous to vectors of disease in that they attract more undesirable outcomes to a location, so that order maintenance is like immunization. The problem-solving approach that has been adopted in place-based policing is also clearly rooted in public health – defining the problem, identifying risk and protective factors, and developing strategies for prevention, implementation, and systematic analysis.

Methodological Contributions from Public Health. Place-based public health research has also informed methodological considerations in the study of crime at place. One important contribution of public health researchers with an interest in violence is the introduction of different sources of data and measurement at the microlevel. Warburton and Shepherd (2006), for example, examined the possibility of incorporating hospital injury data into a problem-oriented policing approach to identify and intervene at criminogenic locations. In their study, emergency room consultants who treated victims of alcohol-related violence mapped the location of incidents involving their patients and identified "hot bars": alcohol-serving establishments at which violence appeared to be concentrated. The consultants worked with police to confront the bar owners with the injury data to back up law enforcement, outreach, and situational crime prevention efforts.

Similarly, Branas et al.'s (2008) and Branas et al.'s (2009) studies of firearm violence and proximity to alcohol outlets involved innovative linking of health and criminal justice datasets to examine how exposure to both individual and microgeographic risk factors is associated with gunshot injuries. They found that the risk of being assaulted with a firearm is as high or higher for individuals who are in close proximity to off-premise outlets (i.e., retailers that sell alcohol for consumption off, rather than on, the premises) as it is for those engaged in heavy drinking, suggesting place-based implications for injury prevention (Branas et al. 2009).

Economics and Place

As a recent review by Bushway and Reuter (2008) discussed, economists have had a very substantial influence on the study of crime and the criminal justice system. This section provides a brief overview of the contributions of economics to place-based criminology specifically, focusing on the development of rational choice/opportunity perspectives for explaining crime in places, and the application of market-based theories such as agglomeration to examining concentration of crime at places. It goes on to examine areas of economic theory and research that may contribute to the development of our understanding of crime in microplaces.

Rational Choice/Opportunity Perspectives. One of the key contributions that economists have made to the study of crime relates to individuals' decision-making processes and situated interactions between parties with different interests as an explanation for criminal behavior (e.g., see Becker 1968; 1993; see also Bushway and Reuter 2008). Criminals are considered to be calculating based on the risks and rewards involved in offending, including the risks conditioned by their immediate environment (see also Clarke and Felson 1993).

The emphasis of these ideas about situated risk and reward have resulted in a growing body of research in criminology concerning how the presence of offenders, suitable targets, and guardians influences offending in microplaces such as street segments and "risky facilities" (e.g., see Clarke and Eck 2007; Eck et al. 2007). As we discussed in earlier chapters, rational choice theories have been an important component of the development of opportunity theories for understanding crime places. In short, because offenders respond rationally to risks and rewards in their immediate environment, crime in places can be predicted by the types of opportunities for crime fostered at specific locations.

Market Perspectives and the Study of Crime. Another important perspective of economics contributing to the understanding of the criminology of place comes from market research. In recent years, there have been a number of location-based market theories in economics that have explored the effects of agglomeration and spatial competition in explaining crime at places. As Bernasco and Block (2011) note, agglomeration and competition are two opposing spatial mechanisms in determining the behavior of markets (see also Fotheringham 1985). Agglomeration economies gather competitors together in a single location, allowing them to share infrastructure, knowledge, and expenses (Getis and Getis 1968). On the other hand, spatial competition processes would imply that market competitors will generally locate themselves as far away from one another as possible.

Research in criminology generally supports the salience of these notions of agglomeration and competition in predicting criminal behavior, particularly in cases of illegal drug markets. Previous research has found that drug markets are highly clustered in places, and that they do not displace easily in response to targeted police interventions (see, for instance, Ratcliffe et al. 2011; Weisburd et al. 2006). Taniguchi and colleagues (2009) found support for the agglomeration economies perspective in illegal drug markets of Philadelphia (see also Johnson et al. 2013). Further, Bernasco and Block (2011) argued that the presence of crime generators on a street segment tends to increase the risk of robbery not only for the given street, but also for the surrounding streets – further supporting the agglomeration effect (see also Bernasco et al. 2013).

Scholars have often noted that economic competition between gangs for control of drug markets produces violent crime. For instance, street corners where multiple gangs sell drugs experience more violence than street corners where only one gang sells drugs (Taniguchi et al. 2011). Levitt and Venkatesh (2000) find that gangs compete directly with one another through gang wars, which occur when a gang is trying to displace demand for drugs from a rival gang's territory, and by pricing drugs below the marginal cost in order to attract customers. Further, drug enforcement can have a number of different consequences for competition for drug market share. For example, enforcement may displace consumers to adjacent markets, increasing both competition and violent crime (Rasmussen et al. 1993) and improving the market share of high-productivity offenders by pricing the low-productivity offenders out of the market (DeAngelo 2012).

Places are also highlighted as a central concern in Kleiman and Young's (1995) economic analysis of the "factors of production" in street-level drug market operations. They suggest that an examination of the factors of production in the process of retail drug transactions can be an aid both to understanding the way drug markets and current drug-control efforts work and to developing new approaches to drug control. The factors necessary for drug markets are a common venue (described as very specific drug-selling locations within neighborhoods); the buyers' access to the venue, desire for drugs, income, and perceived chance of impunity; and the sellers' labor, operating scope within the venue, supply of drugs, ways to spend or save money earned, and perceived chance of impunity. Kleiman and Young (1995) suggest that the optimal drug market disruption strategy for any situation will focus on those factors that can most readily be made scarce relative to the others. Many of their policy recommendations involve manipulating the situational characteristics of drug places to make these locations less attractive to buyers and sellers.

WHAT CAN CRIMINOLOGY LEARN FROM OTHER DISCIPLINES ABOUT PLACES IN THE FUTURE?

The examples described here are by no means a thorough or exhaustive review of the research done in those fields concerning the impacts of places. The examples are presented to illustrate the importance of places in those disciplines and how they have influenced the development of the criminology of place. There are a number of possible ways in which the role of places in other disciplines could continue to contribute to our understanding of crime. In the following sections, we suggest some possible directions that could be used in future crime and place research.

First, psychological research has pointed out that a place not only provides a context for individuals' daily lives, but could also be an object to which a person is emotionally attached or identifies with as a part of personal identity (Jorgensen and Stedman 2006; Low and Altman 1992; McMillan and Chavis 1986; Meinig 1979; Relph 1976; Ryden 1993; Stedman 2002). In order for this to happen, the quality and uniqueness of the places matter. Stedman (2002) surveyed 290 subjects in a region of northern Wisconsin in which there exist more than 1,000 lakes. He found that local residents tend to have identified with "a lake of their own" in their mind. Consequently, the conditions of the lake greatly affect their happiness and satisfaction with life and impact their emotional well-being. "The lake" and the concepts associated with it have become an important part of their lives. People not only develop a strong sense of territoriality for "their" places, but also incorporate personal places as part of their identity (Meinig 1979; Relph 1976). This phenomenon is best illustrated by Ryden's comments: "the place has become a shaping partner in our lives, we partially define ourselves in its terms, and it carries the emotional charge of a family member or any other influential human agent" (Ryden 1993, 66). However, some people take a more utilitarian perspective and treat their environment simply as a place to live. Their satisfaction with places comes from the convenience of the location or other amenities offered at the place rather than a sentimental attachment (Greider and Garkovich 1994; Mesch and Manor 1998). We think this idea of "emotional" bonds to places should be integrated more directly into the criminology of place.

Characteristics of places also determine whether local residents are likely to be "bonded" with a place. Psychologists have argued that residents are more bonded and more likely to choose to permanently live in a good community with a strong sense of belonging. McMillian and Chavis (1986) argued that there are four necessary elements for a place to be considered as a good community: (1) clear membership that distinguishes between insiders and outsiders; (2) resident influence on public affairs within the community; (3) active incorporation of residents' goals into community action plans and fulfillment of the various needs of the residents; and (4) an emotional connection and shared experiences between residents. This sense of community ties in with the concepts of informal social control and collective efficacy to emphasize the importance of social bonds among residents (see Bursik and Grasmick 1993b; Sampson et al. 1997). We think that this concept can also apply to the microgeographic communities we examine. The psychological perspective informs the criminology of place through its suggestion that a place with a strong sense of community will also have a strong mechanism of social control, and in turn a lower probability of crime problems.

Psychologists also find the way people perceive their surroundings is affected by factors such as their gender, stage of life, and cognitive errors[3] (Moore 1979; Tversky 1993). Perceptions about places and the psychological outcomes associated with these perceptions are therefore important topics for examination. For example, Innes (2004) has noted that not all physical disorder sends the same signals; how disorder is perceived varies by the preconceived behavioral expectations a person has for an area (Millie 2008). Thus, research on fear of crime, territorial research, and personal space should focus more on people's perceptions and psychological reactions about places rather than the objective features of places (Bottoms 2009; Sampson 2010; Taylor 1987; Taylor and Harrell 1996).

Similarly, from the public health perspective, the growing focus on small place effects recognizes that the local context not only contributes to global processes that are relevant to health, but also directly impacts people's health and lifestyles. For example, research on HIV transmission suggests that the spatial diffusion of the disease occurs both within and across microplaces, according to interactions between carriers in close proximity to one another and along the lines of transportation routes that allow carriers to move from place to place (see Crooks and Andrews 2009). The correspondence between microgeographic features and individual characteristics and behavior can both explain disease and health inequalities and provide opportunities for prevention. For example, higher-income individuals can afford to live in "healthier" places, away from pollution and violence and closer to health care and health promotion resources, leaving low-income populations more exposed to threats to health (Elliott and Wartenberg 2004).

Thus, the role of small places in public health has moved beyond documenting the distribution of disease to a more sophisticated analysis of the complex relationships and synergies between people, culture, and setting (Kearns and Moon 2002). The recognition that social and cultural processes can occur at microlocations renews focus on health promotion and care (primary prevention) in addition to understanding disease (secondary and tertiary prevention). These ideas are only just beginning to emerge in the criminology of place (see Weisburd et al. 2012; Weisburd et al. 2014), and the public health framework may provide direction for future inquiry. Indeed, criminologists have recently begun to look at health inequalities at crime hot spots (Weisburd et al. 2013; see also Weisburd et al. 2014). Such places are not simply places with high crime; they are behavior settings that are characterized as well by heightened physical and mental health problems (Weisburd et al. 2014).

The contributions of economists to the study of crime places can be expanded by including studies of knowledge spillover and institutional–cultural research in the study of crime at places. Knowledge spillover occurs in places when "high concentrations of people and firms in cities create an environment in which ideas move quickly from person to person and firm to firm" (Carlino 2001, 17). The amount of shared knowledge about particular practices may vary significantly between places because of variations in firm location, the proximity to firms, and the types of firms present at particular locations (e.g., see Audretsch and Feldman 1996; Audretsch and Keilbach 2008). Jacobs (1969) suggests that dense and heterogeneous populations, such as those that occur within urban areas, are likely to produce higher rates of knowledge spillover.

Significant place-based research has been directed toward market-based offenses such as illegal drug offending and prostitution (e.g., see Green 1995; Lawton et al. 2005; Mazerolle et al. 1998; Taniguchi et al. 2009; Weisburd and Green 1994; 1995b). However, relatively little research has been directed toward, for instance, how particular practices surrounding drug dealing differ between cities, or how the concentration of different types of offending (for instance, robbery, burglary, and drug offending) influences how offenders use high-crime areas. Examining how concentrated offending in places produces "knowledge spillover" among offenders might be important in designing effective strategies for particular types of offending.

Institutional–cultural research in economics focuses on the variation in economic activity that occurs across space as a result of complex local and historical processes and existing networks of industries (Martin and Sunley 2003). According to this perspective, economic activity is influenced by a system of relations between business, government, and other social actors who both actively shape and are influenced by the local institutional context (Boggs and Rantisi 2003; North 1990; Overman 2004). For instance, significant economic research has focused on zoning and land planning decisions, and in particular how different groups of economic elites attempt to shape land use policies toward their desired ends (e.g., see McCann 2002). Decisions about the use of microgeographic space in urban areas have a significant impact on the value attached to land, housing, and industries at a particular location (e.g., see Bolt et al. 1998; Logan and Molotch 2007; Palmquist 2005).

These investigations into land use and property value may also have strong implications for the study of crime and crime prevention at places. Offenders may themselves attempt to change how places are used for both legal and illegal purposes to further facilitate offending, or block potential guardians from accessing locations; however, relatively little research has been concerned with how offenders select and shape the use of spaces. Further, relatively little research has been focused on longitudinal changes in crime at places over time. We do know that most places change very little in terms of the amount of offending that they host, generate, and attract (e.g., see Weisburd et al. 2004; 2012). However, little attention has been paid so far to the institutional and cultural shifts in these microplaces that accompany changes in crime and disorder. It seems likely that microlevel changes in land use and investment, driven by the interests of institutional actors, may contribute to these changes in crime at places.

CONCLUSIONS

In this chapter we showed how concern with the role of microgeographic environments in producing the crime problem has come to influence not just study of crime at place, but traditional criminological theorizing about why people become involved in crime and deviance. This is an important trend, and one that shows the growing influence of the criminology of place on criminology more generally. Place matters in criminology today, which represents an important change in the interests of criminologists.

We also demonstrated that place matters in other disciplines, using the examples of psychology, public health, and economics, and how those perspectives have influenced the development of the criminology of place. Criminologists have already adopted many concepts and ideas from these disciplines in both theory development and crime prevention practices. We believe that criminology, as an interdisciplinary science, can learn more from the knowledge of places in these and other disciplines. Mainstream criminology can also benefit from bringing place into a broader array of theoretical and empirical inquiries.

5

Methods of Place-Based Research[1]

The growth of interest in the criminology of place has generated key developments in the data and methods used in identifying and understanding geographic concentrations of crime. Ron Clarke noted in 2004 that "quite soon, crime mapping will become as much an essential tool of criminological research as statistical analysis is at present" (Clarke 2004, 60). This means, of course, that criminologists will have to develop methods of analysis that meet the new problems that geographic data present. Moreover, with ever-improving data quality and resolution, there is a constant need to evolve better research methods, practices, and statistical approaches.

This chapter will outline the imperative for a robust analytical framework that incorporates measures of adjacency in any spatial analysis, and articulate the problems that can befall an aspatial approach to geographic data. The chapter then identifies some of the unique characteristics of spatial analysis before providing an overview of new and innovative approaches to spatial criminological research.

THE IMPORTANCE OF THEORY IN DEVELOPING METHODS

We want to note at the outset that theory is key to any discussion of analytic approaches associated with spatial analyses. While this chapter highlights the roles of both analytic methods and the policy implications that may result from spatial analyses, the theories we discussed in Chapter 3 provide a framework for developing analytic results that provide a greater understanding of places, and the people who use those places, and for policy implications that can be linked to the agencies and locations that will best be served by them.

While various methodologies and techniques have been developed to examine and measure the role of place, these analytical approaches provide little practical value without also considering the reason *why* these places matter.

Methods of Place-Based Research

A simple example of this would be to consider a black box model where we have no information on what occurs within the box, but are merely aware of the outcome of an event. This example, applied to geographic units of analysis, effectively limits the criminal justice system and agency providers to the role of responders with little knowledge or ability to understand why events are occurring and what role, if any, the location itself plays in these events.

As we have noted in previous chapters, traditional criminological theories have focused on the person, suggesting that characteristics of the individual are ultimately responsible for the person's involvement, or lack of involvement, in criminal behavior. These individual factors could be biological, psychological, or sociological, to name just a few. While research has in the past emphasized the role of place (Burgess 1928; Guerry 1864; Quetelet 1831), only in the last thirty years have theories emphasizing the context of the individual taken center stage.

These theories, while highlighting the role of place, have emphasized different aspects of contexts and the manner in which individuals interact with them. Anselin et al. (2000, 215) have noted, for example, "[t]heoretical concerns focus on how place might be a factor in crime, either by *influencing* or *shaping* the types and levels of criminal behavior by the people who frequent an area, or by *attracting* to an area people who already share similar criminal inclinations" (italics added).Theoretical foci, such as the rational choice perspective (Cornish and Clarke 1986), routine activities (Cohen and Felson 1979), and crime pattern theory (Brantingham and Brantingham 1984), have provided a framework for us to understand the influencing, the shaping, and the attractive aspects of these areas.

Further emphasizing the contribution of theory is the manner in which theories have highlighted aspects of these locations for practical considerations. Hot spots policing (Sherman and Weisburd 1995; Weisburd and Green 1995b) has provided a framework for law enforcement agencies to consider best practices for the allocation of resources, supported by inferences of the rational choice perspective and routine activities theory. Geographic profiling (Rossmo 1999) uses considerations of the rational choice perspective, crime pattern analysis, and routine activities to organize the understanding of criminal behavior within a spatial context. Situational crime prevention (Clarke 1980) uses all three theoretical foci to identify techniques for decreasing the likelihood of criminal behaviors that make the act more difficult to complete, more likely to result in an arrest, less likely to be profitable, less likely to incur provocation, or less likely to be excused by ignorance of the act.

The prior examples are not intended to be an exhaustive list; rather, they serve to highlight the application of theory to our understanding of spatial patterns and the resulting spatial analyses (see Chapter 3 for a broader discussion of theories in this area). Of note here is the natural inclusion of spatial influences within criminological theory, suggesting that an aspatial theoretical framework will be unable to inform practitioners or researchers. This chapter highlights several new and innovative analytic methods of spatial analyses from predictive patterns research to qualitative geographical information systems (GIS) techniques, among others. The development of new analytic methodologies will naturally lead to the development of theory and a more complete understanding of the role of place.

THE IMPORTANCE OF METHODS

Alongside the development of appropriate theories to explain spatial patterns of crime, it is necessary to use or develop appropriate methods to test them. Theories can be used to generate testable expectations or hypotheses, but these can only be tested appropriately with suitable methods. While methods developed to test aspatial hypotheses may be suitable sometimes, much of the time they will not.

To illustrate, consider a study concerned with risk factors associated with offending. For such a study, a researcher may develop a theory and then collect data to test it. The data collected may be for a random sample of individuals, and data may be collected on a variety of factors thought to influence the likelihood of them committing crime. Inferential statistical tests may then be used to determine if such factors are correlated with offending rates. For such analyses, a central assumption of the approach is that the observations (in this case people) are independent of each other. Though, as we noted in Chapter 1, individuals may be linked to each other as coffenders, when appropriate sampling is used the assumption of independence will generally be a plausible one, and the statistical methods used to test hypotheses will most likely generate valid results that can be used to inform theory and policy.

Consider this issue in the case of spatial patterns of crime and ask yourself if the assumption of the independence of observations is plausible or whether it would be useful to consider how what happens at one place influences what happens at another. To take a spatial crime pattern example, accepting the assumption of independence would be like saying that the presence of a drug market on one street corner has no effect on the rate of crime or the likelihood of there being a drug market at adjacent street corners. Often this assumption is unrealistic, as research quite clearly demonstrates that crime in general is spatially clustered (for a review, see Johnson 2010). This presents a potential problem for theory testing and policy development, as any analyses that are conducted using statistical methods that assume observations are independent are likely to lead to errors of inference. It means, as we note in the following, that researchers must take into account the spatial correlations of events at places close to each other.

In terms of analytic approaches, there exists no complete listing of systematic tactics to test various kinds of hypotheses. Instead, methods develop and evolve if enough researchers ask the same or similar questions. At this point in time, there is a growing interest in the types of methods that can be used to address some of the theoretical questions raised in this book, and hence the methods are constantly being developed and refined, but relative to some other areas of research, these methods are in their infancy.

In the case of the study of spatial patterns of crime, it is not only the case that the assumptions of what might be described as traditional statistical tests will be violated (recall the assumption of independence described earlier), but also that the types of processes that are believed to generate spatial variation in crime are themselves spatial. This requires that the statistical models used are constructed in such a way that these influences can be explicitly modeled and their effects estimated. This brings challenges that are not encountered in research that is aspatial, and requires the development of appropriate models that explicitly couple the theoretical and statistical model. A failure to do so is likely to lead to researchers coming to incorrect conclusions and the influences of aspatial factors being under- or overstated.

Policy

In the 1990s, the growth of the new public management movement brought private-sector ideas of efficiency, competition, and accountability to public-sector areas of service delivery, such as crime prevention and front-line policing (Crawford 1997). Notwithstanding the capacity of police departments to resist these changes (Ashby et al. 2007; Loveday 1999) or the temporary influx of cash to many police departments in the United States in the wake of the 9/11 terrorist attacks, the period since the early 1990s has been one of relative frugality for the police. This is especially the case for U.S. police departments where funds that once might have been available for community policing programs were diverted to homeland security (Braga and Weisburd 2010). Now police services everywhere are expected to do more with less, and to demonstrate efficiency in the process (Audit Commission 1993). When this level of expectation is coupled with the explosion in availability of cheap digital processing and storage of information, it was perhaps inevitable that information-driven business models, such as intelligence-led policing (National Criminal Intelligence Service 2000), would come to the fore.

Certain characteristics dominate the language of this strategic redirection, with terms that have direct implications for the types of statistical analyses conducted and the methods that are applied. When a new business model is described as "strategic, future-oriented and targeted" (Maguire 2000, 316) and a "proactive" (Sheptycki 2009, 168) system that is more intelligence-led and offender-focused (Audit Commission 1993), then analysts will favor techniques that are more place-based than aggregate, more focused on individuals than groups, and more informative about predicting crime in and around places than explaining past crime patterns across large areas.

These changes have affected policy-oriented spatial analyses. Aggregate information regarding occupants of large areas, such as census tracts, is by virtue of area size more homogenous and will mask much of the heterogeneity and variance of patterns within (see Chapter 2). For the purposes of anonymity for national censuses, this is an attractive characteristic, but it is a negative trait for more focused and targeted crime prevention responses. The new paradigm is about location-based responses to crime and designing out crime at the exact place where an offender may take advantage of an opportunity. Microgeographical analysis of places has the potential to allow policy makers to argue their programs are targeted to achieve the most effective return on investment possible by limiting the application of programs to areas that should benefit from them.

Furthermore, the growth of more nodal forms of governance in the security arena has moved police to a more collaborative model of risk mitigation, bringing in partners from the public and private sectors (Wood and Shearing 2007). This has encouraged more third-party solutions to crime problems (Buerger and Mazerolle 1998; Mazerolle and Ransley 2006), and legislative responses tend to be specific regarding locations and impact on the surrounding environment. For example, many places have increased penalties for people caught dealing illegal drugs within 1,000 feet of a school, and Camden, New Jersey, for example, has experimented with a city ordinance preventing fast food eateries from opening after midnight if they are within 200 feet of a residential area. The growth of high-quality geolocated information about the urban environment is now driving a preference for knowledge regarding the specific spatial spillover (Hakim and Rengert 1981) of crime from noxious environments. It is slowly being recognized that improvements in the quality of data and tools are having implications for the Fourth Amendment to the U.S. Constitution. Reasonable suspicion regarding a person's behavior can include whether or not they are in a known high-crime area, but questions have arisen as to how to specifically define such an area (Ferguson 2011; Weisburd 2008). The range of possible ways that a high-crime area can be defined (e.g., see Eck et al. 2005) is likely to require revision for legal purposes at some point in the future. A greater specificity regarding distances, journey to crime, and the spillover effect of nuisance places will find favor with policy makers in the future.

EVOLUTION TO SPACE

The current trend toward smaller and smaller units of analysis "implies that we need to consider more closely the interactions between adjacent and nearby units, but also gives rise to additional statistical challenges" (Weisburd et al. 2009, 24). Research that naively examines criminal behavior from an aspatial perspective is hampered in two main ways: it is likely to be statistically flawed and it runs the risk of being conceptually incomplete due to the absence of important contextual information.

The incorporation of a spatial dimension is fundamental to many criminological studies that employ statistics to determine causality (or at least theoretically meaningful correlation). As stated earlier, the statistical issue lies within the requisite assumption of independence of observations. This requires that the observed data have not been acted on by an external influence that is common to a number of the observations, with the corollary that knowing one datum gives you no information about any other datum nearby. This is the case when any measured variables are immune from the effect of individual ordering or spatial arrangement of the units under study.

From a technical perspective, studies that do not incorporate any component of spatial proximity are assuming a condition of equality or anonymity that may not be valid (May 1952). The key assumption that measured variables are constant under any spatial permutation is not borne out by the expanding literature on measures of *spatial autocorrelation* (Mencken and Barnett 1999; Messner et al. 1999).

Within a crime context, spatial autocorrelation occurs when the frequency of crime in one spatial area makes its presence in an adjoining area more or less likely. More formally, assume x_i represents the crime count in n areal units as separate observations on X, and each x_i is drawn from the same crime population. If the measurements of x_i are pairwise correlated, then the crime data exhibit spatial autocorrelation (Cliff and Ord 1969). This commonly occurs with contiguous spatial units. When the frequency of crime in an adjoining area increases with the count in the original area then the data are said to exhibit *positive spatial autocorrelation*, a common occurrence with crime data. One regular cause of this spatial autocorrelation occurs when individual crimes are counted to administrative zones, such as census areas, city boroughs, or police districts. Failing to consider the spatial arrangement of the administrative areas and their relationships within statistical models assumes that the underlying phenomena driving the crime patterns are arranged on the same spatial mosaic. The problem with this assumption can be demonstrated with a noncrime example. Consider rainfall measurements conducted hourly at various locations within a city. The spatial scale of large weather patterns, such as cold fronts and their associated rain and thunderstorms, operates at a considerable scale, and therefore the individual rainfall measurements are not independent of the measurements at nearby locations, being influenced as they all are by the same larger phenomenon.

Within the context of crime, there is a growing body of research that finds certain characteristics of socioeconomic status and residential stability are relatively reliable predictors of community crime levels. The most consistent predictors of community crime rates, at least in the United States, appear to be socioeconomic factors and race (Pratt and Cullen 2005), though other researchers have identified residential stability, mainly for its role as a precursor to the formation of local supervisory controls (Bursik 1988). Resource inequality and concentrated disadvantage are also variables that have been found to significantly predict crime (Morenoff et al. 2001). All of these characteristics are available to researchers; however, they are usually accessible from summative units that are not conducive to research without alteration or adaptation. Political or topological features rarely mimic the underlying causal conditions and are a poor basis on which to combine crime counts. They are usually measures of convenience (so as to incorporate census measures in statistical models) rather than realistic spatial arrangements of underlying causal processes.

SPATIAL AUTOCORRELATION

The existence of spatial autocorrelation is a fundamental requirement of many current crime-mapping applications. For example, kernel density surface estimation (a hot spot mapping approach discussed in greater detail later in this chapter) allows an analyst to cover a whole study region with an estimate of the crime density in the local area through a process of spatially interpolating estimated values between crime points. As Goodchild (2009, 414) notes, "[s]patial interpolation, the widespread practice of inferring the values of fields from sample points, relies entirely on the almost universal existence of positive spatial autocorrelation in such phenomena ... Again, spatial autocorrelation is not a problem, but the basis of a solution."

In the absence of the geographic context, aspatial studies assume that geographic proximity is irrelevant to criminal behavior. In other words, offender behavior is assumed to be based on whatever measured characteristics exist within the study area, independent of the characteristics of neighboring places. The limitation of this approach was demonstrated by Rice and Smith's (2002) examination of vehicle theft. Moving from simple ordinary least squares regression models to a model that incorporated a measure of spatial autocorrelation, they concluded from their statistically significant spatial lag variable that "auto theft on a face block is affected not only by the structures and social traits characterizing that particular face block, but also the structures and social characteristics of the face blocks surrounding it" (Rice and Smith 2002, 328).

The characteristics of neighboring areas are therefore vital for a number of reasons. Neighboring places may have features (such as bars or schools) that draw offenders to the general area, they may be the target of a policing operation that displaces offenders, they may have crime-prevention activities that spread a diffusion of benefits, or they might be undergoing sociodemographic changes that impact the equilibrium in neighboring places. With the specific practitioner concerns regarding *displacement* (Barnes 1995; Eck 1993b) and the complementary concept of *diffusion of benefits* (Clarke and Weisburd 1994; Guerette and Bowers 2009; Weisburd et al. 2006), a complete analysis requires not only an explicit examination of crime transfer to and from different areas, but also the researcher must clearly articulate the spatial extent of any expected crime deflection (Barr and Pease 1990; Ratcliffe and Breen 2011).

Methods of Place-Based Research

This places the onus on the researcher to either create a custom geography, or to determine a specific geographic unit and number of units (e.g., face blocks, census areas, police beats) to model crime transfer. Only in this way can criminal behavior and decision making be modeled within a realistic framework where crime prevention activities have offender behavior consequences.

WHAT IS THE APPROPRIATE CONE OF RESOLUTION?

When researchers such as Adolphe Quetelet (1842) and Andre-Michel Guerry (1833) were studying crime across France, the unit of measurement was predetermined by the availability of data: the region was the only level available. Over time, as we detailed in earlier chapters, however, the *cone of resolution* (Brantingham et al. 1976) has moved from the national and regional level down to the routine availability of individual event data located with the accuracy and precision necessary to distinguish crime events at individual properties (Weisburd et al. 2009).

The move to place-based research raises new problems for the analyst to address. Within place-based research, methods have to adjust for the fact that while individual crime events can be identified as point locations, the explanatory context of the crime scene environment is often only available for analysis at larger units. These spatial units include neighborhood watch zones, business districts, police beats, or political boundaries. Even census data, which originate as a myriad of individual datum measurements, are distributed in cumulative format for anonymity purposes. Along with the challenges of working with spatial arrangements that do not follow the underlying causal conditions, other challenges include addressing edge effects of bounded space and the myriad issues surrounding the modifiable areal unit problem (MAUP). Like the ecological fallacy criticism raised by Robinson (1950), the MAUP concerns itself with the fact that you will gain a different understanding of a problem depending on the geographic units used. Sometimes that will occur simply because you are examining units such as census block groups versus census tracts, or clusters of street segments within a certain distance versus street segments themselves. Other times it will be the result of how boundaries are drawn, for example using a radius distance versus a square distance from a certain point.

As Rengert and Lockwood (2009) point out, researchers tend to accept the spatial divisions available to them uncritically and rarely create their own spatial units of analysis. They note that the purpose of creating analytical regions is to reduce the variance within each area and maximize the between-area variance. As such, it is generally the case that administrative boundaries created for noncrime purposes, such as administrative convenience, almost inevitably violate this fundamental research objective (to minimize internal variance and maximize between-unit variance). What is convenient for census officials is inconvenient for crime scientists.

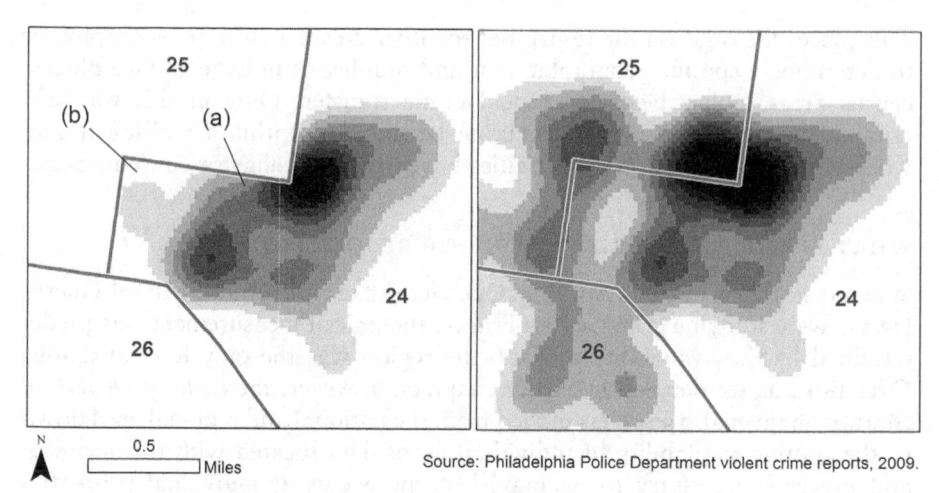

FIGURE 5.1. Impact of edge effects on crime hot spot surfaces.

Edge effects are one of the two symptoms of boundary effects (the other being a problem of the shape of an object affecting how its interaction with other objects is perceived). Edge effects occur when the result of an analysis within a study region would change if data from adjacent areas were made available. For example, Figure 5.1 shows a kernel density surface created from 2009 violent crime reports at the intersection of three police districts in Philadelphia, Pennsylvania. On the left side, the hot spot surface (with darker shading indicating a greater density of crime) is created from only crime reports in the 24th district and is constrained (clipped) to indicate only the crime hot spots within the 24th district. In the right-hand map, point data from surrounding districts were included in the analysis. Area (a) from the first map increases significantly in crime intensity with the inclusion of proximal data, and the area indicated at (b) also changes significantly. Overall, the images are but one example of the impact of edge effects removing neighboring context from a spatial analysis.

The MAUP is a spatial analysis concern caused by the use of discrete (and often arbitrary) boundaries to constrain data that are realized in an unbounded manner. For example, when point data are aggregated to spatial units, the scale and arrangement of the units can influence the outcome of the perception of the cumulative data as well as impact on the validity of statistical tests. The MAUP has a *scale problem* (where data variance is lost as the number of aggregation units is reduced) and an *aggregation problem* (when the variety of different possible aggregation outcomes affects a study). Andresen and Malleson (2011) recently compared two point data sets (from Vancouver, British Columbia, Canada) when these data were aggregated to a variety of areal units: census tracts, dissemination areas (equivalent to a U.S. census block), and street segments. They found that as the size of the areal unit is reduced, the similarity of crime concentration over a five-year period increased, suggesting more stability in chronic crime street segments and indicating that the results are a facet of the choice of aggregation unit.

While Andresen and Malleson's (2011) research supports the value of smaller areal units, there can be a tendency for crime researchers to aggregate to relatively large units. This is because crime is a somewhat rare event and therefore larger units of aggregation are preferable in order to achieve sufficient counts for statistical purposes (Brantingham et al. 2009). The downside of this aggregation is the reduction in variance between units, with the corollary that adjacent places are more likely to be spatially autocorrelated. As aggregation increases, variance decreases (Rengert and Lockwood 2009).

The ability to vary the cone of resolution is one of the great strengths of spatial criminology, but it also requires a varied and detailed skill set on the part of the researcher. Within crime science (Laycock 2005), the concept of place has now become not just fluid but also temporally dynamic. For example, the spatial influence of a nuisance bar can change in moments. When closed, the influence of the bar is largely constrained by the physical dimensions of the building (though house buyers might be wary of living close by). When open, the bar might influence crime both within the establishment as well as on the street immediately outside. If the bar employs poorly trained door staff, or has few rules about restricting service to drunken patrons, then the associated problems can spill onto the sidewalk. A case study of violent crime around 1,282 bars in Philadelphia reveals that violence is highly clustered within 85 feet, then dissipates rapidly, a pattern that is not replicated when fire stations are examined as control sites (Ratcliffe 2012). When a bar closes for the night, problems do not necessarily dissipate. It is possible that the influence of the bar spreads beyond its operating hours and location, as drunken patrons move through local streets potentially in search of cars, food, drugs, or public transportation. These problems of spatiotemporal fluidity pose significant problems for crime analysts, and it is likely that there is no ideal arrangement of rigid areal units that can perfectly encapsulate this dynamic environment. Therefore, when it is necessary to aggregate data, researchers should seek out the best imperfect choice of data units, and use appropriate analytical techniques to control for any problems resultant from these choices.

THE DEVELOPMENT OF NEW GEOGRAPHIES

As Waldo Tobler (1970, 236) articulated, "everything is related to everything else, but near things are more related than distant things." Within this simple statement lurks a problem for spatial criminologists in that much of the available research does not examine point location of data (places) but instead focuses on aggregate/areal units of information (spaces) (Rengert and Lockwood 2009).

As stated earlier, crime analysts and researchers alike often rely on the secondary nature of their data, and are restricted to using geographies as defined by other individuals or agencies. And the use of these administrative boundaries may then lead to significant issues with the resultant analysis. One possible response to these concerns is the commitment to examining these spatial distributions at multiple units of analysis, and in doing so learning how sensitive any results are to spatial scaling. Another potential response, and one that is now possible with modern GIS, is to focus on the smallest unit of analysis (microplace) and from here to generate new geographies. Of course, theoretical definition is key as well. Weisburd and colleagues (2012) focus on street segments, as we noted earlier, because they represent behavior settings and can be viewed as microcommunities. In this case the level of analysis is determined by a theory of the importance of the specific areal unit for defining the crime problem. Unfortunately, many studies begin simply with the spatial unit, usually relatively large, that is available from administrative sources (see Rengert and Lockwood 2009).

Brantingham et al. (2009) highlight the role that *computational criminology* has played in our current studies of crime analysis and the utility of GIS. The availability of GIS and of personal microcomputers has provided a capability that ten years ago would simply not have been possible. With the increased availability of big data, researchers now have an unprecedented ability to merge new tools with large data sets. This availability allows for the development of new geographies within the framework of theory (Brantingham et al. 2009; Caplan et al. 2011; Ratcliffe et al. 2009), or based on distance.

One of the most common distance metrics that has received widespread use is the GIS buffer. This tool allows for the development of a defined area surrounding a point at a set distance, and has been a standard tool available within most GIS software programs since their inception. While there is a great deal of evidence (Groff et al. 2009; Oberwittler and Wikström 2009; Weisburd et al. 2012; Zorbaugh 1929) to suggest that smaller units are more appropriate for analysis, it is also clear that it is not always appropriate to seek smaller and smaller levels of geography. As Rengert and Lockwood (2009) remind us, the unit of analysis needs to be discrete and should reflect the area necessary for the purposes of the analysis, and should not be a measure of convenience.

INNOVATIVE DATA APPLICATIONS OF GIS

The traditional implementation of GIS is characterized by the generation of maps demonstrating quantitative data from a single source alongside descriptive data from one or two variables simultaneously. However, as the availability of GIS has increased and the inclusion of crime analysts has become increasingly common in criminal justice agencies, innovative new techniques and methodologies have developed to take advantage of the information management capabilities of GIS, as well as the popularity of the graphical representation of information. Highlighted in the following are several examples of nontraditional applications of GIS technology.

Most applications of GIS highlight spatial patterns of quantitative data represented by a series of points, lines, or shapes. While the field of criminal justice has accepted this positivistic paradigm, critiques in other fields have raised concerns about this perspective (Curry 1997; Treves 2005). Notably, objections have been raised that oftentimes complex incidents, interactions, and social situations are reduced to dots on a map, and that computerized aggregation of these dots results in the loss of important information, as well as generating a false understanding that these incidents are comparable based on a single common characteristic (e.g., type of location, type of call for service, or type of criminal behavior).

In response to this, a series of efforts have been made to apply a mixed methods approach to the use of GIS, and in the development of its map-generating capabilities. Cope and Elwood (2009, 3) document this journey by focusing on what constitutes qualitative data within a GIS context: "data may be qualitative in part by virtue of the rich contextual detail they provide about social and material solutions ... data may also be qualitative if they contain or provide interpretations of the situations or processes that they describe."

Pavlovskaya (2009) argues for the role of GIS in understanding power relations and considers GIS in the context of being "constantly remade through the politics of its use, critical histories of it, and the interrogation of its concepts that underlay its design, data definition, collection and analysis. In other words, futures of GIS are contested and openings exist for new meanings, uses and effects" (Pavlovskaya 2006, 2004). She continues in this vein to consider seven contradictions or openings (Pavlovskaya 2009, 18–24) that are present in the current applications of GIS:

1. GIS origins are mainly nonquantitative,
2. Computerization is not quantification,
3. Spatial analysis in GIS is nonquantitative,
4. Digital data are not always for counting,
5. Database management and querying are based upon geographic location,
6. Mathematical modeling and statistics are still outside GIS, and
7. Visualization can be a qualitative analytical technique.

The implications of these ideas for the field of criminal justice are unclear, as the rush to new techniques and methods often obscures discussion of more conceptual issues. There are two that have at least been more widely discussed, notably contradictions 5 and 7. In regard to geographic location, there have been consistent calls for careful consideration of the decision on appropriate units of analysis (Openshaw 1984; Ratcliffe and McCullagh 1999) in regard to misspecification or the MAUP. In addition, a number of researchers have called for careful consideration with the use of spatial boundaries designated for administrative purposes (see, e.g., Bailey and Gatrell 1995; Ouimet 2000; Rengert and Lockwood 2009).

Perhaps most compelling of Pavlovskaya's contradictions is with regard to the qualitative nature of data visualization. A body of research has demonstrated the appeal of GIS in visualizing increasingly complex data in a simple and engaging way (Crampton 2001; Kwan 2007; Lewis 1998). Many researchers recognize the moment in a presentation when a map is displayed, and the audience is lost in the effort of finding their homes, their businesses, their current locations, or hot spots known to them. For those brief moments, the audience member is immersed in the area being represented, not necessarily the data being presented.

These qualitative efforts in GIS can take a number of forms. Elwood (2009) demonstrates the utility of a qualitative understanding of GIS, as maps are interpreted and reinterpreted in different ways by those who use them. The maps play a part in shaping the meaning that individuals apply to places. Knigge and Cope (2006) outline the basis for grounded visualization, which introduces the grounded theory perspective into the exploratory understanding of GIS data and maps. Pain et al. (2006) take a mixed methods approach by using qualitative interviews to support quantitative responses to questions of fear and safety in Northeast England, while Summers et al. (2010) use the same approach to study offender spatial decision making.

While it may be the case that a qualitative approach is not applicable to all research efforts by crime analysts or researchers in the field of criminal justice, it is clear that this approach could be applied to an increasing number of topics in the field even as the mixed methods approach to analyses continues to grow in popularity (Pain et al. 2006). Currently, most GIS software programs contain the ability to construct user-defined boundaries, as well as to incorporate images and aerials views into the GIS database, allowing for the potential that a qualitative visualization of the data can play an important role in our understanding of place and the people and behaviors that occur there.

Three-Dimensional Data in GIS

The field is replete with examples of GIS efforts that report and draw conclusions based on the representation of two-dimensional data; however, the inclusion of elevation data has garnered less attention from the field of criminal justice. Noteworthy exceptions to this include the work of Rengert and Lowell (2005), which examined the location of crime incidents within university buildings, and Wolff and Asche (2009), who focused on crime hot spots and crime scene investigations (see Figures 5.2 and 5.3).

Major GIS software providers, as well as a litany of websites, advertise the ability to examine crime and hot spots within three-dimensional spaces. Two challenges are faced in the context of moving from two-dimensional to a three-

Methods of Place-Based Research

FIGURE 5.2. Overlay of floors in Gladfelter Hall, the hot spot of crime identified within a building.
Original source: Rengert, G.F. and Lowell, R. (2005). *Police Foundation crime mapping news: A quarterly newsletter for crime mapping, GIS, problem analysis, and policing.* Washington, DC: Police Foundation.

dimensional crime analysis approach: the first is recognizing the challenges of how data are represented in this third dimension, and the second is the limited availability of valid data with the necessary level of detail.

Albrecht (2007) outlines three-dimensional GIS within the context of terrain modeling and highlights three different ways in which data may be visualized: (1) a wire frame model, (2) using triangulated irregular networks (TINs), and (3) through the use of raster surfaces. While users of computer-aided design (CAD) are no strangers to these techniques, their application in GIS, particularly in the field of criminal justice, has been largely overlooked. What each of these three approaches requires is a reliable measure of elevation, information that has largely been ignored except by those in civil engineering and geological surveying. Data generated by police practitioners (i.e., arrests, incidents, calls for police service) have become increasingly accurate in two dimensions. The next stage for police departments is the development of data models that

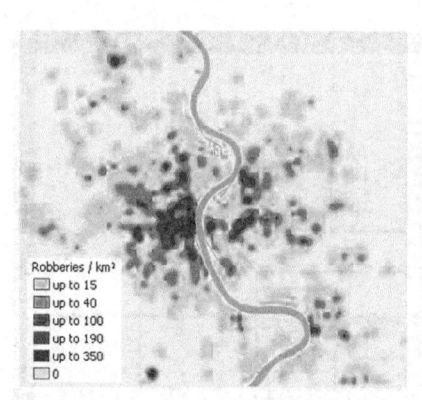

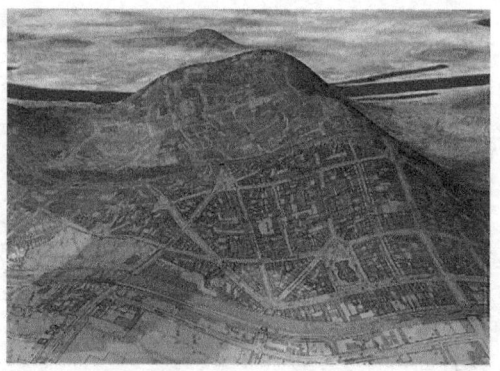

FIGURE 5.3. Hotspot grid with robber densities defined as number of incidents per square kilometer represented in form of a two-dimensional thematic Map (left image) and in form of a three-dimensional "information landscape" (right image).
Original source: Wolff, M. and Asche, H. (2009). "Exploring crime hotspots: Geospatial analysis and 3D mapping." In M. Schrenk, V. Popovich, D. Engelke, and P. Elisei (eds.), *Cities 3.0-smart, sustainable, and integrative* (pp. 147–156). Sitges, Spain: Competence Center of Urban and Regional Planning, Figure 3. With kind permission from Springer Science and Business Media.

record building floors in heavily urbanized environments, alongside the development of accompanying analytical and visualization techniques.

One concern that may be raised about investment in this area is the lack of generalizability due to the often low number of crimes occurring at particular locations within the interior of a building. Rengert and colleagues (2001) dealt with this issue by collapsing multiple floors of data to examine the distribution of the cases within the framework of a single floor. While this limits some of the unique benefits of using three-dimensional analysis, it did allow for a greater understanding of crimes occurring within similar areas on different floors, which identified a weakness in building design and in turn suggested a crime prevention solution.

In short, the utility of three-dimensional GIS in the field of criminal justice has been largely untested; however, with the increasing availability of tools to implement this type of analysis and the plethora of security issues that could benefit from this type of analysis, three-dimensional crime GIS approaches are likely to garner a great deal of attention in the future.

CCTV Camera Viewsheds

With the increasing implementation of closed-circuit television (CCTV) systems worldwide, there has been a greater scrutiny of CCTV effectiveness, leading to evaluations and increased examination of the effectiveness of this crime-prevention technology. Recent research (Caplan et al. 2011; Piza 2012; Ratcliffe et al. 2009) had identified the importance of considering more than the mere placement of a CCTV camera; the viewshed of the CCTV camera, or where the camera can "see," must also be considered in the scope of its crime-prevention capabilities. In short, offenders are less likely to be deterred if they believe that the camera cannot effectively view their behaviors.

Consideration of viewsheds is not unique to the field of criminal justice. Bettinger and Sessions (2003) report on an early application of viewsheds in determining locations of timber harvesting that would go unobserved. Albrecht (2007) highlights the use of viewsheds in the 1990s in determining the optimal placement of cellular towers. These efforts are the result of addressing limitations of the typical buffer analysis. In short, a buffer analysis makes the assumption that all behaviors, activities, and locations within a set distance from a point of interest are to be included in the analysis. This limitation has the potential to include areas that the presence of a CCTV camera or other intervention would be unlikely to impact.

In a study of crime in Philadelphia, Ratcliffe et al. (2009) worked with members of the Philadelphia Police Department to both map the location of CCTV cameras and develop a GIS overlay indicating the viewshed of the area that each CCTV camera could observe. Caplan et al. (2011) conducted a quasi-experiment to compare the impact of strategically placed cameras and randomly placed cameras. For both implementation types, a viewshed was constructed using a two-block radius and using Google Earth maps to identify obstacles that would block the line of sight of the camera. Piza (2012) developed this work further by considering how viewsheds of fixed locations may change over time rendering a camera ineffective at particular times.

In short, the inclusion of camera viewsheds is a step forward in better understanding the place-based decision making of offenders in locations where CCTV is present, a vital development in moving from traditional geography to using new methods to explore new geographies with improved spatial resolutions.

CRIME HOT SPOTS

As discussed earlier, researchers often perform analyses using data that are aggregated to areal units. A number of problems associated with this approach have been discussed, and one of the main risks with such an analytic strategy is that the theory to be tested and the approach to analysis may be disconnected (or only loosely coupled), with the corollary that research conclusions may be misleading. As noted, in the past some researchers have aggregated data in this way for statistical reasons – sometimes because crimes are so rare that failing to do so would make it difficult to use appropriate analytic models; however, it can also be because the statistical models found in software packages of which researchers are aware do not allow analyses at the level of resolution they would like.

In recent years, there have been advances in the types of analyses undertaken and the level of resolution at which the analyses are focused. For instance, instead of analyzing patterns at the area level, researchers increasingly analyze patterns at the street segment level (e.g., Groff et al. 2010; Johnson and Bowers 2010;

Weisburd et al. 2012), or the point level, where the point could represent an individual residential dwelling (see Farrell 1995) or a particular type of facility (e.g., Eck et al. 2007). In terms of analytic approaches, ever-increasing computing power has facilitated the use of more sophisticated and computationally intensive approaches, and researchers increasingly borrow techniques from the expanding library of techniques from other disciplines or develop their own.

In the case of home-grown approaches to new techniques, researchers are increasingly using *permutation approaches* to test hypotheses. The advantage of such tests is that, because they can be programmed by a researcher, they can be used to answer very specific research questions. To take an example, one might want to know if burglary locations are spatially clustered such that crimes tend to occur closer to each other than would be expected on a chance basis. A nearest neighbor analysis can be used to answer such a question, and the approach to analysis is to simply calculate the distance between each crime and that nearest to it. An average nearest neighbor distance can then be calculated and compared with what would be expected if the pattern were random. In the past, the latter would be calculated by assuming that burglaries might occur anywhere. This is an unrealistic assumption that can easily lead to erroneous conclusions.

Using a permutation test, however, it is simple to calculate what the expected nearest neighbor distances would be if the researcher knows where all of the homes that *could* be burgled are located (see Johnson 2010). Increases in the availability of such data make this type of analysis easier. Similar analyses can be conducted to examine whether spatial clustering occurs at the street segment level (Andresen and Malleson 2011; Johnson and Bowers 2010) or any other level. Using these techniques, it has been shown that crimes such as burglary do cluster in space, with some street segments and some neighborhoods experiencing a disproportionate volume of offenses – volumes that significantly exceed what would be expected if the risk of crime were evenly distributed.

This has clear implications for those engaged in crime reduction, such as the police. If some locations experience more crime than others, crime reduction resources should be allocated accordingly – being deployed to those locations where they are most needed. In support of this, research concerned with hot spots policing – whereby police patrols focus on high crime locations – demonstrates the effectiveness of such a deployment strategy (see Chapter 6).

Spatiotemporal Hotspots

As well as demonstrating that crime clusters in space, research shows that it clusters in time. Such patterns can be examined in a number of ways. For example, one can examine if and how the risk of crime varies over the course of a typical day or year. In addition, one can examine how it varies from one day to the next, and if and how patterns of crime on one day influence those on the next.

Considering how the risk of crime typically varies over the course of a day, distinct patterns are to be expected as people's routine activities generally vary over the course of the day. This means that people themselves have a varying exposure to being a victim of crime at certain times of the day, and their homes are more likely to be unprotected by their presence at particular times (see Cohen and Felson 1979; Ratcliffe 2006). One complication with examining how patterns of crime vary over the course of the day is that for many crimes, the actual time of an offense will be unknown. For example, burglary victims may be on holiday or away from home when an offense occurs. Ratcliffe and McCullagh (1998) have developed a technique known as *aoristic analysis* to cope with such issues, and the technique allows an analyst to produce a profile for a set of offenses that estimates how the risk of crime varies throughout the day. Combining this type of analysis with an analysis of where crimes typically occur provides a more precise way of determining where *and* when to deploy crime reduction resources (see Ratcliffe 2004b).

However, while some crimes occur in relatively high volumes, the rate of crime per day in any particular neighborhood, or along a particular street segment, will typically be low. Thus, while assigning resources to the riskiest locations at the riskiest times of the day will be a substantial improvement over random deployments, it will sometimes mean that resources are allocated to places at times when no crime can be expected to occur. Therefore, an understanding of the days on which crime is most likely, would be of clear benefit. More recent analytic advances are of value in this respect.

To elaborate, research concerned with repeat victimization indicates that some people, facilities, and households are at a greater risk than others. Moreover, when repeat victimization occurs it tends to do so swiftly (see Farrell 1995; Pease 1998), and this timing differs significantly from what would be expected if the timing of events were random (e.g., Johnson and Bowers 2004b). This is important in that it offers insight into not just *where* crimes might next occur, but *when* they might do so. From a policy perspective, this suggests that to prevent repeat victimization – and hence crime more generally – any responses need to be implemented quickly. A number of strategies designed to reduce repeat victimization have been implemented and evaluated, and the best available evidence suggests that they are effective at reducing repeat victimization, and offending in the neighborhood more generally (Grove et al. 2012). Importantly, preventing repeat victimization does not simply lead to offenders displacing their activity and targeting nearby homes that do not receive the intervention. In fact, in some studies that have focused on the crime of burglary (e.g., Forrester et al. 1988; Webb 1996), reductions in burglary (measured at the area level) have exceeded 50 percent.

As discussed, the research concerned with repeat victimization suggests that victims of crime are at an elevated risk of crime in the future. This knowledge can inform predictions as to when and where crime will occur in the future, but it offers no insight for those as yet not victimized; however, understanding why repeat victimization occurs might. While repeat victimizations of the same person or home may occur for a number of reasons (see Johnson 2008; Pease 1998), one of the most likely explanations is that offenses committed against the same victim are the work of the same offender. Most detected repeat burglaries are the work of a returning offender (e.g., Bernasco 2008; Johnson et al. 2009), as are thefts from motor vehicles (Johnson et al. 2009).

Inspired by this type of reasoning, researchers have argued (e.g., Johnson and Bowers 2004b; Townsley et al. 2003) that having burglarized one home, a successful burglar should not only be more likely to revictimize that home but – because homes that are near to each other tend to be similar to each other – he or she should also target those nearby, committing what have been referred to as *near repeats* (Morgan 2001). As things may change over time, bringing uncertainty in the eyes of the offender, it has also been predicted that where offenders return to homes they have already victimized or those nearby, they would be most likely to do so quickly. To test this hypothesis, researchers have adapted techniques from the field of epidemiology, originally designed to detect disease contagion. A number of approaches have been developed, but a variant of the Knox (1964) test is the most commonly employed technique. For this test, each crime (usually of a particular type) is compared with every subsequent crime and the distance and time between these pairs of events calculated. In the case of burglary, if offenders do in fact swiftly target homes that are near to those that they have previously victimized, then we would expect to find that more burglaries occur near to each other in space *and* time than would be expected. Estimating how many crimes would be expected to occur near to each other in time and space if offenders do not adopt the types of strategy discussed can be achieved in a number of ways. However, researchers typically do this in such a way that the same spatial hot spots of crime observed in the actual data are present in the expected distribution. Moreover, any seasonal or daily variation in the level of crime observed in reality is preserved in the patterns expected. This is accomplished through the use of a permutation test (Johnson et al. 2007).

A series of studies (e.g., Johnson et al. 2007; Townsley et al. 2003) has shown that burglary does cluster in space *and* time in a way that is consistent with the near repeat hypothesis. Moreover, studies have shown that other offenses such as theft from motor vehicles (Johnson et al. 2009), shootings (Ratcliffe and Rengert 2008), and robberies (Grubesic and Mack 2008) exhibit near repeat patterns.

PREDICTIVE TECHNIQUES

We noted earlier in the chapter the policy movement toward finding predictive tools in policing. The technique most commonly used is kernel density estimation (KDE). Such maps use simple algorithms to produce a smoothed crime intensity surface estimated from existing crime reports. From a predictive perspective, the assumption underpinning the use of such maps is that the areas that were most at risk in the past will continue to be so in the future.

An alternative approach is to identify those features of the environment that have been found to be associated with crime risk – such as where offenders are believed to live, where bars are located, and so on – and to then generate a map that identifies where these features are located and where there are concentrations of them (see Groff and LaVigne 2001). The theory behind this approach is that, regardless of whether crimes have previously been observed in an area, if particular combinations of features are found there, then the *potential* for crime to occur in that area will be higher than it is in areas without such features. Risk terrain modeling (RTM; e.g., Caplan, Kennedy, and Miller 2011) is an example of this type of approach. To generate an RTM map, the researcher first produces a series of map layers, one for each criminogenic feature of interest. These individual layers are then combined to produce a composite map that identifies where high concentrations of features thought to be criminogenic coalesce. It is in such areas that crime is anticipated to most likely occur. This approach has been used to study crimes including shootings (Caplan et al. 2011), as is illustrated in Figure 5.4. The results are encouraging, showing that these approaches outperform KDE maps, at least for long-term predictions.

Neither of the aforementioned approaches, KDE and RTM, currently incorporates what is known about the space-time dynamics of crime (see previous section). Prospective crime mapping (e.g., Bowers et al. 2004; Johnson et al. 2007) was a first attempt to do this. To generate such maps, a simple mathematical equation is used to mimic the near repeat process. That is, when a crime occurs, that crime is assumed to lead to an elevation in risk at the location at which it occurred and those nearby, but this elevation in risk is assumed to decay over time. When a series of crimes occurs near to each other, the risk of crime is assumed to be elevated in an additive fashion such that if two crimes occur, the risk of crime will be temporarily doubled. Figure 5.5 illustrates the process. As well as the risk of crime *diffusing* over time, it is assumed to diffuse across space so that the risk of crime will be most elevated where the crime occurred but that the risk will also be higher for nearby locations, with the strength of this elevation decaying the further one is from the crime event.

A further approach takes account of the joint influences of the space-time dynamics of crime and features of the environment that do not change but may increase the potential for crime to occur. Johnson et al. (2009) reported a model (referred to as *ProMap*) for the crime of burglary, which develops the prospective mapping approach by including in the model features of the environment that likely affect this type of crime. Such features included variation in housing density, the presence of major roads (see Johnson and Bowers 2010), and a variety of sociodemographic factors. This model was shown to significantly

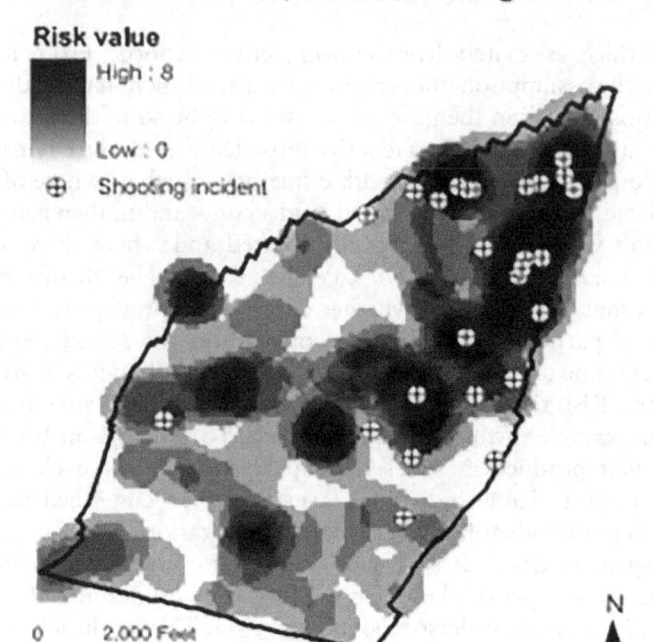

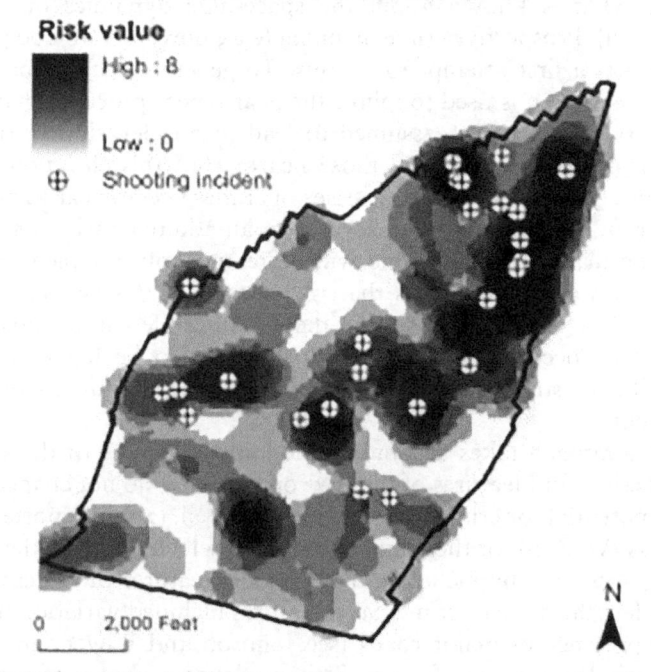

FIGURE 5.4. Risk terrain and shooting overlay.
Original source: Caplan, J.M., Kennedy, L.W., and Miller, J. (2011). "Risk terrain modeling: Brokering criminological theory and GIS methods for crime forecasting." *Justice Quarterly*, 28(2), 360–381. Reprinted with permission of Taylor & Francis Ltd.

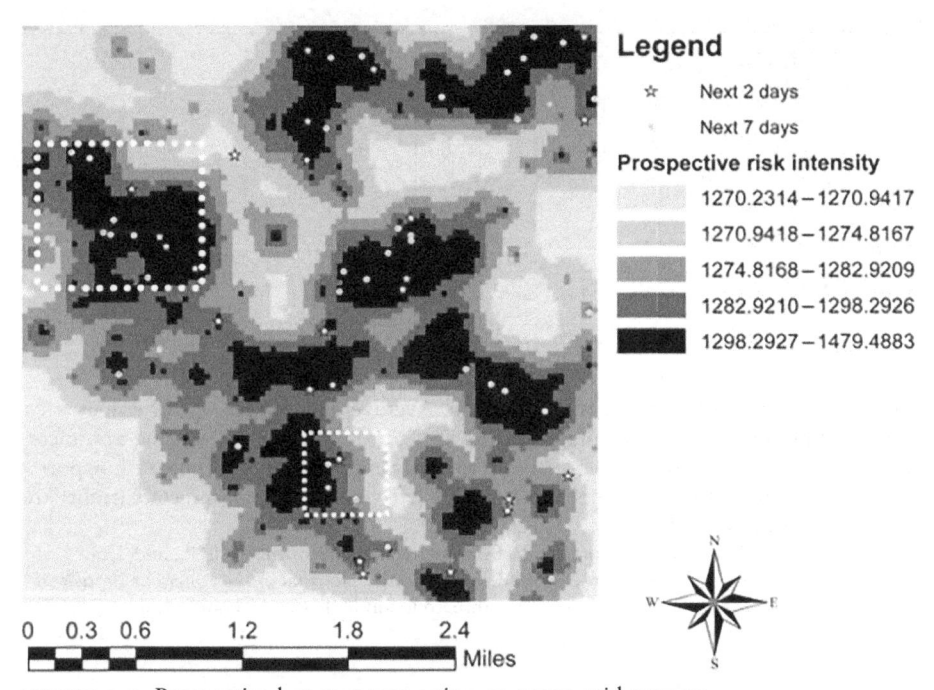

FIGURE 5.5. Prospective hot spot map using 50-meter grid squares.
Original source: Bowers, K.J., Johnson, S.D., and Pease, K. (2004). "Prospective hot-spotting the future of crime mapping?" *British Journal of Criminology*, 44(5), 641–658. By permission of Oxford University Press.

outperform predictions based on KDE maps and the standard prospective mapping approach.

Mohler et al. (2011) adopt a similar approach, but use a slightly different method that also captures the space-time dynamics of crime and estimates the influence of other factors to produce predictions of where crime might next occur. To do this, they first use a statistical model known as a *self-exciting point process* to estimate the extent to which a near repeat process contributes to future patterns of crime, and the degree to which other factors that do not change over time have a part to play. In the case of the latter, the particular features concerned are not specified – instead their collective influence is estimated using the statistical model. Having estimated the influence of each type of factor, the model can then be used to generate predictions as to where crime is most likely to occur in the future (see Figure 5.6). This approach has been shown to outperform KDE and standard prospective maps, but has not yet been compared to *ProMap* predictions.

On the basis of the findings presented here, it would appear that those forecasting methods that model both the space-time dynamics of crime and

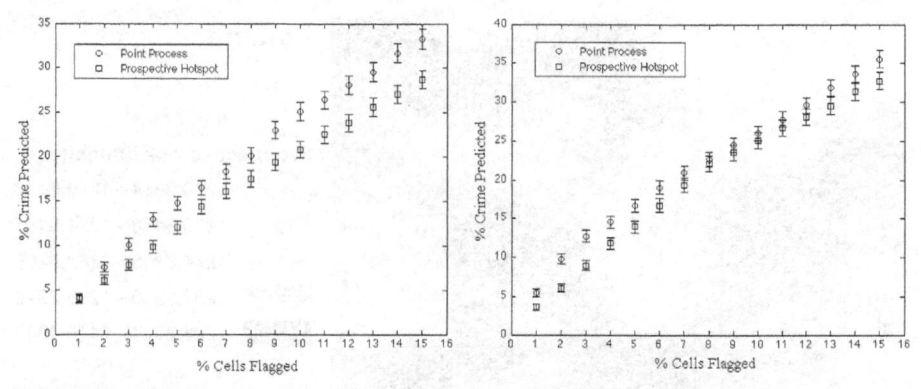

FIGURE 5.6. Forecasting strategy comparison. Average daily percentage of crimes predicted plotted against percentage of cells flagged for 2005 burglary using 200-meter by 200-meter cells. Error bars correspond to the standard error. Prospective hotspot cutoff parameters are 400 meters and 8 weeks (left) and optimal parameters (right) are 200 meters and 39 weeks.
Original source: Mohler, G.O., Short, M.B., Brantingham, P.J., Schoenberg, F.P., and Tita, G.E. (2011). "Self-exciting point process modeling of crime." *Journal of the American Statistical Association*, 106(493), 100–108. Reprinted with permission of Taylor & Francis Ltd.

the influence of features of the environment that do not change (at least on a short time scale) are those that are most accurate in predicting future crime locations. The precise extent to which the use of such methods will offer improvements in police practice requires investigation, but it would seem imprudent not to aspire to use the best available tools to reduce crime.

COMPUTER SIMULATIONS

The types of models so far discussed are those that seek to predict where crime is most likely to occur over the next few days or months. Computer simulations represent a different approach that can be used to answer different types of questions. While such models have been around for some time, it is only in the last decade that they have really been embraced by those involved in the study and prevention of crime. They are generally used for one of two purposes. The first is to see if a model can be developed that is able to reproduce patterns of crime as observed in the real world (e.g., see Birks et al. 2012; Groff 2007a,b). Thus, such simulation models – which are based on theoretical explanations of crime – allow researchers to test how good a job their theory does in explaining a phenomenon of interest. Second, simulations can be used to ask "what if?" questions, such as whether a particular policy intervention might reduce crime and, if so, by how much. The advantage of the latter is that experimental trials of particular interventions are generally costly, and a simulation allows a researcher to test the plausibility of whether it is likely to work prior to implementation, and how a range of different approaches might affect outcomes. Simulations also allow the researcher to estimate how intense an intervention might need to be for it to have an observable impact on crime levels.

A number of different types of computer simulation models exist (for a review, see Gilbert and Troitzsch 2005), but three types of models in particular have been applied to the study of spatial patterns of crime. These are *cellular automata*,[2] *microsimulation*, and *agent-based models* (ABMs), the latter two of which will be briefly discussed here. In the case of microsimulations, the researcher identifies a population of interest (e.g., residents of a city) and then represents it in a model. Each member of the population is given a set of attributes and these may change over time in systematic ways and/or on a chance basis. Consider a burglary simulation implemented by Johnson (2009). In this model, every home in one U.K. county was identified and allocated a risk of burglary – calculated using data recorded by the police and census information. Each home was also allocated a number of physical security measures that would reduce the risk of burglary. The aim of the study was to determine if, in the absence of a simulated intervention, patterns of near repeats as observed in the real world could be generated in the simulation if the only thing that determined whether a home was burgled were the general risk to that home, or whether it was necessary to temporarily boost the risk to burgled homes and those nearby. The results of that study demonstrated that realistic patterns of near repeats could only be generated by modeling the long-term risk to homes and a temporary boost that diffused in space and time.

ABMs represent a more sophisticated type of computer simulation. Such models are made up of two components: (1) agents that represent the actors whose behavior the model is intended to simulate and (2) an environment within which the agents operate and interact. Agents can represent any type of actor the researcher is interested in, and they can be given a variety of characteristics that influence their behavior. Agents' behavior is typically governed by a set of condition action rules that specify their decision making for a range of situations. As such, agents are usually rational decision makers considering the costs and benefits of their actions (but they need not be). Rather than being deterministic – which is to say that an agent will consistently make the same decision under the same circumstances – ABMs are usually stochastic, which means that while an agent will make rational choices, an element of randomness is introduced to ensure that choices vary across situations. Making the simulation stochastic in this way also helps model other factors that might affect an actor's behavior but that are not explicitly included in the simulation. An important feature of ABMs is that the choices one agent makes can affect those made by another, and the environment that the agents inhabit, and this can lead to the emergence of complex behaviors (spatial or otherwise) that might not be expected. For most models of this kind, the proximity of one agent to another is a key determinant of how they influence each other's behavior.

Moreover, as with spatial analyses of crime in the real world, a key factor in building such models is how to best represent and divide up the spatial environment to best test the theory of interest.

A number of examples have been published that illustrate the sorts of what-if questions ABMs can be used to examine. For example, Epstein (2002) described an ABM model of civil violence that reproduces patterns observed in the real world, and that can be used to estimate what the effects of different police strategies might be in dealing with such problems. Batty and colleagues (2003) described an ABM of the Notting Hill Carnival in London (United Kingdom). This was designed to examine what effect changing the route and the physical layout of the event would have on the likelihood of people being injured during the carnival. Johnson (2009) used an ABM to simulate the possible effects of hot spots policing on reducing crime.

In the case of each example, an advantage of using simulations is that the models can be tested time and time again. This is useful for two reasons. First, it enables the researcher to see how the outcomes of the simulation vary from one run of the model to another. In some cases, a simulation model may generate similar results every time, whereas in other cases the outcomes of the model may be very unpredictable. Where model outcomes for a particular simulated policy are very unpredictable, one may wish to tread carefully when considering whether to adopt such a policy in the real world. Second, being able to run the model many times allows the researcher to make slight changes to the model and observe how these affect model outcomes. For example, Johnson (2009) examines how increasing the number of police involved in a hot spots policing simulation influences the level of simulated crime, and how this compares with a model in which police patrols move randomly. The results indicate that for the hot spots policing simulation, increasing the number of officers decreases the level of crime in a linear way. However, the same is not true for simulated random patrolling strategies, for which increasing the number of police does not always reduce crime.

OPERATIONAL DECISION MAKING WITH NEW GEOGRAPHIES

The change in geographical focus down to the street block level and individual location will change the focus of decision making at the policing and policy level. For example, former Police Chief Jim Bueermann (2012) reported how the Redlands Police Department dispensed with traditional beat boundaries and instead assigned officers to patrol hot spots determined directly from KDE analysis of crime patterns. The Philadelphia Foot Patrol Experiment identified violent hot spots with a local Moran's I analysis of Thiessen polygons centered on street intersections (Ratcliffe et al. 2011). These new methods and techniques will enable a more focused government and policy response to problems that do not manifest at the census tract level, or at the level of police districts, but instead are microplace problems.

The issue of crime-specific locations, such as bars and nightclubs, is a further example of the need for governmental responses that are more place-specific and focused. New analytical approaches that enable examining the extent of violence around places, such as bars, can help policy makers determine the spatial extent of any crime spillover and craft a suitable response. Block-based analysis (Groff 2011), or the use of microbuffers around criminogenic places (Ratcliffe 2012) can drive specific distance metrics that can maximize policy outcomes while minimizing impacts on unaffected locations.

The next challenge will be a process of continued spatial analysis development on microplace methods and practice, aligned with a knowledge transfer campaign to educate policy makers and decision makers in the public safety industry about the place-specific, focused tools that are available. The challenge for policy makers is to develop confidence in the resultant analyses and respond with appropriate targeted policies.

CONCLUSIONS

There has been an explosion in new methods and practices to understand the microlevel crime problem at places and small spaces. The development from larger aggregate studies at the census tract level to the new paradigm has been rapid and vigorous, but at the same time, there remain challenges of cohesion and normalization. At present, there are too few reviews of various techniques, and many scholars and practitioners are adopting approaches to spatial research with little appreciation for the benefits and limitations of the analytical approach in question. For example, RTM is increasingly popular yet at present the benefits over other analytical approaches have rarely been independently verified. Ongoing evaluation will assist the analytical community with robust measures of confidence in various activities, as is currently underway in the geographic profiling community (Kent et al. 2006; Rich and Shively 2004).

A second limitation of the current paradigm is a data limitation. Within the last few years, the quality and precision of available crime data have lagged behind the analytical progress to where there remains a very real concern that future analytical development will be hampered by poor data quality that will inhibit confidence in further data exploration. The data quality that currently exists, especially for crime recorded by police departments, was satisfactory a decade ago, but the new techniques (many of which are discussed in this chapter) are rapidly starting to outstrip the quality of the existing data. New development needs to progress on multiple fronts if spatial criminology is to continue moving the boundaries at the current rate.

All this being said, there has been an explosion of new spatial criminological techniques for analyzing spatial data over the last decade, many of which we have reviewed in this chapter. Not only are we able to analyze crime at individual locations, but many techniques actively consider the influence of nearby locations. As Townsley (2009, 456) predicts, "adjacency will become a fundamental feature in any spatial analysis, independent of theory."

In this chapter, we have emphasized the importance of methodological advances in the development of the criminology of place. As we have noted, methods have emerged to meet the theoretical developments in the field, as well as practical crime-prevention efforts. Just as the focus on place has demanded rethinking of traditional understandings of the crime problem, it has also called for new innovations in the methods we use to analyze crime.

6

Reducing Crime at High-Crime Places[1]

Practice and Evidence

The fact that crime and disorder are concentrated at a few places is interesting and deserves an explanation. It is also interesting that places show up in other criminological theories and in other disciplines. And it is useful to understand the methods for studying places. However, a primary reason we are interested in high-crime places is that it might be possible to do something about crime by addressing these places. We are convinced that focusing on places can substantially reduce crime and disorder. Our conviction is not a matter of faith, but is based on over twenty-five years of accumulating evidence.

This chapter summarizes the research evidence examining whether focusing on crime places reduces crime. We first discuss a broad range of place-based prevention strategies examined by Eck and Guerrette (2012). This review provides strong evidence for a place-based approach to crime prevention. We then turn to a specific form of place-based crime prevention – hot spots policing (Sherman and Weisburd 1995). Again, we have a strong body of evidence supporting a place-based approach. Having reviewed hot spots policing, we turn to the importance of place managers and third parties in controlling problem places. We then examine an extension of the third-party approach to argue that a place-based approach to crime may free crime control policy from the police monopoly. Then we describe how a place-based approach to crime could be incorporated in community corrections to improve probation and parole outcomes. Finally, we review the larger body of research on the potential threat of crime displacement, and its opposite, the diffusion of crime control benefits. Consistently, the evidence described in this chapter clearly shows the substantial utility of a place-based approach for reducing crime.

SITUATIONAL CRIME PREVENTION AT PLACES

In Chapter 3 we argued for the importance of social disorganization theories for understanding crime places. This is an area where basic research suggests promise (e.g., see Weisburd et al. 2012; Weisburd et al. 2014), but where there is little evidence of effectiveness of specific practices. Such evidence is beginning to be developed,[2] but we can say little at this juncture. In contrast, the evidence regarding opportunity reduction and crime has grown systematically over the last few decades.

Summarizing this evidence, Eck and Guerette (2012) conducted a systematic review of 149 evaluations of the effectiveness of situational crime prevention at places. Seventy-seven percent of these interventions were effective and only 7 percent were ineffective (the remaining evaluations had mixed or inconclusive findings). Over two-thirds of these evaluations used moderate to strong designs to rule out most alternative explanations for the outcomes. This gives us reasonable confidence that intentionally created changes in opportunities often result in crime or disorder changes. With some variation, these results are true over a wide variety of place types (residential, retail sales, transport, public ways, and recreational).

We have extracted from Eck and Guerette's (2012) paper results dealing with important opportunity-based constructs – offender, target, guardianship, physical environment, and place management. We only examine programs that explicitly manipulated aspects of routine activity theory (n = 112). We ignored evaluations that manipulated other opportunity characteristics (e.g., rapid cleanup to address the rewards offenders receive from graffiti), and evaluations of combinations of interventions (e.g., security guards and physical redesign). Thus, this summary is very conservative.

Table 6.1 summarizes their results. For each construct more interventions were successful than were not. The worst performers were interventions that manipulated targets, but here we have the fewest evaluations to compare. Fourteen projects implemented some form of access control designed to keep possible offenders out. All but one were clearly effective. Of the five target interventions, three were effective (the one target removal evaluation showed clear success, but property marking to prevent burglaries is of dubious value). Sixty percent of the guardianship interventions were effective (and only 13 percent were obviously ineffective). Twenty-two evaluations looked at some form of physical redesign of buildings or streets. Eighty-six percent of these interventions were effective, according to the studies' authors. Finally, evaluators have examined nine place management interventions, two of which were randomized experiments. Eight of the nine evaluations showed place management to be effective, and the ninth had mixed results.

Scientists often claim that the ability to control nature is the ultimate achievement of a scientific theory. We have just reviewed evidence that opportunity theories give policymakers this ability. Most of the evaluations reviewed

TABLE 6.1 *Effectiveness of Opportunity-Based Interventions at Places*

Intervention	Effective	Not Effective	Mixed Results	Inconclusive Results	Percent (row n)
Offender					
Access Control	93 (13)			7 (1)	8 (14)
Target					
Removal	100 (1)				1 (1)
Devaluing*	50 (2)	50 (2)			4 (4)
Guardianship					
CCTV	59 (22)	14 (5)	24 (9)	3 (1)	33 (37)
Lighting	55 (11)	15 (3)	15 (3)	15 (3)	18 (20)
Patrols & Surveillance	80 (4)			20 (1)	4 (5)
Physical Environment					
CPTED	94 (15)			6 (1)	14 (16)
Street Redesign	67 (4)		17 (1)	17 (1)	5 (6)
Place Management	89 (8)		11 (1)		8 (9)
Total	71 (80)	9 (10)	13 (14)	7 (8)	100 (112)

* Property marking (3) and use of ink tags (1)
Original source: Eck, J.E., and Guerette, R.T. (2012). "Place-based crime prevention: theory, evidence, and policy." In B.C. Welsh and D.P. Farrington (eds.), *The Oxford Handbook of Crime Prevention* (pp. 354–383). New York: Oxford University Press, Table 8 and modified using information from Tables 3–7 and the Appendix. By permission of Oxford University Press.

by Eck and Guerrette (2012) were at least moderately strong, and very few were cross-sectional or correlational designs. These results provide strong indication that crime prevention at places can be very effective. The implications for theory are also straightforward. This evidence rules out the possibility that disorganization characteristics alone produce crime place hot spots. If disorganization were the sole explanation, the opportunity blocking evaluations would not have been so clearly successful. This suggests any explanation for high-crime or-disorder places must involve opportunity, either alone or in combination with addressing social disorganization.

POLICE EFFORTS TO CONTROL CRIME HOT SPOTS

Researchers have developed a narrower, but very persuasive, literature on crime prevention at places with regard to police interventions (Braga and Weisburd 2010). Hot spots policing is the application of police interventions at very small geographic units of analysis. The first formal evaluation of hot spots policing, a test of concentrated police patrol in crime hot spots in Minneapolis during the early to mid-1990s (Sherman and Weisburd 1995), spawned a series of rigorous hot spots policing studies.

In the Minneapolis Hot Spots Patrol Experiment (Sherman and Weisburd 1995), computerized mapping of crime calls was used to identify 110 hot spots of roughly street-block length. Police patrol was doubled on average for the experimental sites over a ten-month period. Officers in Minneapolis were not given specific instructions on what activities to engage in while present in hot spots. They simply were told to increase patrol time in the treatment hot spots, and the activities they engaged in ranged a good deal from more proactive problem-solving efforts to simply sitting in the car parked in the center of a hot spot street segment. The study found that the experimental as compared with the control hot spots experienced statistically significant reductions in crime calls and observed disorder. The significant decline in calls for service was driven largely by a decline in soft crime calls (e.g., disturbances, drunks, noise, vandalism). While soft crime calls declined 7.2 to 15.9 percent in the treatment group relative to the control group, depending on the time period examined, hard crime calls (e.g., burglaries, auto thefts, assaults) declined a nonstatistically significant 2.6 to 5.9 percent.

The results overall, though, suggested increased police presence could have a significant effect on crime, particularly disorder and less serious crime. This marked a major change from the conventional wisdom about the impact the police could have on crime. The most influential prior study of police patrol at the time was the Kansas City Preventive Patrol Experiment (Kelling et al. 1974), which found that neither doubling nor removing preventive patrol in a beat had a significant impact on crime or victimization. The finding that police randomly patrolling beats is not an effective crime deterrent makes sense based on the review of the crime concentration literature in Chapter 2. Since crime is very concentrated across cities, it makes little sense from an effectiveness and efficiency standpoint to respond with a strategy relying on the random distribution of police resources across large geographic areas.

While the initial Minneapolis study did not include a systematic examination of officer activities in the hot spots, subsequent analyses by Koper (1995) provide some insight into how much time officers should be spending in hot spots to maximize residual deterrence. Koper analyzed observational data on nearly 17,000 instances when police drove through or stopped at a hot spot and examined the time from when the officer(s) left the location until the next occurrence of criminal or disorderly behavior. Using survival analysis techniques, he found that each additional minute of time officers spent in a hot spot increased survival time by 23 percent. Survival time here refers to the amount of time after officers departed a hot spot before disorderly activity occurred. The ideal time spent in the hot spot was fourteen to fifteen minutes; after about fifteen minutes, there were diminishing returns and increased time did not lead to greater improvements in residual deterrence. This phenomenon is often referred to as the "Koper curve" as graphing the duration response curve shows the benefits of increased officer time spent in the hot spot until a plateau point is reached at around fifteen minutes (see Figure 1 in Koper 1995). As Koper (1995, 668) notes, "police can maximize crime and disorder reduction at hot spots by making proactive, medium-length stops at these locations on a random, intermittent basis." Koper argues for an approach in which police travel among hot spots, spending about fifteen minutes in each hot spot to maximize residual deterrence, and moving from hot spot to hot spot in an unpredictable order, so that potential offenders recognize a greater cost of offending in these areas because police enforcement could increase at any moment.

Koper's (1995) recommendations were applied to the design of a more recent hot spots policing experiment in Sacramento, California. Officers were explicitly instructed to rotate between treatment group hot spots and to spend about fifteen minutes in each hot spot. Results suggest the Koper (1995) approach to hot spots policing had a significant impact on crime. Treatment group hot spots had significantly fewer calls for service and Part I crime incidents than control group hot spots when comparing the three-month period of the experiment in 2011 to the same period in 2010 (Telep et al. 2014).

Significant crime and disorder declines are also reported in a series of randomized controlled experiments that tested a more tailored, problem-oriented approach (see Goldstein 1990) to dealing with crime hot spots (see Braga and Weisburd 2010). In the Jersey City Problem-Oriented Policing in Violent Places experiment (Braga et al. 1999), for example, the exact response varied by hot spot, but the responses all included some aspect of aggressive order maintenance and most included efforts to make physical improvements to the area (e.g., removing trash, improving lighting) and drug enforcement. Strong, statistically significant reductions in total crime incidents and total crime calls were found in the treatment hot spots relative to the control hot spots. Social and physical observation data showed improvement in visible disorder in ten of the eleven treatment areas compared with the control sites after the intervention.

In the Jersey City Drug Market Analysis Program experiment (Weisburd and Green 1995b), a step-wise problem-solving model was compared with generalized enforcement in drug hot spots. The treatment group received a three-stage intervention. In the planning stage, officers collected data on the physical, social, and criminal characteristics of each area; in the implementation stage, officers coordinated efforts to conduct a crackdown at the hot spot and used other relevant responses to address underlying problems; and finally, in the maintenance stage, officers attempted to maintain the positive impact of the crackdown. The experimental sites had significantly smaller increases in disorder calls compared with the control sites. In particular, the project had a positive impact on calls related to public morals and suspicious persons.

In Lowell, Massachusetts, a problem-oriented policing intervention to address disorder was associated with a statistically significant 20 percent reduction in crime and disorder calls for service at the treatment hot spots compared with the control hot spots (Braga and Bond 2008). Systematic observations confirmed the official crime data results, showing significant reductions in social and physical disorder at the treatment places relative to the control places.

The Braga and Bond (2008) experiment also included a mediation analysis to assess which hot spots strategies were most effective in reducing crime. Results suggested that situational prevention strategies had the strongest impact on crime and disorder. Such approaches are often a prominent part of hot spot interventions, particularly those involving problem solving and include actions such as securing lots, razing abandoned buildings, and cleaning up graffiti. Increases in misdemeanor arrests made some contribution to the crime control gains in the treatment hot spots, but were not as influential as the situational efforts. Social service interventions did not have a significant impact on crime and disorder. These findings suggest not only the importance of situational crime prevention as a strategy for addressing crime facilitators in hot spots, but also that aggressive order maintenance through increases in misdemeanor arrests may not be the most effective way of addressing high-disorder places (see Braga et al. 2015).

More recently, an experimental study in Jacksonville, Florida, (Taylor et al. 2011) was the first to compare different hot spot treatments in the same study with one treatment group receiving a more standard saturation patrol response and the second receiving a problem-oriented response that focused on officers analyzing problems in the hot spot and responding with a more tailored solution. Results showed a decrease in crime (though not a statistically significant decrease) in the saturation patrol hot spots, but this decrease lasted only during the intervention period and disappeared quickly thereafter. In the problem-oriented policing hot spots, there was no significant crime decline during the intervention period, but in the ninety days after the experiment, street violence declined by a statistically significant 33 percent. These results offered the first experimental evidence suggesting that problem-oriented approaches to dealing with crime hot spots may be more effective than simply increasing patrols in high-crime areas. They also suggest that problem-solving approaches may take more time to show beneficial results, but any successes that come from a problem-oriented framework may be more long-lasting in nature.

This series of rigorous evaluations of hot spots policing has led to a series of scientific reviews of the overall hot spots policing practice and evaluation evidence. We summarize the three main reviews of the literature in the following.

University of Maryland Report to the United States Congress (1997, 2002). In 1996, the United States Congress commissioned the Department of

Criminology and Criminal Justice at the University of Maryland to provide an independent, scientific assessment of more than $4 billion worth of federally sponsored crime-prevention programs. Lawrence Sherman and his colleagues (1997) reviewed scientific evaluations of programs intended to prevent crime in seven settings in which crime prevention takes place: families, schools, communities, labor markets, places (e.g., urban centers, homes), police, and courts/corrections. Programs were evaluated on the Scientific Methods Scale, which ranked scientific studies from 1 (weakest) to 5 (strongest) on overall internal validity. Properly implemented randomized experiments were rated highest on the scale and nonexperimental correlation studies lowest. The scale was one of the first attempts in crime and justice studies to rank studies scientifically and to communicate quality in science more effectively to policy makers, practitioners, media, and the general public. The findings of the original 1997 report were updated in a 2002 book (Sherman et al. 2002).

In the policing section of the updated Maryland report, Lawrence Sherman and John Eck (2002) examined eight major hypotheses about policing and crime. These hypotheses examined a variety of police crime prevention strategies, including increasing numbers of police, rapid response to 911, random patrols, directed patrols, reactive arrests, proactive arrests, community policing, and problem-oriented policing. Sherman and Eck distinguished directed patrols from traditional random patrols by observing that the advent of computerized crime analysis allowed greater precision in the identification of crime patterns. In turn, the police used this precision to focus police resources on the times and places at greatest risk of serious crime. Sherman and Eck suggested that the police were operating under the hypothesis that the more precisely patrol presence is concentrated at the "hot spots" and "hot times" of criminal activity, the less crime there will be in those places and times.

To be included in the directed patrol program category, the studies had to focus on high-crime places, times, or areas. Sherman and Eck (2002) identified nine studies in this review. All nine studies reported crime reductions in response to the directed patrol strategy. Using a standard of at least two consistent findings from level 3 methods score (well-measured, before–after studies with a comparison group) studies and a preponderance of the other evidence in support of the same conclusion, the review concluded that increased directed patrols in street-corner hot spots "works" in preventing crime.

National Research Council's Committee to Review Research on Police Policy and Practices (2004). As part of their considerable investment in law enforcement practice and research, the U.S. Department of Justice requested the National Research Council to establish the Committee to Review Research on Police Policy and Practices (National Research Council 2004). The committee assessed police research and its influence on policing as well as the influence and operation of the community policing philosophy (National Research Council 2004).

The committee was charged with a number of specific tasks including evaluating the effectiveness of police activities in reducing crime, disorder, and fear (see also Weisburd and Eck 2004). In reviewing the existing evaluation literature on police crime prevention programs, the committee used internal validity as a primary criterion for assessing the strength of the evidence provided. As such, the findings of more rigorous research designs, such as randomized experiments, were given greater credibility than the findings of research designs such as quasi-experimental or correlation studies (National Research Council 2004; Weisburd and Eck 2004). Since randomized field experiments can be compromised by implementation difficulties, the committee also considered the integrity of the implementation design in their assessment of research evidence.

As part of their review of focused policing efforts to reduce crime, the committee closely examined the research evidence on the crime-prevention effectiveness of hot spots policing. The committee's assessment drew strongly on preliminary results from a systematic review of hot spots policing conducted for the Campbell Collaboration (Braga 2001). Findings of the completed Campbell systematic review are presented in the next section of this chapter. The committee reported that a series of randomized field trials and quasi-experimental research studies showed that policing focused on crime hot spots can result in meaningful reductions in crime and disorder (National Research Council 2004; Weisburd and Eck 2004). The committee also considered the issue of crime displacement in their assessment of the crime prevention value of hot spots policing and concluded these approaches did not simply cause crime to move elsewhere. The National Research Council report was not ambiguous in its conclusions regarding the effectiveness and importance of hot spots policing. The committee concluded:

There has been increasing interest over the past two decades in police practices that target very specific types of criminals, and crime places. In particular, policing crime hot spots has become a common police strategy for addressing public safety problems. While there is only weak evidence suggesting the effectiveness of targeting specific types of offenders, a strong body of evidence suggests that taking a focused geographic approach to crime problems can increase policing effectiveness in reducing crime and disorder. National Research Council 2004, 246–247

Campbell Collaboration Systematic Review and Meta-Analysis of Hot Spots Policing Programs. The third set of reviews of place-based police efforts are the systematic reviews of hot spots programs conducted for the Campbell Collaboration.[3] There is consensus among those who advocate for evidence-based crime policy that systematic reviews are an important tool in reviewing evidence for effective crime-prevention strategies. In systematic reviews, researchers attempt to gather relevant evaluative studies in a specific area (e.g., the impact of correctional boot camps on offending), critically appraise them, and come to judgments about what works "using explicit, transparent, state-of-the-art methods" (Petrosino et al. 2001, 21). As part of the Campbell Collaboration Crime and Justice Group's efforts to build a scientific knowledge base on effective crime-prevention practices, a systematic review has been conducted on an ongoing basis on the crime prevention effects of hot spots policing programs (Braga 2001; 2005; 2007). The most recent iteration of the Campbell hot spots policing review identified nineteen methodologically rigorous evaluations involving twenty-five tests of hot spots policing programs (Braga et al. 2014). Ten eligible studies used quasi-experimental research designs (52.6 percent) and nine eligible studies used randomized controlled trials (47.4 percent) to evaluate the effects of hot spots policing on crime. The nineteen eligible studies were (asterisk indicates randomized controlled trial):

1. Minneapolis Repeat Call Address Policing (RECAP) Program (Sherman, Buerger, and Gartin 1989)*
2. New York Tactical Narcotics Teams (Sviridoff et al. 1992)
3. St. Louis Problem-Oriented Policing in 3 Drug Market Locations Study (Hope 1994)
4. Minneapolis Hot Spots Patrol Program (Sherman and Weisburd 1995)*
5. Jersey City Drug Markets Analysis Program (DMAP) (Weisburd and Green 1995b)*
6. Kansas City Gun Project (Sherman and Rogan 1995b)
7. Kansas City Crack House Police Raids Program (Sherman and Rogan 1995a)*
8. Beenleigh Calls for Service Project (Criminal Justice Commission 1998)
9. Jersey City Problem-Oriented Policing at Violent Places Project (Braga et al. 1999)*
10. Houston Targeted Beat Program (Caeti 1999)
11. Oakland Beat Health Program (Mazerolle et al. 2000)*
12. Pittsburgh Police Raids at Nuisance Bars Program (Cohen et al. 2003)
13. Buenos Aires Police Presence after Terror Attack Study (DiTella and Schargrodsky 2004)
14. Philadelphia Drug Corners Crackdowns Program (Lawton et al. 2005)
15. Jersey City Displacement and Diffusion Study (Weisburd et al. 2006)
16. Lowell Policing Crime and Disorder Hot Spots Project (Braga and Bond 2008)*
17. Jacksonville Policing Violent Crime Hot Spots Project (Taylor et al. 2011)*
18. Philadelphia Foot Patrol Program (Ratcliffe et al. 2011)*
19. Boston Safe Street Teams Program (Braga et al. 2011b)

A majority of the hot spots policing evaluations concluded that hot spots policing programs generated significant crime-control benefits in the treatment areas relative to the control areas. Eighty percent of the twenty-five tests (20) of hot spots policing interventions reported noteworthy crime-control gains

Combined Effect Sizes for Study Outcomes

Study name	Outcome	Std diff in means	Standard error	p-Value
KC Gun	Gun crimes	0.866	0.275	0.002
Phila. Drug Corners	Combined	0.855	0.258	0.001
Buenos Aires Police	Motor vehicle theft incidents	0.617	0.169	0.000
JC Disp. Prost.	Prostitution events	0.525	0.149	0.000
JC Disp. Drug	Drug events	0.441	0.131	0.001
Minn. RECAP Resid.	Total calls	0.369	0.132	0.005
Boston SST	Total violent incidents	0.341	0.020	0.000
Oakland Beath Health	Drug calls	0.279	0.056	0.000
JC DMAP	Combined	0.147	0.270	0.585
Lowell POP	Total calls	0.145	0.034	0.000
JC POP	Combined	0.143	0.043	0.001
Phila. Foot Patrol	Violent incidents	0.143	0.021	0.000
Pittsburgh Bar Raids	Drug calls	0.125	0.038	0.001
NYC TNT 67	Combined	0.087	0.077	0.257
Minn. Patrol	Total calls	0.061	0.015	0.000
KC Crack	Total calls	0.051	0.039	0.188
Minn. RECAP Comm.	Total calls	0.015	0.137	0.913
Jacksonville POP	Combined	-0.005	0.092	0.959
NYC TNT 70	Combined	-0.027	0.080	0.739
Jacksonville Patrol	Combined	-0.055	0.096	0.568
		0.184	0.035	0.000

FIGURE 6.1. Campbell review of hot spots policing program main effects.
Original source: Braga, A.A., Papachristos, A.V., and Hureau, D.M. (2012). "Hot spots policing effects on crime." *Campbell Systematic Reviews*, 8(8).

associated with the approach. The five tests that did not report crime-control benefits were the Minneapolis RECAP treatment at commercial addresses, the New York Tactical Narcotics Team in the 70th Precinct, the Beenleigh Calls for Service Project, the Houston Targeted Beat Program's problem-oriented policing intervention, and the Jacksonville direct-saturation patrol intervention. Due to limited information in the original evaluation reports, the Campbell Collaboration review meta-analysis[4] only included effect sizes for twenty main effects tests and thirteen displacement and diffusion tests in sixteen eligible studies. All thirteen displacement and diffusion tests were limited to examining immediate spatial displacement and diffusion effects; that is, whether focused police efforts in targeted areas resulted in crime "moving around the corner" or whether these proximate areas experienced unintended crime-control benefits.

The forest plots in Figure 6.1 show the standardized difference in means between the treatment and control or comparison conditions (effect size) with a 95 percent confidence interval plotted around them for all tests. Points plotted to the right of 0 indicate a reduction in crime or disorder. Points to the left of 0 indicate a backfire effect: control conditions improved relative to treatment conditions. The meta-analysis of main effect sizes found a statistically significant overall mean effect in favor of hot spots policing strategies (0.184).

Combined Effect Sizes for Displacement and Diffusion Outcomes

Study name	Outcome	Std diff in means	Standard error	p-Value
Phila. Drug Corners	Combined	0.580	0.065	0.000
JC Disp. Prost.	Combined	0.395	0.019	0.000
JC DMAP	Combined	0.161	0.269	0.550
Oakland Beat Health	Drug calls	0.160	0.035	0.000
JC Disp. Drug	Combined	0.124	0.015	0.000
Buenos Aires Police Protect	Combined	0.051	0.082	0.540
JC POP	Combined	0.049	0.001	0.000
Lowell POP	Total calls	0.013	0.001	0.000
Boston SST	Violent incidents	0.009	0.000	0.000
KC Gun	Gun crimes	-0.044	0.263	0.868
Jacksonville POP	Combined	-0.050	0.167	0.766
Phila. Foot Patrol	Violent incidents	-0.057	0.000	0.000
Jacksonville Patrol	Combined	-0.088	0.196	0.654
		0.104	0.016	0.000

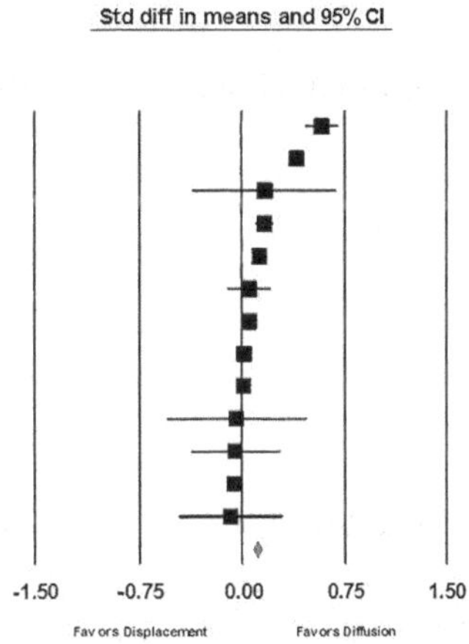

Meta-Analysis Random Effects Model, Q = 22699.482, df = 12, p<0.000

FIGURE 6.2. Campbell review of hot spots policing program displacement and diffusion effects.
Original source: Braga, A.A., Papachristos, A.V., and Hureau, D.M. (2012). "Hot spots policing effects on crime." *Campbell Systematic Reviews*, 8(8).

Displacement and diffusion effects are reported in Figure 6.2. Points plotted to the right of 0 indicate a diffusion of crime control benefits effect; in this case, the test showed a reduction in crime or disorder in the areas surrounding the targeted hot spots. Points to the left of 0 indicate a crime displacement effect. Nine tests reported effect sizes that favor diffusion effects over displacement effects. Only the Philadelphia Foot Patrol experiment reported a statistically significant displacement effect. The meta-analysis suggests a modest but statistically significant overall diffusion of crime-control benefits effects (0.104) generated by the hot spots policing strategies.

The Campbell systematic review revealed that police departments use different approaches to control crime hot spots. Figure 6.3 presents a continuum of strategies, ranging from traditional to innovative, that police can use to control crime at hot spot locations (Braga and Weisburd 2006). At one extreme, police departments use traditional, incident-driven strategies to control crime in the community. Although these activities coincidentally cluster in space and time, these opportunistic enforcement strategies are not specifically targeted at crime hot spots and the limitations of this approach are well known (Greenwood et al. 1977; Kelling et al. 1974; Spelman and Brown 1984). The Braga and Weisburd (2006) continuum divides hot spots policing efforts into "enforcement" and "situational" problem-oriented

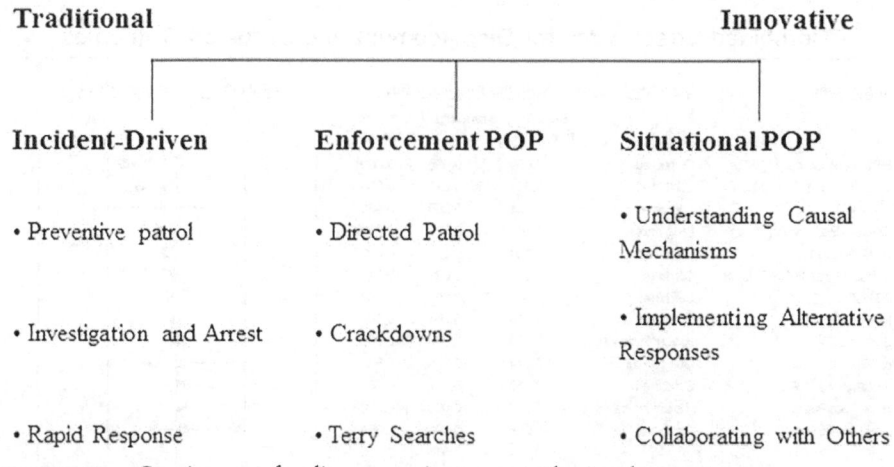

Traditional		Innovative
Incident-Driven	Enforcement POP	Situational POP
• Preventive patrol	• Directed Patrol	• Understanding Causal Mechanisms
• Investigation and Arrest	• Crackdowns	• Implementing Alternative Responses
• Rapid Response	• Terry Searches	• Collaborating with Others

FIGURE 6.3. Continuum of police strategies to control crime hot spots.
Original source: Braga, A.A., and Weisburd, D. (2006). "Problem-oriented policing: The disconnect between principles and practice." In D. Weisburd and A.A. Braga (eds.), *Police innovation: Contrasting perspectives* (pp. 133–154). New York: Cambridge University Press.

policing programs (see also Eck 1993a). Problem-oriented enforcement policing interventions move the police response forward by focusing mostly traditional tactics at high-risk times and locations. These focused police enforcement efforts include directed patrol and heightened levels of traffic enforcement, as well as alternative strategies such as the aggressive enforcement of laws and ordinances regulating disorderly behavior in public places.

In essence, these enforcement-oriented approaches seek to modify the criminogenic routine activities of places by increasing actual and perceived risks of detection and apprehension in a very small area. Offenders seeking to commit crimes at particular places may be deterred by increased police presence and action. Increasing patrol car presence in high-crime locations may be the simplest way to generate crime-prevention gains. Increasing police contact with serious offenders, through disorder enforcement, conducting Terry stops,[5] and implementing crackdowns – a massive short-term swamping of law enforcement resources in a specific area – may extend these crime-prevention gains. Although these programs are "problem-oriented" in a global way, their tactics do not employ the individualized treatments for crime problems advocated by Herman Goldstein (1990). Problem-oriented enforcement policing interventions tend to concentrate mainly on the time and location of crime events, rather than focusing on the characteristics and dynamics of a place that make it a hot spot for criminal activity. The innovative end of the continuum fits Goldstein's (1990) vision of "situational" problem-oriented policing, in which police agencies undertake thorough analysis of crime problems at places, collaborate with community members and other city agencies, and conduct a broad search for situational responses to problems.

The most recent Campbell Collaboration systematic review of hot spots policing programs used meta-analysis to compare these two different police approaches to controlling crime at hot spots. The analysis revealed that problem-oriented policing programs produced a larger overall mean effect size (0.232) that was twice the size of the increased traditional policing overall mean effect size (0.113). Relative to simply increasing police visibility and making additional arrests in crime hot spots, problem-oriented interventions that attempted to alter place characteristics and dynamics produced larger crime-prevention benefits. Innovative problem-oriented policing strategies require that police departments engage a broad range of partners in their development of strategies to ameliorate the underlying conditions that cause problems at crime places to persist over time.

Next Steps in Hot Spots Policing

While our review of the hot spots policing literature suggests overall strong evidence for the effectiveness of police focusing their attention on small geographic areas with high levels of criminal activity, there still remain important questions for future research on hot spots policing (see Weisburd and Telep 2014). First, there are a number of hot spots strategies that have not been rigorously tested. As Koper (2014) reports, a survey of agencies of various sizes indicated a wide variety of strategies they use to address high-crime places. While some of the most popular strategies used by respondents have been well evaluated (e.g., problem solving and directed patrol), other common responses have not been the subject of extensive rigorous research. For example, many agencies identified targeting known offenders as an effective strategy for shooting and homicide hot spots. To date, only limited research has evaluated a focus on known offenders as a hot spots strategy, but the results for this approach are very promising (see Groff et al. 2015). Buy-and-bust and reverse sting operations were identified by a number of respondents as effective approaches in drug violence hot spots, but these strategies have not been rigorously evaluated thus far. Other strategies frequently used by agencies that have not yet been researched extensively include community partnerships, checks on probationers and parolees, and using warrant service operations to target wanted offenders.

Second, we need to know more about which strategies are most effective in what contexts. Clearly, the effectiveness of strategies will depend on the specific types of crimes and types of places that are the focus of police attention. But we still do not have enough studies to provide detailed answers to these types of questions. Such detail is needed for the real world application of hot spots policing. Survey responses described by Koper (2014), for example, revealed that agencies frequently use different types of strategies to address different types of violent crime, but research to date has not extensively examined if and how the effectiveness of hot spots strategies varies across crime type.

Third, a number of scholars have recently argued that intensive police interventions such as hot spots policing may erode citizen perceptions of the legitimacy of the police (e.g., see Kochel 2011; Rosenbaum 2006). Rosenbaum (2006), for example, argues that enforcement-oriented hot spots policing runs the risk of weakening police–community relations. Aggressive tactics can drive a wedge between the police and communities, as the latter can begin to feel like targets rather than partners. This is particularly relevant in high-crime minority communities where perceptions of the police already tend to be negative (see Gau and Brunson 2010). This has potential implications for the crime-control effectiveness of hot spots policing as Tyler (1990) has argued that legitimacy is an important predictor of long-term compliance with the law.

Despite arguments that intensive interventions such as hot spots policing will have negative impacts on police legitimacy, there is very little empirical evidence to date to support this position. There is some evidence that residents of areas that are subject to focused police attention welcome the concentration of police efforts in problem places (e.g., Chermak et al. 2001). A separate examination of the Kansas City Gun Project (Sherman and Rogan 1995b) found that the community in the treatment sites strongly supported the intensive patrols and perceived an improvement in the quality of life (Shaw 1995). Research from a randomized field trial in three cities in San Bernardino County, California, found that a broken windows-style intervention in street segments had no impact on resident perceptions of police legitimacy (Weisburd et al. 2011), although the authors note the surveyed residents may not have noticed nor had contact with the police during the treatment period. Most recently, Kochel (2013) found a limited impact of hot spots policing treatments on resident perceptions of police legitimacy in a randomized experiment in St. Louis County, Missouri. The problem-oriented policing treatment in that study had no impact on legitimacy, while the directed patrol treatment was associated with decreased legitimacy perceptions immediately following treatment, although these declines had disappeared six months later.

Future research should continue to examine the impact of hot spots policing on citizen perceptions of police legitimacy. In particular, future studies should measure how the individuals who were stopped and searched by the police in targeted areas perceive such programs. If hot spots policing does negatively impact perceptions of legitimacy, then not only does this raise important concerns about police fairness, but also crime control gains in the short run may be offset by reduced cooperation and compliance of the public in the long term. Additionally, it is important to understand if police can enhance the effectiveness of hot spots policing by incorporating principles of procedural justice into hot spots strategies. Procedural justice refers to the ways in which the police interact with citizens, including the ways in which police strategies give citizens the sense that they are treated fairly and that their side of the story is heard (see Tyler 2004). Field experiments are needed to test whether a procedurally just hot spots policing approach could increase legitimacy perceptions and enhance crime control effectiveness (see Weisburd and Braga 2013).

THE IMPORTANCE OF PLACE MANAGERS AND "THIRD PARTIES" IN CONTROLLING CRIME PLACES

Another important development in place-based crime prevention policy has been the engagement of noncriminal justice system actors in addressing high-activity crime places. Properties and facilities at places are owned by people and entities other than the police, known as "place managers" (Eck 1994; see Chapter 3). While police can work with or stimulate these individuals to address problems at high-activity crime places (Felson and Boba 2009; Buerger and Mazerolle 1998), place managers play an essential role in the internal dynamics and potential criminal opportunities at places that can attract or ward off likely offenders.

Place managers can include a wide range of individuals such as sales clerks, doormen, apartment managers, business owners, and home owners. Place managers are distinguished from others by their legal authority to act at a place. This authority is based on property ownership and rights associated with ownership. Property owners can delegate some or all of this authority (e.g., the apartment building superintendent has authority by virtue of his or her terms of employment). Neighbors, for example, generally are not mangers of places other than their own homes, unless a homeowner specifically asks a neighbor to "keep an eye on things" while the owner is absent. Some place managers, such as school teachers or bar managers, look after settings that do not persist for the whole day (Felson 2006). While hot spots approaches may lead to short-term deterrence, sustained crime reduction at places ultimately requires the commitment of owners and their delegates. Thus, many of the alternative crime prevention strategies pursued by the police to deal with problem places involve the cooperation of property owners, business operators, and others to suppress local crime and disorder problems. Crime prevention through environmental design (CPTED), for example, must be applied by place managers, even if the police are the institution that stimulated this response.

For instance, in their analysis of violence in bars in Cincinnati, Ohio, Madensen and Eck (2008) suggest that place management decisions were very influential in determining whether or not crime occurs at a particular location. Like previous studies, they found very little support for the hypothesis that high-crime bars are simply the product of high-crime neighborhoods. If the neighborhood hypothesis were true, then problem bars would be concentrated geographically, and nonproblem bars would be located in other neighborhoods. This is not what they found. Rather, problem bars were located near and among nonproblem bars, in the same neighborhoods.

Madensen and Eck (2008) reported that managers created environments at bars that suppressed or facilitated violence through business-related choices. This finding – that the structure and policies of the environment or place can be manipulated to affect crime – also resonates in school environments as well, as Gottfredson et al. (2002) have pointed out. The types of patrons that frequented the bars and the characteristics of the behavior settings were the product of management decisions such as bar themes; property characteristics; bar location; activities and entertainment; staff, training, and security; and market strategies. These decisions are interrelated and dynamic; violence-inhibiting and-facilitating decisions in one area can be mitigated or aggravated by decisions made in another area. For instance, a college bar hosting a "hip hop" night with dancing that brings large groups of intoxicated young men in close proximity to each other will be at far greater risk of violence when compared with a food-serving wine and cigar bar that caters to more mature patrons. In the college bar, subsequent management choices about staffing, such as the presence of trained bouncers, and proactive decisions in dealing with disorderly patrons by halting the serving of alcohol or through their removal from the premises, will importantly influence the amount of violence the establishment experiences when the hip hop event occurs.

Madensen (2007) developed a more general theory of place management decisions and activities that can be applied to other types of facilities, such as banks, retail stores, and even web-based businesses (see Figure 6.4). This perspective on the management of private businesses applies to the management of public places as well. For instance, Madensen (2007, 162–163) describes some of the relevant decisions that managers, such as elected officials and appointed public executives, make that influence the types and likelihood of crime and disorder problems at public parks. The theme of the park (e.g., national forest, playground, recreational) will influence property characteristics and the park location. Parks intended for families will have picnic areas, parks for children will have playgrounds, parks for teenagers will have basketball courts, and parks for the elderly will have sitting areas and shuffleboard (Madensen 2007). Security features may include see-through fencing, locking public restrooms at night, road barricades, lighting, posted rules, and implementation of curfews. If crime or disorder occurs in these locations, managers who have more experience or work with others who have successfully addressed these problems and managers who have access to greater resources (e.g., community or state funds) will have the ability to change these environments more quickly. Managers who are not negatively impacted (e.g., live elsewhere) and cannot be held accountable for the condition of the parks (e.g., appointed rather than elected public officials) will be less likely to aggressively respond to problems in these locations (Madensen 2007).

In many cases, place managers will be proactive in dealing with crime and disorder problems and willing to work with the police to create safe environments. Unfortunately this is not always the case; police officers may need to

Reducing Crime at High Crime Places: Practice and Evidence

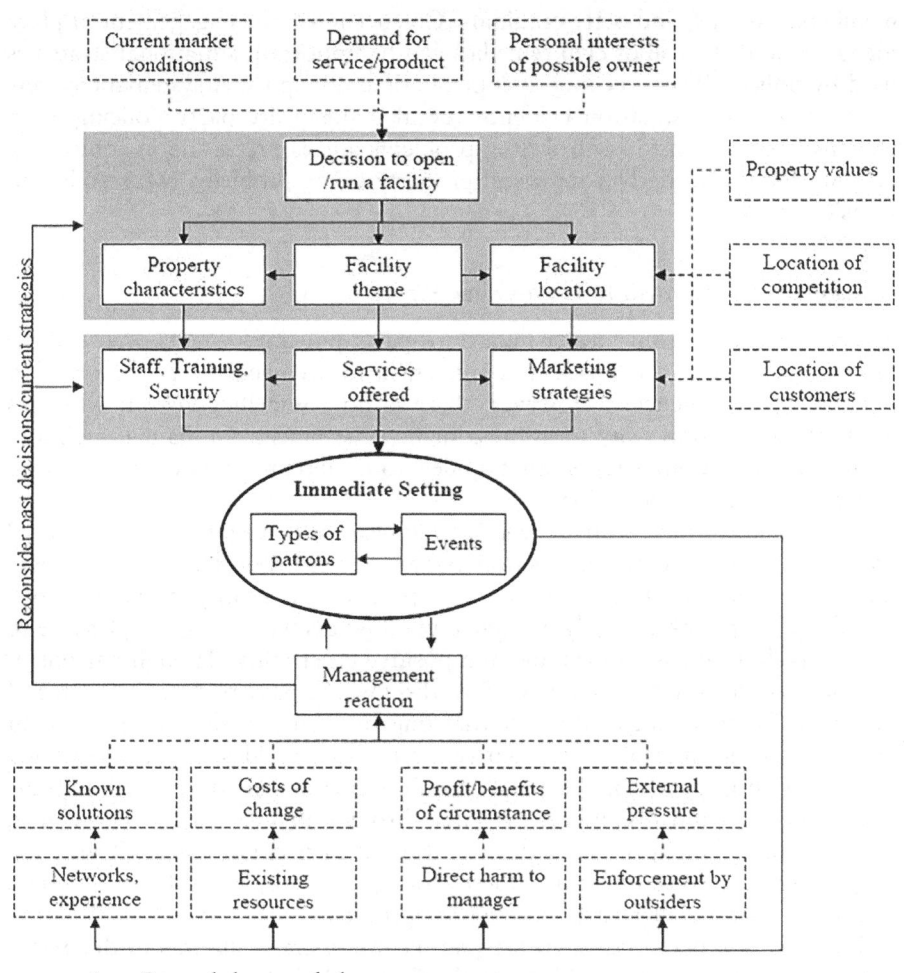

FIGURE 6.4. General theory of place management.
Original source: Madensen, T.D. (2007). *Bar management and crime: Toward a dynamic theory of place management and crime hot spots*. PhD dissertation. Cincinnati, OH: University of Cincinnati.

force irresponsible or negligent parties to take action. Third-party policing is defined as "police efforts to persuade or coerce organizations or non-offending persons, such as public housing agencies, property owners, parents, health and building inspectors, and business owners to take some responsibility for preventing crime or reducing crime problems" (Buerger and Mazerolle 1998, 301). The police use a range of civil, criminal, and regulatory rules and laws to engage or force third parties into taking some crime control responsibility. The ultimate targets of third-party policing efforts are the people engaged in deviant and criminal behavior at the place, typically drug dealers, gang members, vandals, and petty criminals (Green 1996). The engagement of place managers and the use of civil remedies can be important situational strategies used by police officers seeking to control crime hot spots. A systematic review of the available evaluation evidence revealed that third-party policing is an effective mechanism to control drug problems and is promising in controlling violent crime, disorderly youth, and property crime problems (Mazerolle and Ransley 2006).

A Regulatory Approach to High-Crime Places

It is possible to go even further than third-party policing. To date, most of the place-based policies proposed and studied have involved the police or other criminal justice agencies. However, there is no compelling reason why this needs to be the only way to address high-crime places. Graham Farrell and John Roman (2006) suggest that under some circumstances crime can be treated as a form of pollution.

Pollutants are one form of what economists call "negative externalities." Externalities are effects of production that are not incorporated into the price of the good or service being produced. A positive externality provides a free benefit. A shop with a highly attractive window display that gives pleasure to passing pedestrians is an example of a positive externality. Though patrons of the shop pay for the cost of the window display, the passersby get it for free. If they paid for this benefit, thus internalizing the benefits, shop keepers might produce more such displays. A negative externality provides an uncompensated cost. If the shop owner places his trash on the curb, where dogs break into the bags, and the wind distributes the litter throughout the neighborhood, then people in the area experience a deterioration of their environment. If the shop keeper were forced to internalize these costs (perhaps by a stiff fine), he would secure his trash better and avoid the litter problem.

From a place perspective, crimes and disorders are pollutants to the extent that management practices facilitate them. As this is being written, police in Waco, Texas, are investigating a shootout among motorcycle gangs that left nine dead and numerous injured. A local restaurant had sponsored this get-together of motorcycle groups, including outlaw motorcycle gangs. Police had warned the restaurant of the potential for violence, and had asked them to stop the meetings, according to news reports. A neighboring restaurant is suing the owners of the site of the shootout, claiming a loss of revenue due to irresponsible business practices (Dennis 2015). This suit illustrates the point that how a place is managed can influence the potential for crime externalities at the location, and this idea is recognized in law.

But this is a dramatic example of only one of four ways place management can create externalities by facilitating crime: imposing costs on the environment around the place. A large body of research examines the impact of facilities on crime in their neighborhoods (Wilcox and Eck 2011). The second form of negative externality is imposed on crime victims. A hotel where a lack of security makes it possible for a stranger to enter and rape a guest has created this form of negative externality. Third, as a consequence of reported crimes, the police and other agencies must spend money to address the aftermath. This cost is borne by taxpayers. Finally, the place-facilitated crime can have negative consequences for the family and friends of the offender (Eck and Eck 2012).

John Eck and Emily Eck (2012) showed how the very same portfolio of regulatory approaches that have been used to reduce air, water, and other forms of pollution can be, and often have been, used to reduce crime at places. A recent example comes from Chula Vista, California, where the city council adopted a regulatory approach to reduce police calls from motels in the city. The city council placed a cap of 0.5 calls for service per room from motels. Motels that failed to comply were required to enter into a memorandum of agreement to take actions to reduce calls, or risk losing their operating license. Gisela Bichler and colleagues (2013) evaluated the impact of the regulations and found it reduced calls for service at the targeted motels, and also at nearby motels in adjacent cities not affected by the regulations.

Drawing on the literature describing regulation of industry to curb pollutants, Eck and Eck (2012) describe five forms of regulation (policy instruments) that can be used to address places with extreme numbers of crime or disorder events. The first are command and control policies. These are the most commonly applied form of regulation, and encompass the type of regulation most people think of when arguing for more regulation. Command and control regulation prescribes mandatory procedures and conditions, or prohibits particular conditions. A city ordinance requiring convenience stores open after dark to employ two clerks is an example (Clifton 1987).

Subsidies are a form of regulation that rewards place managers for using particular forms of technology or procedures. Examples of subsidies include dispensing door or window locks below their market costs, providing free training in crime prevention, and even responding to alarm calls. Like command and control regulation policies, subsidies focus on the way place managers reduce crime. The other forms of regulation are increasingly indifferent to how crime reduction is achieved (within broad limits), but focus on achieving some crime reduction.

Legal liability is a policy instrument that may induce place managers to use more and better prevention. The principle here is that if place owners believe they will be sued because of crime on their property, and the plaintiffs will prevail in court, place managers will employ more effective prevention than they otherwise would. It is important to distinguish between private suits, where there is a lack of evidence of effectiveness (Eck 1996), and public suits, where there is considerable strong evidence of effectiveness (Eck 2002; Mazerolle and Ransley 2006).

User fees, taxes, and fines can impose costs for crimes over some prescribed limit, or cap. Policies to charge place owners for excessive calls to the police

(Payne 2015) are of this type. Places are permitted some crimes, on the principle that random variation alone creates a general crime risk all places must face, and place owners pay taxes to address these rare circumstances. However, the local government charges place managers for crimes over this limit. It might seem odd that places are given permits to have crimes up to a cap. However, one must remember that in most jurisdictions, for most crimes, places have an informal permit to have any number of crimes. So permitting crimes up to a limit is far more restrictive than current practice. It is also important to recall that the permit goes to the place, not to offenders. Offenders are still subject to legal sanctions, whether their particular crime was within the limit for the crime place or outside it.

There are real examples of each of the regulatory approaches to crime at places described so far. The last form of regulation has not been tried, though in principle it appears promising. This is the use of a tradable permit policy, much like the current policy to control sulphur dioxide emissions (Stavins 2007). Like the preceding regulatory policy, local government sets a cap for the number of crimes permitted. Owners of places with fewer crimes than permitted can sell their unused permits to place managers who cannot abate crime by other means. This rewards very safe places and imposes a cost on high-crime places. The cap assures a global crime reduction for the jurisdiction (Eck and Eck 2012).

Each of these types of regulatory instruments is suitable for some conditions, but not for others. There are numerous examples of their use to control crime, but the evaluation literature is meager. Consequently, there is limited evidence-based guidance as to which specific instrument should be used where.

Though the police have often had some role in such regulation, this is more of an accident of history than a necessity of the approach. Eck and Eck (2012) point out that it is not clear that the police are the best regulators of places. In Cincinnati, for example, the police had been given regulatory authority over apartment buildings to curb nuisance places, but after community complaints that the police efforts were insufficient, the city council shifted the authority to the city attorney's office.

Rather than treating high-crime places as "police problems," a regulatory approach treats such places as the problem of the place owner. It shifts the responsibility for crime reduction to the place manager. The place manager is held accountable for police having to return to the place to deal with troublesome behaviors. This, potentially, has two positive consequences. First, it shifts the cost burden from the taxpayer to the place managers who create criminogenic conditions. Second, it reduces the need for criminal enforcement, with its attendant social and financial costs (Eck and Eck 2012). Though regulations have long been used to reduce crime, there is only a small body of evidence supporting them. Consequently, it is a strategy that needs to be pursued with robust research and evaluation support to determine if it can live up to its potential.

COMMUNITY CORRECTIONS AND CRIME PLACES

Another area in which criminal justice practice taking place-based approaches can be promising is in community supervision of offenders. Community corrections efforts, despite the "community" label, have not been geographically focused in similar ways as policing crime hot spots. Rather, community corrections focus on reforming or monitoring the *individual* in the community (the term "community" simply meaning "outside prison"). The focus on individuals and not places in community corrections is also reflected in the evaluation research on community corrections, as Byrne (1989) and Mears et al. (2008) have pointed out, which primarily evaluates the impact of treatment and supervision on an individual offender's recidivism. Further, community corrections often fails to address criminal opportunities in the community (Cullen et al. 2002). Targeting places with high concentrations of parolees or probationers, or implementing (and evaluating) place-based approaches to supervision or treatment, are relatively new developments in community corrections research and practice.

However, as with policing, the importance of places in community corrections cannot be understated. As with crime, individuals on probationary supervision, or who have reentered society after imprisonment, concentrate geographically (Byrne 1989; 2008; La Vigne 2007). These places also are bereft of resources that might facilitate offender rehabilitation, or may have high levels of crime opportunities that might further inhibit successful offender reintegration. As Davis and Tunks (1990–1991) have argued, these places can contribute to increased likelihood of recidivism and drug availability for probationers and parolees (see also Kubrin and Stewart 2006; Mears et al. 2008).

There are a number of ways community corrections practice might benefit from a place-based perspective. The first is in considering the role that geographic and environmental factors play in the successful outcomes of those on probation and parole supervision. For example, could probation agencies be more geographically accessible to improve chances of successful supervision? Perhaps if probation officers were more easily accessible, or transportation was provided to reduce the time and distance between probationers and resources, the likelihood of successful probation might be increased. There is a growing body of literature that suggests geographic factors can have an impact on successful treatment (see Archibald 2008; Jacobson 2004; Mason et al. 2004; Stahler et al. 2007). For example, how accessible drug or psychological treatment is for those on probation, or how near supervision offices are to people, may be key factors in their rehabilitation (see Beardsley et al. 2003; Davis and Tunks 1990–1991; Friedmann et al. 2001; Schmitt et al. 2003). But there is limited evaluation work to draw from in community corrections on how place-based interventions that use these concepts and findings might improve recidivism rates for those under correctional supervision.

Perhaps the solution for successful probation and reduction of recidivism might rely not only on closeness to supervision, treatment, life skills, and job training services, but also on nearness to places with reduced opportunity for offending. Placement of offenders back into communities that facilitate their offending by providing many opportunities to offend, or that have low levels of collective efficacy and social control (formal or informal), might be more detrimental than the lack of nearness to probation services. A place-based perspective in community corrections might also view places as potential targets for organizing crime prevention interventions. Schaefer and colleagues (2015) provide a variety of practical efforts that community corrections officials can take to block crime opportunities for their charges. These include identifying the places where people on probation or parole get into trouble, developing supervision plans that take into account criminogenic places, working with place managers to help monitor offenders, and enlisting prosocial friends of offenders to help keep them out of trouble at high risk places.

A place-based orientation opens up a variety of possibilities for reducing recidivism, but many questions need to be answered. Are hot spots of trouble for individuals on probation and parole different from hot spots for other offenders? Are special interventions for those under correctional supervision effective at crime places? Can state and local jurisdictions adjust environmental factors in places with high concentrations of probationers to improve their life chances? How can place managers be enlisted in these efforts? Can law enforcement act as a prophylactic for probationers in high-crime-opportunity communities by assisting with informal supervision to keep individuals out of trouble, or reduce the opportunity for offending by acting as a guardian and deterrent? This may be more difficult than thinking about how places influence offender recidivism, given that unlike policing, the function of probation officials and the courts is to specifically supervise individuals, not implement crime-prevention programs more generally at specific places.

The answers to these questions are largely unknown. Whether parolees and probationers placed in better-resourced and low-crime areas fare better with regard to their reoffending remains underevaluated, as does targeting places with probation-specific interventions. However, as Janetta (2009) argued to a congressional subcommittee, a place-based supervision approach, where parole officers and their cases are geographically concentrated, may be a starting point. Janetta cites Arizona's Legacy Project and Maryland's Proactive Community Supervision (PCS) model as examples (see Taxman 2008), but also states that such geographically focused efforts are not the norm. For example, Maryland's current approach, the Violence Prevention Initiative,[6] focuses probation efforts on the highest-risk offenders, which has shown some success, rather than on high-risk places. Given limited resources, and given that such offenders are likely concentrated in space, targeting specific high-crime places, where these high-risk offenders are located, could be a force multiplier.

CRIME DISPLACEMENT AND DIFFUSION OF CRIME-CONTROL BENEFITS

The research reviewed so far in this chapter reveals there is strong evidence that the police and other social control agents can have a significant impact on crime at place (see Braga et al. 2012; Lum et al. 2011; Sherman and Eck 2002; Weisburd and Eck 2004). However, if such efforts only shift crime or disorder to other places then these interventions may not be socially beneficial. Shifting crime is commonly referred to as displacement, and it has traditionally been a reason for skepticism about the efficacy of place-based interventions (see Reppetto 1976). It has also been a key factor in discouraging criminologists from focusing on microgeographic places. While displacement can take many forms (e.g., spatial, temporal, target, tactical, offense, offender), most research has focused on spatial displacement. If an intervention reduces crime by simply pushing it elsewhere, this raises serious concerns about the overall effectiveness of efforts at high-crime places. The available evidence on hot spots policing programs reviewed earlier suggests that proximate areas are more likely to experience noteworthy decreases in crime rather than crime increases. Nevertheless, concerns over the potential for crime displacement persist in contemporary discussions of place-based crime prevention efforts (e.g., see Black and Park 2012).

The traditional argument for displacement is perhaps best summarized by Reppetto (1976, 167) who noted:

> The police, however, cannot be everywhere; all houses and commercial establishments cannot be secured with attack-proof doors and windows, and all neighborhood environments cannot be altered. A different level of protection between various potential targets, both human and nonhuman, will always exist. Given the differential and no reduction in the offender population, will not the foreclosure of one type of criminal opportunity simply shift the incidence of crime to different forms, times and locales?

In other words, the opportunities for crime were believed to be too numerous to make place-based interventions effective and efficient. In this model, highly motivated offenders would easily shift their offending to nearby places with ample crime opportunities (see Clarke and Felson 1993; Trasler 1993). Gabor (1981, 391) notes that the displacement hypothesis fits in well both with a model of criminals as rational actors seeking to minimize costs and maximize benefits and with the hydraulic model, where offenders compulsively seek out criminal activities. While recent research has challenged these traditional views (see the following), Guerette and Bowers (2009, 1332) note, "the burden of proof clearly has been placed on disproving earlier (and arguably still prevailing) suppositions about the inescapability of crime displacement."

In contrast to a belief that displacement is inevitable, Clarke and Weisburd (1994) argued that another phenomenon that indicates "the reverse of displacement" is a common outcome of focused crime-prevention efforts. They defined this "diffusion of crime control benefits" as "the spread of the beneficial influence of an intervention beyond the places which are directly targeted, the individuals who are the subject of control, the crimes which are the focus of intervention or the time period in which an intervention is brought" (Clarke and Weisburd 1994, 169). These unintended benefits had been described by others as the "multiplier" effect (Chaiken et al. 1974), the "halo" effect (Scherdin 1986), "free rider" effects (Miethe 1991), and "free bonus" effects (Sherman 1990). The Chula Vista regulation of motels, mentioned earlier, is an illustration of the production of unintended benefits: motels in adjacent cities, not subject to the Chula Vista regulations, also reduced their calls for police services (Bichler et al. 2013).

Since 1990 there have been six main reviews of empirical studies that report on displacement: Barr and Pease (1990); Eck (1993a); Hesseling (1994); Guerette and Bowers (2009); Bowers et al. (2011); and Telep et al. (2014). We focus in particular on two of the three most recent reviews, because of their comprehensiveness, focus on microunits of geography, and inclusion of both displacement and diffusion effects. All of these reviews, though, arrive at some basic conclusions. First, displacement is not an inevitable outcome of place-based interventions. Second, displacement, when it does occur, is usually less than the amount of crime prevented. In other words, even when there is evidence of displacement, the intervention still tends to be worthwhile in terms of total crime prevented. And third, for reviews that assess displacement and diffusion effects, a diffusion of crime control benefits is generally more likely than crime displacement.

Guerette and Bowers (2009) assessed displacement and diffusion in situational crime-prevention interventions. Overall, they found some displacement in 26 percent of the 574 observations from the 102 studies they examined (though in none of these cases was the amount of displacement greater than the direct crime prevention benefits of the program) and a diffusion of crime control benefits in 27 percent of the examined studies. Focusing only on spatial displacement and diffusion, they found that 37 percent of the observations showed evidence of spatial diffusion while only 23 percent showed evidence of spatial displacement. As they conclude, "the findings provide continued support for the view that crime does not simply relocate in the aftermath of situational interventions" (Guerette and Bowers 2009, 1357).

Bowers et al. (2011) conducted a Campbell Collaboration systematic review on displacement and diffusion effects in geographically focused policing interventions. They found forty-four eligible studies overall, sixteen of which were used in a meta-analysis. The meta-analysis found, when examining crime in catchment areas surrounding target sites, there is little evidence of displacement and some evidence of a diffusion of crime-control benefits, although the results overall are not statistically significant. They conclude that "the message from this review is a positive one to those involved in the sort of operational policing initiatives considered, the main point being that displacement is far from inevitable as a result of such endeavor, and, in fact that the opposite, a diffusion of crime control benefits appears to be the more likely consequence" (Bowers et al. 2011, 4). Telep et al. (2014) conducted a Campbell review assessing the likelihood of displacement and diffusion in interventions in large-scale geographic areas. Their findings suggest that there are few rigorous studies examining displacement at large geographic units, but at mesounits (e.g., neighborhoods, police precincts), displacement only occurs in a small proportion of studies, and a diffusion of crime-control benefits is just as likely to occur.

These results must be taken with some important caveats. The amount of displacement depends, in part, on the type of intervention being used and the type of crime or disorder being prevented. Additionally, because most of the studies examined did not set out to examine displacement, it was rare that evaluators were able to use a methodologically sound research design for detecting it (see Weisburd and Green 1995a). This is the case in part because researchers must make decisions about the allocation of scarce research funds and resources. Additionally, as Barr and Pease (1990) note, displacement is inherently difficult to measure because it can take so many different forms and can occur at multiple levels of geography.

As described earlier in this chapter, one area where the evidence regarding spatial displacement is particularly strong is hot spots policing. There is little evidence of displacement of crime to areas nearby targeted hot spots. One of the hot spots studies included in the most recent iteration of the Campbell hot spots policing systematic review (Braga et al. 2014) was explicitly concerned with measuring displacement and diffusion. In Weisburd and colleagues' (2006) examination of hot spots policing interventions at drug and prostitution markets in Jersey City, New Jersey, spatial displacement and diffusion were primary outcomes. The study employed analyses of more than 6,000 twenty-minute social observations at the research sites, supplemented by interviews with arrestees from the target areas and ethnographic field observations. Quantitative findings indicated that for the crime hot spots examined, crime did not simply move around the corner in response to intensive police crime-prevention efforts at places. Indeed, the study supported the position that the most likely outcome of such focused crime-prevention efforts is a diffusion of crime-control benefits to nearby areas.

Displacement is not inevitable, in part, because geographic areas, such as hot spots, tend to have specific features that make them attractive targets for criminal activity, and these same features may not exist on neighboring blocks. For example, in the Weisburd et al. (2006) study, the prostitution hot spot targeted by police had few homes and many vacant buildings, making it an attractive site for prostitution activity. In contrast, one of the catchment areas near the target site had many more residences, making it more likely that the police would be called when prostitution occurred. In this context, prostitutes could not easily move their illegal activity to areas nearby.

Weisburd and Telep (2012) point to the "tight coupling" of crime and place as an explanation for the frequent absence of displacement. They note the concentration and stability of crime at place, and the evidence of spatial heterogeneity across large geographic areas (see Weisburd et al. 2012), to suggest there are specific characteristics that couple crime to places. The displacement hypothesis is based on an assumption that people and crime are loosely coupled to place and will move easily to other places. The empirical literature on crime places suggests just the opposite. Focusing again on the Weisburd et al. (2006) study, for example, a number of offenders in the drug-market hot spot complained in interviews about the time and effort it would take to reestablish their activities in other areas as a reaction to the police intervention. An additional explanation for the resistance to spatial displacement is simply that offenders, like nonoffenders, come to feel comfortable with their home turf and the people that they encounter. In this case tight coupling is due to a very human desire for the familiar. Moving crime locations can be seen by offenders as uncomfortable or even dangerous.

Clarke and Weisburd (1994) point to two potential explanations for diffusion effects, deterrence and discouragement. Deterrence refers to situations where offenders overestimate the risk associated with a particular intervention, and accordingly avoid offending in areas not targeted by the initiative. Crime-control benefits would therefore diffuse because of offender fear of arrest. Discouragement focuses more on costs and benefits and refers to situations where the police intervention makes the effort required to offend greater than the benefit acquired from the crime. This reward reduction can lead to a general benefit for a community that expands beyond the initial target.

Weisburd and Telep (2012) expand upon these notions to examine nonpsychological explanations for why diffusion may be more likely to occur than displacement. Taniguchi and colleagues (2009), for example, use the economic theory of agglomeration economies to explain why targeting illegal drug markets may lead to a diffusion of crime control benefits rather than displacement. They find that removing the largest and most profitable site from an illegal drug market will reduce the size of the overall market by making drug dealing in the surrounding area less profitable. The logic here is similar to the economics of the legitimate retail sector where closing a major department store in a mall may negatively impact the profits of smaller surrounding stores.

CONCLUSIONS

Overall, there is strong and broad evidence of the effectiveness of place-based approaches to crime and disorder reduction. We have evidence showing that reducing crime opportunities at places will reduce crime. We have specific evidence of the effectiveness of hot spots policing. Evidence for engaging place managers to control crime is increasing. Indirect evidence suggests applying a place-based approach to community corrections could be beneficial.

Importantly, the overwhelming evidence shows that place-based approaches do not necessarily move crime to other locations. Indeed, it is more likely that nearby locations benefit from crime reduction at crime hot spots. In short, the evidence base for place-based prevention is persuasive.

Further, the evidence supporting a place-based approach is more consistent than that for "person-based" prevention. Lum et al. (2011) provide a direct comparison of place versus person strategies using studies in the Evidence-Based Policing Matrix.[7] Their work shows that close to 70 percent of place-based policing evaluations show significant crime prevention impacts. This is in contrast to less than 40 percent of person-based approaches. We think more generally that it is time to recognize the promise of places for public crime-control policies.

7

Crime Places in the Criminological Imagination

We began this book by noting that criminologists have largely ignored the involvement of microgeographic places in crime. Mainstream criminologists have focused on "who done it?" and not "where done it?" (Sherman 1995). At least for the last century the key inquiries of crime and the key prevention approaches have looked to doing something about criminal motivation (Sutherland 1947; Reiss 1981). Why people commit crime has been the main focus of criminology (Brantingham and Brantingham 1990; Weisburd 2002), and catching and processing offenders has been the main focus of crime prevention (Weisburd 2008). In contrast, the criminology of place (Sherman et al. 1989; Weisburd et al. 2012), which began to develop in the 1980s and 1990s (Brantingham and Brantingham 1981; 1984; Eck 1994; Eck and Weisburd 1995; Roncek and Bell 1981; Weisburd and Green 1995a), provides an alternative vision of how we can understand crime and the crime problem. Like the emergence of community criminology during the same period (Bursik 1988; Morenoff et al. 2001; Sampson 2008; Sampson et al. 1997) the criminology of place has offered a new set of mechanisms for crime study and a new set of methods for doing something about the crime problem.

Theory has been a driving force in criminological study, and as we note below, we think that more not less attention to theory is important for advancing the criminology of place. However, theories are about something and try to explain something. When we change the unit of analysis, we are changing the target for theory. The criminology of place proposes a new target. It focuses on places, rather than people. Its goal is to explain the criminal involvement of microgeographic units rather than trying to explain the criminal involvement of people. This does not mean we ignore the role of individuals in the crime problem. But it does mean that we begin our inquiries with the place and see the individuals as only one part of the crime equation at places.

We have illustrated in the preceding chapters the extent to which theory, method, and empirical evidence about crime places have been developing over the last three decades. In this concluding chapter, we want to draw from our review of what is known some key themes that we think our work has identified, and key questions that still need to be answered.

THE LAW OF CRIME CONCENTRATION AND THE FUTURE OF CRIME AND PLACE STUDIES

Crime is concentrated at microgeographic units of analysis. This "law of crime concentration at places" (Weisburd 2015a; see also Weisburd et al. 2012; Weisburd et al. 2014) is perhaps the key empirical grounding of the criminology of place. As we noted in Chapter 2, similar concentrations of crime at place are found across time in cities, and across cities. About 5 percent of places in a city produce 50 percent of crime and about 1 percent of places produce between 20 and 25 percent of crime (see Chapter 2). This concentration is so ubiquitous, having been found in every type of place examined, that Wilcox and Eck (2011, 476) have also called it "the iron law of troublesome places." It is this concentration that has raised the interest of criminologists in understanding crime at place. It has become the key underlying logic behind such crime prevention programs as hot spots policing (Braga and Weisburd 2010; Braga et al. 2014; Sherman and Weisburd 1995). It is central to the successful application of much situational crime prevention (Eck and Guerrette 2012). And it has much potential for improving community correctional rehabilitation (Cullen et al. 2002; Schaefer 2013).

We expect that as new findings emerge, this law of crime concentration will continue to be the foundation of research interest and crime prevention in this area. What might lead to this consistency in levels of crime concentration? It is important to note at the outset that the concentration of crime follows patterns of concentration in many other areas of scientific inquiry (e.g., see Bak 1994; Eck et al. 2007; Hill et al. 2007; Richter 1935; Sherman 2007; Simpson 1949). The concentration of human activity has been noted for well over a hundred years (e.g., see Allport 1934; Dalton 1920; Gini 1912; Hirschman 1945; Lorenz 1905; Zipf 1949). Joseph Moses Juran (1951) noted this concentration in looking at economic activities, coining the phrase "the vital few and the trivial many." Juran sought to emphasize to managers that they should focus on the small number of events or cases that produce the majority of relevant business activities, for example the small number of defects that cause most complaints about products, or the small number of clients that are responsible for a majority of revenue. Juran termed this phenomenon the "Pareto Principal" after Vilfredo Pareto (1909), who first brought attention to what is sometimes referred to as the 80–20 rule (see also Koch et al. 1999). Pareto observed that a number of distributions seem to follow this specific pattern of concentration.

For example, in studying land ownership in Italy he found that 80 percent of the land was controlled by just 20 percent of the population. He also observed that 20 percent of the pea pods in his garden produced 80 percent of the peas. The 80–20 rule is generally seen only as an approximation, and indeed there are other concentration rules that have been noted – for example, the 90–10 rule as applied to computer processing (Lipovetsky 2009).

Given the concentration of humans and other events, the concentration at places should not be surprising. However, it still calls out for an explanation. There are several explanations competing for our attention. One is simply that populations vary across places, and the density of populations at places is strongly related to places being chronic crime hot spots (Weisburd et al. 2012). If repeat offenders pick on a few places, then this concentration might arise. Similarly, if a few repeat victims hang out in a small subset of places, this too could give rise to place concentration. Brantingham and Brantingham (1995) called places that have numerous targets "crime generators," thus suggesting that size and number of targets can play an important role. They also called places that attract offenders "crime attractors," thus addressing the offender role. By implication, they suggest that explanations for high-crime places might be place specific – some are due to targets and some to offenders, and some might be due to both.

However, there might be more comprehensive processes at work; processes that could subsume offenders, targets, size, and other place characteristics. One explanation goes back to Durkheim's classic proposition that the level of crime is stable in society, or rather that there was a "normal level" of crime in society (Durkheim 1895). For Durkheim, this meant that crime was not necessarily an indication of an illness or pathology in society, but rather that healthy societies would inevitably have some normal level of crime. Crime waves and crime drops in this context can be seen as the result of some "abnormality" in society that results from crisis or dramatic social change.

Underlying Durkheim's proposition is his understanding of crime as a product of social definition. Kai Erikson (1966) was to build upon this idea in his classic study *Wayward Puritans*, where he sought to show that the definition of crime had a social function. By defining others as deviant, society can help draw the boundaries between acceptable and unacceptable conduct (see also Adler and Adler 2009; Becker 1968). Defining people as criminal in this sense serves a function in defining the moral boundaries of society. We can know the boundaries of acceptable behavior by observing "deviants" who are sanctioned for violating societal norms.

As we noted in Chapter 2, crime rates over the last few decades would seem to strongly contradict Durkheim's conception of normal levels of crime in society. Between 1973 and 1990 violent crime doubled (National Research Council 1993), and in the 1990s the United States experienced a well-documented "crime drop" (Blumstein and Wallman 2000). Weisburd et al. (2012; Weisburd and Amram 2014) argued, however, that there is indeed a "normal level of crime" in cities, but one that relates to the concentration of crime at place and not to the overall rate of crime. But if there is a law of crime concentration at places in the sense that Durkheim had originally postulated, then it means that we should be able to identify places where such concentrations are not found. There should be places where crime is not very concentrated and spread throughout areas in a city. There should be cities where crime is much more heavily concentrated than has been observed in prior studies. A normal level of concentration suggests that there will be communities where social or other problems cause crime concentrations at places to violate the normal crime hypothesis. So far, we have little evidence of this, which raises the specter of whether the crime concentrations observed follow a statistical rather than a social rule, as suggested by Pareto and others. But our lack of such data may be because studies so far have focused upon situations where there has not been social or economic crisis. A key avenue of inquiry in future studies must be perhaps low income countries, or cities in the midst of significant social or economic crises.

If we can assume that the law of crime concentration reflects an underlying reality of modern cities, can we use Durkheim's initial insights to consider possible reasons for this law of crime concentration at places? If we follow Durkheim and other theorists who built on his work, we would look to the role of crime at place in defining normative boundaries in society. In this case, we might argue that a certain number of places in the city with severe crime problems serve as lessons for the city more generally. This would fit well with the finding that crime hot spots are found throughout the city. Accordingly, we all have direct visceral experiences with the "bad places" in the city, and perhaps that serves to define for the rest of us the "moral boundaries" of place. The normal level of crime concentration in this context would relate to the proportion of problem places that are needed to bring the lessons of moral boundaries to the city's residents.

Another possible explanation for a law of crime concentration at places comes from the concentration of other characteristics of places in the city. For example, Weisburd et al. (2012) note that the concentrations of bus stops or number of public facilities, like crime, stay relatively stable over long periods. Perhaps the law of concentration of crime is related to the overall distribution of social and environmental characteristics of places in cities. Does the stability of patterns of business and employment in a city, for example, reflect more general patterns of concentration that are related to the growth and development of urban areas? Certainly cities regulate such concentrations, by defining commercial, business, and industrial use of property. Perhaps the normal concentrations of crime are simply a reflection of the normal concentrations of other social activities in the city. The law of crime concentration at places may simply be a reflection of a more general law of the stability of concentrations of specific aspects of social and economic life in the city. This is suggested by Juran (1951).

But this brings us back to Durkheim, because crime is a social phenomenon and its tolerance is a social construct. Is society willing to tolerate crime at only a certain proportion of the landscape of a city? Is the law of concentration a result of the boundaries of crime at place that citizens are willing to tolerate? Will people become worried and call for action when crime hot spots increase beyond a specific proportion of places in the city, and will they become more lax when the concentrations are below that level? We think that these questions need to be central to the next generation of studies in the criminology of place.

We have a specific explanation involving the economic life of cities, which we think also may help scholars to begin to understand the law of crime concentration in cities. Eck (1994) and Madensen and Eck (2008; 2013) propose a theory of property management that provides insight to why specific places in a city produce so much of its crime. They see places – owned parcels of real property – as loci of control. Property rights confer on place managers (owners, and the people they delegate to exercise these rights) legal powers to organize space, regulate conduct, control access, and acquire resources at their places. Place managers exercise these rights in ways that suit them, within the legal restrictions (zoning, health and safety, other regulations).

Place management, in essence, is less about crime than the normal day-to-day use of space by the people who own the property and have legal control over it. Crime is typically an unwanted byproduct that place managers work to prevent. This is because crime often inhibits their use of the place – the place manager's property can be stolen or damaged, the place manager might be injured or killed, or others who place managers would like to use their property might be frightened away. A store owner, for example, has an incentive to prevent crime on her premises because it drives off customers and raises the costs of doing business. A homeowner has an incentive to prevent crime because it interferes with his enjoyment and safety, and the enjoyment and safety of his family.

What do place managers do to curb crime? Madensen (2007) proposed a complex model, spanning several time scales, showing how place managers adjust their behavior and the characteristics of their sites to events and outside interventions (e.g., market forces and government regulation). She proposes that place management is largely about adjusting four things within this context: the organization of space, the regulation of conduct, the control of access, and the acquisition of resources (ORCA). For business properties, the last can be summarized as profits. However, all property owners need resources. So a nongovernmental organization acting as a charity (e.g., a soup kitchen or church) must convince people to donate time and money. Access control involves a form of selective invitation – some people (e.g., customers, people of the right faith, family members) are encouraged to enter the property, while others are not. While on the property, people are encouraged to behave in certain ways, and discouraged from other activities. And the physical space surrounding the activities, from the edge of the property to the center, is designed to facilitate the desired activities and inhibit the undesired activities. Place managers have at least partial control over every mechanism proposed for high levels of crime: they control access by offenders and potential victims; they control the physical design; they can create both formal and informal social control on their property; they control the number of physical targets at the place and how they are protected; and they can regulate the level of explicit guardianship. Whether a place manager understands how to do these things, and whether he or she chooses to do them, is variable.

Place managers are not uniform in their abhorrence of crime or their ability to do something about it. And their incentive to do something about crime depends on the crime. So a small grocery store might have a strong interest in driving down shoplifting and robbery, but have less interest in dispersing drug dealers who use the store and parking area. Eck and Wartell (1998) suggest that owners of commercial property, including rental housing, have a stronger incentive to suppress crime if they are getting a high rate of return from the property compared with similar businesspeople whose property is barely showing a profit. And when the place costs more to own than the place manager can afford, he or she has an incentive to walk away from it, as we saw in the recent economic downturn. So it is not surprising that high-crime places tend to concentrate in some neighborhoods, as these are the neighborhoods where the ability to gain a profit from property is lowest. And it is not surprising that in these same neighborhoods, most places still have very little crime, because crime is still costly to owners. In a particularly interesting pair of studies, Troy Payne and John Eck examined owners of rental property in Cincinnati in 2006. Crime is highly concentrated in these properties, as it is in every other type of facility studied (Wilcox and Eck 2011), and the ownership of firms is also known to be highly concentrated (Axtell 2001).

Would crime be highly concentrated among property owners? Using public records, they aggregated crime events to their apartment complex addresses and then aggregated the addressed crime to the property owner. The answer turns out to be "yes"; a relatively few apartment owners own most of the apartment crime (Payne and Eck 2007). Specifically, 10 percent of the apartment complex addresses had 31 percent of the serious crime, while 10 percent of the owners had 47 percent of the serious crime. A related study in Hamilton, Ohio, found similar results (Payne et al. 2013). One of the prime reasons crime is so concentrated among owners of property is that owners probably use similar management practices across their properties, and ownership itself is highly concentrated: 8 percent of the apartment complex owners in Cincinnati held over 51 percent of these properties (Payne and Eck 2007).

One way to see the significance of ownership is to look at ownership changes. Clarke and Bichler-Robinson (1998), in an early test of the ownership thesis, examined several case studies of property ownership and crime and showed how change in ownership can shift crime up or down. Troy Payne examined the relationship between ownership change in apartment complexes and crime throughout Cincinnati, from 2002 to 2009. He found that "Ownership change and crime are associated with each other in a feedback system. Ownership change is more likely at apartments with a history of past crime, and ownership change is associated with a 10 percent increase in future crime counts" (Payne 2010, 1).

Though these descriptive studies are consistent with Eck and Madensen's thesis that how property is managed influences crime at places, the most compelling evidence for the importance of place management comes from experimental and quasi-experimental evaluations of interventions at properties. Police get much of the credit for interventions at places, but when it comes to proprietary places, police cannot intervene to change the place except through the owner. Either the owner must voluntarily agree to the changes and help in their implementation or the police must seek legal authority to compel such changes. Consequently, any evaluation of a prevention effort at an address provides evidence about the efficacy of place management. As we saw in Chapter 6, there is considerable evidence that address-level interventions using situational crime prevention often reduce crime.

So according to place management theory, if the concentration of crime is normal, then it is, in part, due to the normal operations of property owners and their employees. Most place managers, either by fortune or hard work, are reasonably good at keeping crime low and have incentives to do so. Some place managers have less incentive or do not know how to do this. Rana Sampson and colleagues (2009) suggest that the network of "super controllers" within which place mangers are embedded will have a strong influence on whether they succeed at keeping crime low or whether they fail. Since network structures and feedback have been strongly implicated in the creation of concentrated human activity (Axtell and Epstein 1996; Bak 1996), the place management thesis is a strong contender for explaining crime concentration at places.

BROADENING THEORETICAL DEVELOPMENT

Empirical studies are not enough if we are to advance our understanding of crime at place. Theory is key to the development of any area of study. The criminology of place has its theoretical roots in opportunity theories. Many of the scholars that have pioneered opportunity theories of crime have been focused on crime prevention rather than advancing criminological theory. Situational crime prevention (Clarke 1980; 1995; 2000; Cornish and Clarke 2003), for example, simply by its name identifies the primary interest of its originators. Routine activity theory (Cohen and Felson 1979) would seem to respond more directly to theoretical concerns. Indeed, place management theory is a subset of routine activity theory (Madensen and Eck 2008). But its development over time has also reflected a strong concern with preventing crime rather than with developing criminological theory (Felson 1995).

One of the strengths of the criminology of place is that it has sought not simply to talk about crime but to do something about it. One reason for the strong evidence of crime prevention effectiveness in this area is likely the enduring interest in crime prevention that has motivated it. In contrast, many traditional criminological theories have little connection to the reality of crime prevention, and often deal with prevention problems only as an afterthought (Gottfredson and Hirschi 1995; Hirschi 1993).

"Opportunity theories" (Cullen 2010; Wilcox et al. 2003) have become the central explanation for why crime trends vary at places and are used as a basis for constructing practical crime prevention approaches (e.g., see Eck 1995; Sherman et al. 1989; Weisburd et al. 2004). As we noted earlier, Sherman et al. (1989, 30) argued in introducing the idea of a criminology of place that "(t)raditional collectivity theories [termed here "social disorganization theories"] may be appropriate for explaining community-level variation, but they seem inappropriate for small, publicly visible places with highly transient populations." Nevertheless, there may be important factors that influence the likelihood of crime occurring at places, which cannot be marshaled for crime prevention. We recognize the importance of opportunity theory for the criminology of place, but other explanations may work in collaboration with opportunity theories or are competitors. We noted in Chapter 3 that social disorganization theory has relevance for place-based study. This introduction of social disorganization theory (see Weisburd et al. 2012; Weisburd et al. 2014) broadens the variables and mechanisms that are brought to the study of microgeographic places and crime. We think it should be part of a larger broadening of theoretical inquiry in this area (see also Braga and Clarke 2014).

In Chapter 3 we argued for greater "theoretical integration" (Bernard and Snipes 1996) in the study of crime and place (e.g., see Elliott 1985). It likely that as the theoretical breadth of crime and place studies increases, it will lead to a richer and more comprehensive understanding of crime. And in this sense the crime prevention focus of many scholars in this area will help to advance this approach. Criminological scholars sometimes seem to argue for the primacy of particular theoretical perspectives. This theoretical competition approach was dominant in criminology for many years (Bernard and Snipes 1996). But in a practical sense there is little reason for becoming embroiled in such theoretical battles in the criminology of place. A focus on crime prevention naturally leads to the integration of whatever tools are best in doing something about the crime problem.

Integration can bring with it, however, its own set of problems. Travis Hirschi (1989) forcefully suggests that one of the major strengths of treating theories as if they were in opposition is that it can bring clarity to the theories. Proponents of alternative theories must clarify their constructs, processes, and research methods. Competition, in short, breeds clarity and forces us to pay close attention to the quality and quantity of evidence. Integration, therefore, brings with it the risk of fuzziness. If we are not careful, integration can serve mostly a social function among a community of scholars: reducing uncertainty and conflict among peers. If the concepts are blurry then the volume of evidence one can cite in favor of one's perspective becomes greater. Researchers who might be forced into a public debate, with all its tension and strain, can avoid such circumstances. Hirschi (1989) points out that some theories, faced with conflicting evidence, can find new life by pleading for integration with more empirically successful theories. Therefore, if integration of theories is to serve a scientific purpose, it must be done only if it advances our understanding of the topic under consideration: in this case, the concentration of crime at a few places. Integration must also identify clear gaps in the explanatory power of the theories being considered and will only be successful if the theories under consideration can be fitted together without distorting their original meaning.

It is time in our view to invigorate theoretical investigations at the level of microgeographic places. Such an approach is key to the growing centrality of this area of study and its influence on traditional criminology. We think it is also key for developing more effective crime prevention policies at places.

THE IMPORTANCE OF INTRA- AND INTERDISCIPLINARY PERSPECTIVES

In Chapter 4 we showed how place-based studies have begun to influence traditional theorizing about both offender motivations and crime. It is interesting that crime and place scholars have from the outset tried to integrate offender decision making into their perspectives. This is most pronounced, for example, in Brantingham and Brantingham's (1984; 1993a) development of crime pattern theory, which is very much concerned with how offender decision making is influenced by the physical environment. More recently Wikström and colleagues (2010) have tried to integrate offender-based and place-based perspectives in their development of situational action theory. But often when the environment is recognized (see Gottfredson and Hirschi 1990), the offender is still very much at the center of the crime equation. The criminology of place perspective sees offender motivations as simply one part of an equation to understand crime at place.

There is some disagreement among those who study crime places (including among authors of this book) about the role of criminal motivation. Some think it is unimportant for understanding and preventing crimes at places. Others feel that criminal motivation might be useful. In the original formulation of situational crime prevention, a critique of traditional criminological focus on offender motivations was a key underlying idea (Clarke 1980; 1995). Situational crime prevention scholars argued that changing opportunity structures would allow on its own for crime prevention. This was the case because offenders were assumed to engage in rational choices (Clarke and Cornish

1985). Assuming rational choices meant that irrespective of offender motivation, by manipulating such factors as levels of effort or likelihood of apprehension crime levels could be lowered at places. Cohen and Felson (1979, 589) also argued in their groundbreaking article on routine activities that they "take criminal inclination as given and examine the manner in which the spatio-temporal organization of social activities helps people to translate their criminal inclinations into action." Scholars who have followed this approach have generally assumed a likely offender and have had little interest in examining the problem of offender motivation. Weisburd et al. (2012) contend that crime is "coupled" to place, relying on both opportunity and social disorganization theory. But the coupling of crime to place draws very little from knowledge about offender motivation.

Those who are agnostic about the value of criminal motivation offer several reasons for their skepticism. First, studying places or situations focuses scholars on characteristics of places, not characteristics of offenders, just as some physicists study quarks and others study dynamical systems of macroscopic mater. These skeptics simply believe that these are two interesting but only distally related crime topics and, for the most part, progress in either can be made without reference to the other. Another argument is that offender motivation has been studied a great deal but has not yielded much explanatory power (Weisburd and Piquero 2008). Rather than continue to re-plow what appears to be infertile soil, motivation skeptics in this area suggest we should look to theories that explain concentrations of crime at place.

The third argument motivation skeptics offer is that the monopoly that offender motivation researchers have had on the field has not yielded much by way of practices – by governments or private institutions – that could reliably reduce criminality. Scholars who study crime at place, as we and others have pointed out, fundamentally believe that practice is important. So the lack of practical utility deriving from offender motivation research suggests this is not an area worth pursuing.

A fourth argument offered is that when comparisons are made between motivational predictions and those drawn from, for example, examining opportunities for crime at place, the motivational predictions come up short. Weisburd and Piquero (2008) indicate that situational models of crime tend to explain more than motivation-based models. An example of this at a more abstract level is brought by Zimring (2006). He points out that there has been no fundamental change in any motivationally related characteristic of U.S. society in the 1990s, yet crime dropped. Farrell and colleagues (2011) point out that the crime drop could quite plausibly be explained by changes in the opportunity structures for crimes.

Finally, motivational skeptics argue that whether there is a class of individuals who can be called "motivated offenders" or whether most people are generally motivated most of the time is not a question that needs an answer in the study of crime at place. Since science values parsimonious theories over complex theories, in that context, why bother adding motivation to the theory if simpler approaches, such as that offered by opportunity theories, are doing reasonably well? Just as basic theories of physics do not take into account wind speed when looking at gravitational attraction, a basic theory of crime might not have to account for motivation.

Despite these arguments, there may be value in linking motivational research to crime at place study. As we noted earlier, an important contribution in this direction is crime pattern theory (Brantingham and Brantingham 1993a,b), which looks to see how the "back cloth" of crime (i.e., the physical settings where it occurs) influences offender behavior. It is clear that individuals commit crimes. People influence crime at places, and places influence individuals. Recently, scholars interested in both correctional rehabilitation and crime places have posited that offender rehabilitation and probation/parole success might be aided by more attention to crime places (Cullen et al. 2002; Schaefer 2013; Schaefer et al. 2015). Two decades ago, Maltz (1995) suggested that offender development might be influenced by the places to which he or she were exposed. Thus we have more than hints that understanding places might aid in the understanding of offender motivation, and that motivational considerations might aid in explaining high-crime places. This is a new and potentially exciting opportunity for young scholars that the criminology of place opens up. Gaining greater understanding of this interaction will only enrich crime and place study.

Just as criminology of place scholars need to integrate traditional criminological perspectives into their thinking about the crime problem, they need to continue to reach out to other disciplines for theoretical and empirical insights. We covered this question in detail in Chapter 4, focusing not only on what has been learned already, but also on promising new ideas from other fields that we think should be considered more directly. But we want to note here another facet of this interdisciplinary interest – the idea that criminology can offer new insight into key questions in other fields.

In recent years there has been criticism of the growing "medicalization" of problems in fields outside health (Conrad and Schneider 2010). For example, public health agencies and scholars have begun to see such problems as gun crime, violence, and drugs as public health problems (Welsh et al. 2014). While such definitions of problems sometimes reflect the competition of disciplines for resources or public visibility, they can as well reflect the simple fact that different disciplinary perspectives can add new ideas and new knowledge to areas of study.

We think that the criminology of place has much potential for this type of insight. For example, there is important research being done today on the ways in which the locations of health services can affect drug use and other antisocial behaviors (Hipp et al. 2009; Hipp et al. 2010). In an ongoing study supported by the National Institute of Drug Abuse, researchers are finding strong relationships between hot spots of crime and hot spots of health problems (Weisburd et al. 2014). For example, depression is found to be twice as likely for residents living at hot spots as at cool spots. Posttraumatic stress syndrome diagnoses are three times as likely to be found among residents living on the hottest crime streets. It is too early to draw causal conclusions regarding these correlations, but it does suggest that criminologists may have much to say about public health problems in cities. We suspect that criminologists can also add to knowledge of other problems that may have place-based elements that are often studied from a narrow disciplinary perspective.

THE IMPORTANCE OF ADVANCES IN DATA, METHODS, AND STATISTICS

Continued focus on data, methods, and statistics is crucial for the continued advancement of the criminology of place. This has already been a key factor in development and lack of development of work in this area. We believe the first detailed empirical examination of the distribution of crime across microgeographic places is Shaw's identification of the home addresses of delinquents in Chicago in 1929 (see Figure 1.1). As we noted in Chapter 1, the figure produced by Shaw looks like a modern crime map. Shaw (1929, 5), in turn, argued after completing this work that "study of such a problem as juvenile delinquency necessarily begins with a study of its geographical location."

But Shaw's work did not lead to an explosion of microplace studies; indeed, it stands alone among studies of the period. Part of the reason for this is, of course, the enduring interest of Chicago sociologists in communities (Weisburd and McEwen 1997). But clearly the technical difficulties of carrying out the task of hand mapping offenders to addresses must have discouraged other criminologists from taking Shaw's lead. Imagine if Shaw had mapped crime as opposed to addresses of delinquents. The sheer magnitude of such an enterprise is one simple reason for the failure of Shaw's innovation to influence study of crime.

The emergence of microgeographic study in the 1980s and 1990s can be seen similarly as strongly related to the new ease with which crime information could be captured and analyzed (see in particular Weisburd and McEwen 1997). The idea of automated crime mapping emerged in the late 1960s. Early applications (Carnaghi and McEwen 1970; Pauly and Finch 1967) showed the potential for visual representations of crime patterns through computer-generated maps. Technical considerations again prevented the rapid spread of automated mapping. The maps required large mainframe computers for development and production, and these were not often available to scholars. Using such applications was often a labor-intensive and time-consuming endeavor. Even when the desire for developing maps of crime was present, it was extremely difficult given existing technologies to access crime data. And as difficult as it was to prepare crime data that were under the control of police or other criminal justice agencies, it was that much more difficult to gain information from other agencies. Indeed, in this period there was little sharing of data across public agencies. Problems existed in both the compatibility of systems that were used and the identification of people or places tracked by specific agencies.

Starting with the Apple computer in 1979, the capabilities of microcomputers have increased every year and the costs have decreased. Desktop computers now deliver the power of mainframe computers. What this means is that the hardware necessary to develop computer maps has become available to lone scholars and even the smallest criminal justice agencies. The software has also become cheaper and more efficient. Information systems that accurately record crime events and the processing of offenders have become the rule rather than the exception in American criminal justice agencies. Especially for police, the linkage of such information to places, generally street addresses, has become a central concern. In general, it is the management responsibilities faced by such agencies that have led to this geographic focus. In order to respond quickly and efficiently to emergency calls to the police, accurate coding of street addresses in information systems has become a necessity for modern police departments. Other agencies that want to track the whereabouts of offenders are also concerned that there be accurate identification of where offenders live and work.

In turn, the more general concern for compatibility among systems and data sources has now made it possible for practitioners and scholars to link data about the ecology of crime to a host of other information sources (e.g., census data, hospital records, tax records, land use information). All of this has contributed to development of the criminology of place. Simply stated, the advances in data and methods made it possible for Shaw's original conclusion to become a reality. It is not an accident that the criminology of place begins to develop when it becomes feasible to code and analyze data at microgeographies. Such innovations in hardware, data, and methods are a key part of understanding the emergence of crime and place studies.

In Chapter 5 we examined a number of areas where innovation in methods was particularly important and promising. For example, we emphasized the need to take into account the relationship of places to other places nearby in the context of spatial autocorrelation. We also noted the emergence of "big data" and new techniques such as agent-based modeling. One issue that has continued to hinder study of crime at place is the restrictions imposed by the U.S. Census on use of data at a microgeographic level. Many scholars in this area end up "pushing up" the level of their analyses to census block groups or tracts because social and economic data from the census are not released, even in restricted data environments, to scholars at a lower level. We think this is perhaps the most important barrier today to the advancement of basic research study in this area. And we suspect that there are solutions that can be developed. In a study supported by the Israel Science Foundation, the Israeli Central Bureau of Statistics has agreed to provide data at the street segment level (that can be merged to crime data at street segments) to researchers under the condition that the data be held in a secure room in the Bureau (Weisburd 2014).

IMPLEMENTING PLACE-BASED CRIME PREVENTION IN PRACTICE

In Chapter 6 we reviewed the strong evidence in support of place-based crime prevention. In particular in the case of hot spots policing, there is a persuasive body of studies supporting a microgeographic approach to crime problems (Braga and Weisburd 2010; Braga et al. 2014). An important question to ask is to what extent are practitioners using place-based crime prevention?

We do have data on this question in the case of hot spots policing. Telep and Weisburd (2012) examined data from the 2007 Law Enforcement Management and Administrative Statistics (LEMAS) survey (see Reaves 2010), as well as survey data that asked police agencies about hot spots policing (Koper 2014). While data on specific tactics are limited in the LEMAS survey, there are a number of questions related to police technology. Crime analysis and crime mapping in particular are very important for the successful implementation of hot spots policing. The results overall suggest widespread use of these technologies in larger departments but not in smaller ones. For example, while over 90 percent of the largest agencies were using computers for hot spot identification, just 13 percent of departments overall were. Even in moderately sized cities (population 100,000–249,999), just 56 percent of departments used computers to identify hot spots. When it comes to using computers for crime analysis and crime mapping, results were similar. One hundred percent of the largest departments made use of computers for such tasks, but only 38 percent of agencies overall used computers for crime analysis, and 27 percent used computers for crime mapping. In terms of patrol officer access to crime data, just 31 percent of the largest agencies and 11 percent of agencies overall provided officers access to crime maps in their patrol cars.

The use of computers for crime mapping and analysis has increased since the 2003 LEMAS survey. For example, the percentage of officers working in a department that uses computers for crime mapping jumped from 57 percent in 2003 to 75 percent in 2007 and for hot spot identification the increase was from 45 percent in 2003 to 58 percent in 2007 (Reaves 2010). Research by Weisburd and Lum (2005) suggests that the use of crime mapping diffused quickly across policing from the mid-1990s through 2001. They note that the adoption of crime mapping was closely linked to the use of hot spots policing. When agencies were asked why they developed crime mapping in the department, the largest response category was "to facilitate hot spots policing." Kochel (2011, 352) cites similar statistics, noting "Within 15 years, hot spots policing had diffused almost completely throughout large U.S. police departments." These latest LEMAS data suggest that the use of crime mapping continues to increase, but smaller agencies are lagging behind.

Data on the adoption of hot spots policing also come from a Police Executive Research Forum (PERF) survey of 176 policing agencies of various sizes on their efforts to reduce violent crime (Koper 2014). Responses showed close to two-thirds (63 percent) of agencies used hot spots policing to reduce violent crime. This was by far the most popular response to the question of how to address violence. When asked what sort of places the agency defines as hot spots, the majority of respondents noted addresses or intersections (61 percent) or clusters of addresses (58 percent). However, a majority of respondents (57 percent) also identified neighborhoods as potential hot spots and a sizable minority pointed to patrol beats (41 percent) as the sort of place that would be defined as a hot spot. This suggests that the idea of hot spots policing may not be fully understood by many practitioners.

It is important to note that while the data discussed here provide an estimate of the extent to which police agencies have adopted hot spots policing, they do not make clear how frequently agencies are actually using hot spots policing in practice. In other words, while it appears that a substantial portion of larger agencies are using computers to identify crime hot spots, what percentage of officer time is actually being spent on hot spots policing in these agencies? A recent study conducted in Dallas, Texas, suggests that the level of use of such strategies may in fact be marginal relative to the overall resources of the police. While Dallas had a strong policy of directed patrols at crime hot spots, supported by a Compstat framework, only a small percentage of unallocated time was found to be spent on hot spots patrols (Weisburd et al. 2014).

In turn, most scholars argue that police agencies are still dominated by traditional tactics such as rapid response and random patrol across jurisdictions (Lum 2009; Lum et al. 2011; Sherman and Eck 2002; Telep and Weisburd 2012). And this is not the case because of a lack of recognition of the importance of places in policing and other criminal justice areas. To police and probation officers and other criminal justice street-level bureaucrats (Lipsky 1980), the idea that places are important to their craft seems obvious if not central. For example, the word "geography" is not foreign to police standard operating procedures, and many officers would argue that their patrol is geographically oriented – officers are assigned to specific beats or areas to which they are responsible. Academy as well as subsequent field training emphasize and regularly evaluate officers' understanding of "geography," which usually involves knowing the street layouts of their city or area of responsibility. Police managers and line-level officers are also quite familiar with the particular locations that cause recurring citizen calls for service. Even the notions of crime concentrations and "hot spots" seem obvious to police officers. Researchers focusing on hot spots policing or police deployment have heard time and again some form of the following rebuttal to their efforts: "We already know where the crime is; we don't need a map/criminologist/crime analyst/police commander/civilian to tell us where it is." And, related to this argument: "We already go to where the crime concentrates."

Thus, to practitioners, the meaningfulness of "place" and the connection between crime and geography is obvious, if not straightforward. However, these beliefs often are misaligned with a number of realities of criminal justice practice. In policing, as we already noted, the mainstay of patrol deployment is random preventive patrol and response to 911 calls (Lum 2009). Detectives are rarely assigned geographically or according to specific problem places (Braga et al. 2011). Rather, they are assigned to specific cases by crime type (e.g., homicide, robbery, auto theft) and respond when it is their turn to respond among their squad colleagues. Similarly, probation officers are often assigned caseloads of individuals spread out over wide spaces, and resources available for reentry and supervision are often located far from an individual's home. Probation officers also are not charged with assessing a probationer's immediate surroundings or community that may influence the success or failure of their cases. Instead, they are asked to focus on an individual's drug use or risk of violating the conditions of his or her probation.

Therein results the place-based paradox of practitioners: places matter to criminal justice practitioners, but places are often ignored as a key aspect of their craft. Despite the place orientation of officers, for example, there is more evidence that the regular practice of officers is *not* to focus on crime concentrations, and to be deployed, in their beats, in a random manner. There is little to suggest that the mainstays of American policing or probation – responding reactively to 911 calls or conducting individual case investigations on suspects or specific probationers – are in any way anchored by what both practitioners and researchers have known for some time about the interactions between environment and crime, criminality, and supervision. The misbelief that practitioners already focus on places or already know where crime concentrates can ironically inhibit practitioners from being open to focusing on places in ways that can contribute to crime prevention, crime reduction, or improved monitoring of individuals reentering society.

We believe that places *should be* a priority for criminal justice policy makers and practitioners for three specific reasons. First is a theme emphasized throughout this book, but that needs to be again reiterated: crime concentrates, and that concentration is stable over time (see Chapter 2). And crime is not simply concentrated abstractly (i.e., a "bad neighborhood"), but crime is often concentrated at very specific places – street blocks, alleyways, specific locations and addresses, intersections, or a few street blocks (Weisburd et al. 2012). Even within what people believe are "bad neighborhoods," at most places very little – if any – crime occurs. Yet, the allocation of criminal justice resources does not match the allocation of crime (and victimization) across places. Rather, the allocation of criminal justice resources often takes a broader, random, we-have-to-cover-it-all approach. Contrary to the common rebuttals presented earlier, it does not appear that officers clearly know where the crime is, nor are they being regularly deployed to where crime is as part of their daily activities. The fact that officers continue to be assigned to all places in a city, even places without crime, seems to counter the matter-of-fact belief that police are geographically oriented. Even the rebuttal that citizens will be unhappy with police if they move toward a directed patrol approach is empirically unsupported. The same rings true with probation officers. An understanding of places and their implication for both offender recidivism and treatment is not a regular part of the standard procedures of community corrections practice (Cullen et al. 2002; Schaefer 2013).

Second, place should matter to criminal justice professionals, because as we illustrated in Chapter 6, the strongest evidence that we have with regard to reducing and preventing crime are those interventions that are place-, not people-, oriented. These include directed patrol at crime concentrations proactively targeting places or crime-prone people in places, or addressing underlying environmental and situational causes of problems (Braga et al. 2014; Eck 2002; Weisburd and Eck 2004). Hot spots policing and problem-oriented policing at places remain the most scientifically supported interventions that the police can use to reduce crime. This includes considerations of displacement, which, as discussed in Chapter 6 does not undo the benefits of place-based crime prevention (indeed, the diffusion of benefits often adds to crime prevention outcomes). A growing body of evidence also shows that citizen place managers can be quite influential in determining the level of crime at specific locations. Further, there appears to be new evidence that probation, reentry, and community corrections interventions that are place-oriented also show promising effects.

Finally, not only should place matter because crime concentrates or because prevention programs at places can produce real results (although arguably, those two issues alone should be enough to be convincing), but places should also matter to practitioners because they provide a meaningful point of departure and reference to one's professional activities. Indeed, police and probation officers already organize their professional work around a place – the beat or the area they are responsible for. Yet, that orientation is purely a procedural one related to reactive deployment tactics, such as rapid response to 911 calls. Similarly, for the probation officer, social worker, or others, the area is only a geographic boundary that delineates reactive responsibility. Reorienting their work to address the underlying problems that cause particular places to perpetuate high rates of offending can alleviate the frustration experienced by criminal justice practitioners that they are not impacting crime in a meaningful way by repeatedly focusing on resolving particular crime incidents or managing large caseloads of crime-prone individuals.

Considering places and their role in crime prevention leads to considering policies beyond the criminal justice system. This might seem surprising because crime and place research has been so important for advances in police effectiveness over the last twenty years. The proliferation of hot spots research and analytical methods makes the criminology of place almost synonymous with enforcement at high-crime locations. It would be unfortunate if this continues. Traditional criminologists, to their credit, have always been concerned with the possibility that crime research could bolster the worst aspects of state power. Indeed, as we write, several cities, including New York, have been wracked by controversies over the use of aggressive law enforcement, such as stop, question, and frisks at crime hot spots (Gelman et al. 2007; Ridgeway 2007; Weisburd et al. 2014). Criminologists are rightfully concerned when they complain that the criminology of place may be providing an excuse for the police to practice enforcement practices that are not only aggressive, but also might involve strong racial disparities.

Fortunately, a focus on crime places can point to fewer enforcement-oriented policies. Within policing, problem-oriented policing has the potential to mitigate against hot spots enforcement with racially disparate outcomes. This is because problem-oriented policing can open up police to public involvement in defining problems and formulating solutions, and because it can focus police on changing circumstances that give rise to offending, rather than simply making more arrests. Indeed, when faced with charges of racially biased policing, Cincinnati adopted a problem-oriented approach under the auspices of the federal court (Eck and Rothman 2006). Most of the problems the police addressed using a problem-oriented approach under the collaborative agreement were at places (Eck 2014). Despite the successes of the collaborative agreement to improve community–police relations, the police have struggled with adopting a problem-oriented approach, largely due to turnover at the mayoral, city manager, and police chief levels (Eck 2014). This example demonstrates the promises and difficulties of a problem-oriented approach – it can work when applied (Weisburd et al. 2010), but police have difficulty implementing and sustaining it (Braga and Weisburd 2006).

But the criminology of place can open up even greater opportunities to reduce reliance on the police and the criminal justice system. Eck and Eck (2012) suggest that given the evidence so far – the stable concentration of crime at a relatively few places; the demonstrated effectiveness of place-based interventions involving place managers; and the limited scope of crime displacement – it may be useful to follow the advice of Farrell and Roman (2006) and treat crime as a pollutant and crime places as point source polluters. This opens up a large array of regulatory approaches – some of which have been tried and some of which are potential options – to preventing crime without strong reliance on police enforcement. It is possible, Eck and Eck (2012) contend, that a relatively few regulators could have more effect on crime than numerous officers, largely because a regulatory approach pushes the responsibility for crime prevention back to key members of the public (place managers) rather than relying mostly on publicly financed government institutions to do the work. Though regulatory approaches have worked (see Bichler et al. 2013 for an example), there has been little systematic research on regulation of crime places outside the context of policing (Mazerolle and Ransley 2006). For criminologists interested in exploring alternatives to criminal justice sanctioning, this may be an exciting opportunity.

Weisburd et al. (2012; Weisburd et al. 2014) suggest that crime hot spots can become a locus for social interventions as well. They call for the implementation of economic and employment programs, as well as interventions that seek to increase collective efficacy at the microgeographic level. Successful crime prevention can be seen as operating at two levels. One level responds to the immediate situational components of crime and often relies on deterrence and directly reducing crime opportunities as a method of reducing the likelihood of crime. At another, there are long-term social factors often relating to disadvantage and low collective efficacy. The work of Weisburd and colleagues suggests that it is time to experiment in this latter area at a microgeographic level. There will often be overlap, and the most effective long-term crime prevention will focus on both approaches. Informal social controls that are encouraged by increased collective efficacy will also work to reduce opportunities for crime. Hot spots policing and situational prevention may, by reducing fear of crime and increasing quality of life on streets, also increase collective efficacy and reduce social disadvantage. It is time to examine these possibilities and mechanisms more carefully to develop a fuller repertoire of crime prevention at a microgeographic level.

CONCLUSIONS

We titled our book *Place Matters* because we wanted to draw attention to the importance of microgeographic places for understanding crime and doing something about the crime problem. The criminology of place should become a key part of criminological understandings and of crime prevention. We have tried in this book to summarize why this is the case, and why the integration of the study of crime at place should be integrated more broadly into criminological thinking. Viewing place as the key organizing feature of crime is a radical proposition given the traditional focus of criminology on people. But we think that our review of what is known about the criminology of place suggests that it should be a central focus of criminology in the twenty-first century.

Notes

Chapter 1 Crime Places within Criminological Thought

1. We searched the course catalogs for the top ten criminology programs in the U.S. News and World Report in the fall of 2014 to determine which courses taught criminological theory. The book title and ISBN for every course section that taught criminological theory (n=23) was recorded and each book was then accessed either online or in print to examine whether or not it discussed microgeographic units of analysis. This process included reviewing the table of contents, glossary, index, and reference section for information related to microgeographic units of analysis.
2. X, Y coordinates refer to the latitude and longitude of a crime event and allow crimes to be precisely mapped using geographic information systems (GIS).

Chapter 2 The Concentration of Crime at Place

1. Writing of this chapter was led by George Rengert, Kate Bowers, Joshua C. Hinkle, and Julie Hibdon.
2. This represents the total number of street addresses (i.e., land parcels) for each of the six calendar days.
3. This represents the total demand for police services (i.e., 911 calls, walk-ins, and on-site intervention) with known street addresses.
4. Note that the data in Tel Aviv for Weisburd (2015a) are drawn from a slightly different data source than the data reported in Weisburd and Amram (2014), which accounts for differences observed in the crime concentration statistics.

Chapter 3 Theories of Crime and Place

1. Writing of this chapter was led by John E. Eck, Elizabeth Groff, and David Weisburd.

2. In offender search theory, offenders become aware of crime opportunities as a result of noncriminal day-to-day activities (see Brantingham and Brantingham 1993b; 1995).
3. Braga and Clarke (2014) raise questions about the use of voting behavior as an indicator of collective efficacy. They argue that voting behavior is not a good measure of collective efficacy, pointing to Sampson's (2012) recent findings that voting patterns across neighborhoods were not strongly correlated with measures of collective efficacy. Importantly, the Weisburd et al. (2012) measure and Sampson's measure are substantially different. Sampson examined the proportion of residents in the neighborhood who reported voting in the last mayoral election. Weisburd et al. measure the proportion of active voters on a street, defined by voting patterns over two years. Voting once does not necessarily show strong commitment to involvement in public affairs, but voting consistently over time says more about an individual's commitment (see Coleman 2002; Putnam 2001). More importantly, it reflects a general propensity toward civic engagement that is likely to be even stronger on the home street segment.
4. Note that place managers influence more than guardianship. Importantly, for example, they also control the presence of targets and the physical environment. Consequently, we must not mistakenly assume place management is simply another name for guardianship, or that guardianship is the same as place management. Though connected, and sometimes overlapping, these are distinct practices.

Chapter 4 The Importance of Place in Mainstream Criminology and Related Fields: Influences and Lessons to Be Learned

1. Writing for this chapter was led by Gerben Bruinsma, Sue-Ming Yang, Charlotte Gill, and Breanne Cave.
2. Felson notes that the article was rejected by a number of journals before it was reconsidered and published in the *American Sociological Review* (personal correspondence).
3. For instance, Stevens and Coupe (1978) found that people assign the location of a larger geographic unit, such as a state, to a subordinate geographic unit, such as a city, causing systemic errors in their understanding of the spatial relations between subordinate units when they differ from the superordinate units.

Chapter 5 Methods of Place-Based Research

1. Writing of this chapter was led by Jerry H. Ratcliffe, Brian Lawton, and Shane D. Johnson.
2. For an example of the use of a cellular automata in criminology, see Spicer et al. (2012).

Chapter 6 Reducing Crime at High-Crime Places: Practice and Evidence

1. Writing of this chapter was led by Anthony A. Braga, Cynthia Lum, Cody W. Telep, and Travis Taniguchi.

2. For example, Weisburd, Gill, and Wooditch (2014) are working with the Brooklyn Park Police Department with Bureau of Justice Assistance support to examine whether police can increase collective efficacy at hot spots and through that reduce crime. This randomized experiment is in progress. Weisburd and Wooditch are working with Eric Jester in Pittsburgh in developing a study that would use economic interventions at crime hot spots to reduce crime in hot spots and surrounding areas. These are just emerging efforts that will hopefully yield important evidence in the coming years.
3. Formed in 2000, the Campbell Collaboration Crime and Justice Group aims to prepare and maintain systematic reviews of criminological interventions and to make them electronically accessible to scholars, practitioners, policy makers, and the general public (Farrington and Petrosino 2001; see also www.campbellcollaboration.org).
4. Meta-analysis is a method of systematic reviewing designed to synthesize empirical outcomes of studies, such as the effects of a specific crime-prevention intervention on criminal offending behavior (Wilson 2001). Meta-analysis uses statistical methods to analyze the relationships between findings and study features (Lipsey and Wilson 2001). The "effect size statistic" is the index used to represent the findings of each study in the overall meta-analysis of study findings and represents the strength and direction (positive or negative) of the relationship observed in a particular study (e.g., the size of the treatment effect found) (Lipsey and Wilson 2001). The "mean effect size" represents the average effect of treatment on the outcome of interest across all eligible studies in a particular area, and is estimated by calculating a mean that is weighted by the precision of the effect size for each individual study.
5. In the case of *Terry v. Ohio* (1968), the Supreme Court upheld the right of the police officers to conduct brief threshold inquiries of suspicious persons when they have reason to believe that such persons may be armed and dangerous to the police or others. In practice, this threshold inquiry typically involves a safety frisk of the suspicious person.
6. See www.dpscs.state.md.us/initiatives/kcs/index_KCS_cs-new.shtml.
7. See www.policingmatrix.org.

References

Abelson, E.S. (1992). *When ladies go a-thieving: Middle-class shoplifters in the Victorian department store*. New York: Oxford University Press.

Abler, R., Adams, J.S., and Gould, P. (1971). *Spatial organization: The geographer's view of the world*. Englewood Cliffs, NJ: Prentice-Hall.

Adler, P.A., and Adler, P. (2009). *Constructions of deviance: Social power, context, and interaction*. 6th ed. Belmont, CA: Wadsworth Publishing.

Agnew, R. (2006). *Pressured into crime: An overview of general strain theory*. Los Angeles: Roxbury.

(2013). "When criminal coping is likely: An extension of general strain theory." *Deviant Behavior*, 34(8), 653–670.

Akers, R.L. (1992). "Linking sociology and its specialties: The case of criminology." *Social Forces*, 71(1), 1–16.

Akers, T.A., and Lanier, M.M. (2009). "'Epidemiological criminology': Coming full circle." *American Journal of Public Health*, 99(3), 397–402.

Albrecht, J. (2007). *Key concepts and techniques in GIS*. Thousand Oaks, CA: Sage Publications.

Allport, F.H. (1934) "The J curve hypothesis of conforming behavior." *Journal of Social Psychology*, 5(2), 141–182.

Altman, I., and Chemers, M. (1980). *Culture and environment*. Monterey, CA: Brooks/Cole.

Anderson, E. (1999). *The code of the street: Decency, violence and the moral life of the inner city*. New York: W.W. Norton.

Andresen, M.A., and Malleson, N. (2011). "Testing the stability of crime patterns: Implications for theory and policy." *Journal of Research in Crime and Delinquency*, 48(1), 58–82.

Anselin, L., Cohen, J., Cook, D., Gorr, W., and Tita, G. (2000). "Spatial analyses of crime." In D. Duffee (ed.), *Criminal Justice 2000, Measurement and analysis of crime and justice*, vol. 4 (pp. 213–262). Washington, DC: National Institute of Justice, U.S. Department of Justice.

Appleyard, D. (1981). *Livable streets*. Berkeley, CA: University of California Press.

Archibald, M.E. (2008). "Exploring the reciprocal effects of substance abuse treatment provision and area substance abuse." In D. Richardson and Y. Thomas (eds.), *Geography and drug addiction* (pp. 263–278). New York: Springer.

Ashby, D.I., Irving, B.L., and Longley, P.A. (2007). "Police reform and the new public management paradigm: matching technology to the rhetoric." *Environment and Planning C: Government and Policy*, 25(2), 159–175.

Audit Commission (1993). *Helping with enquiries: Tackling crime effectively*. London: Her Majesty's Stationery Office.

Audretsch, D.B., and Feldman, M. (1996). "R&D spillovers and the geography of innovation and production." *American Economic Review*, 86(3), 630–640.

Audretsch, D.B., and Keilbach, M. (2008). "Resolving the knowledge paradox: Knowledge-spillover entrepreneurship and economic growth." *Research Policy*, 37(10), 1697–1705.

Axtell, R.L. (2001). "Zipf distribution of U.S. firm sizes." *Science*, 293(5536), 1818–1820.

Axtell, R., and Epstein, J.M. (1996). *Growing artificial societies: Social science from the bottom up*. Washington, DC: Brookings Institution.

Bailey, T.C., and Gatrell, A.C. (1995). *Interactive spatial data analysis*. Essex: Longman Scientific and Technical.

Bak, P. (1994). "Self-organized criticality: A holistic view of nature." In G. Cowan, D. Pines, and D.E. Meltzer (eds.), *Complexity: Metaphors, models, and reality.* (pp. 477–495). Reading, MA: Addison-Wesley.

——— (1996). *How nature works: The science of self-organized criticality*. New York: Springer.

Balbi, A., and Guerry, A.-M. (1829). *Statistique comparée de l'état de l'instruction et du nombre des crimes dans les divers arrondissements des Académies et des Cours Royales de France*. Paris: Jules Renouard.

Barker, R.G. (1968). *Ecological psychology: Concepts and methods for studying the environment of human behavior*. Palo Alto, CA: Stanford University Press.

Barker, R.G., and Wright, H.F. (1955). *Midwest and its children*. New York: Harper and Row.

Barnes, G.C. (1995). Defining and optimizing displacement. In J.E. Eck and D. Weisburd (eds.), *Crime and place. Crime Prevention Studies*, vol. 4 (pp. 95–114). Monsey, NY: Willow Tree Press.

Barr, R., and Pease, K. (1990). "Crime placement, displacement, and deflection." In M. Tonry and N. Morris (eds.), *Crime and Justice: A Review of Research*, vol. 12 (pp. 277–318). Chicago, IL: University of Chicago Press.

Batty, M., DeSyllas, J., and Duxbury, E. (2003). "The discrete dynamics of small-scale spatial events: Agent-based models of mobility in carnivals and street parades." *International Journal of Geographical Information Science*, 17(7), 673–697.

Beardsley, K., Wish, E.D., Fitzelle, D.B., O'Grady, K., and Arria, A.M. (2003). "Distance traveled to outpatient drug treatment and client retention." *Journal of Substance Abuse Treatment*, 25(4), 279–285.

Beavon, D.J.K., Brantingham, P.L., and Brantingham, P.J. (1994). "The influence of street networks on the patterning of property offenses." In R.V. Clarke (ed.), *Crime Prevention Studies*, vol. 2 (pp. 115–148). Monsey, NY: Criminal Justice Press.

Becker, G.S. (1968). "Crime and punishment: An economic approach." *Journal of Political Economy*, 76(2), 169–217.
  (1993). "Nobel lecture: The economic way of looking at behavior." *Journal of Political Economy*, 101(3), 385–409.
Beirne, P. (1987). "Between classicism and positivism: Crime and penality in the writings of Gabriel Tarde." *Criminology*, 25(4), 785–820.
Beirne, P., and Messerschmidt, J. (1991). *Criminology*. San Diego, CA: Harcourt Brace Jovanovich.
Bell, P.A., Greene, T.C., Fisher, J.D., and Baum, A. (2001). *Environmental psychology*. 5th ed. New York: Harcourt Brace, Inc.
Bellair, P.E. (1997). "Social interaction and community crime: Examining the importance of neighbor networks." *Criminology*, 35(4), 677–704.
Benson, M.L., Madensen, T.D., and Eck, J.E. (2009). "White-collar crime from an opportunity perspective." In S. Simpson and D. Weisburd (eds.), *The criminology of white-collar crime* (pp. 175–193). New York: Springer.
Bernard, T.J., and Snipes, J.B. (1996). "Theoretical integration in criminology." In M. Tonry (ed.), *Crime and Justice: A Review of Research*, vol. 20 (pp. 301–348). Chicago, IL: University of Chicago Press.
Bernasco, W. (2008). "Them again? Same-offender involvement in repeat and near repeat burglaries." *European Journal of Criminology*, 5(4), 411–431.
Bernasco, W., and Block, R. (2011). "Robberies in Chicago: A block-level analysis of the influence of crime generators, crime attractors, and offender anchor points." *Journal of Research in Crime and Delinquency*, 48(1), 33–57.
Bernasco, W., Block, R., and Ruiter, S. (2013). "Go where the money is: Modeling street robbers' location choices." *Journal of Economic Geography*, 13(1), 119–143.
Bernasco, W, Bruinsma, G.J.N., Pauwels, L.J.R., and Weerman, F.M. (2013). "Adolescent delinquency and diversity in behavior settings." *Australian and New Zealand Journal of Criminology*, 46(3), 357–378.
Bernasco, W., Ruiter S., Bruinsma, G.J.N., Pauwels, L., and Weerman, F. (2013). "Situational causes of offending: A fixed effect analysis of the space-time-budget data." *Criminology*, 51(4), 895–926.
Berry, B.J.L., and Kasarda, J.D. (1977). *Contemporary urban ecology*. New York: Macmillan.
Bettinger, P., and Sessions, J. (2003). "Spatial forest planning: To adopt, or not to adopt?" *Journal of Forestry*, 101(2), 24–29.
Bichler, G., Malm, A., and Enriquez, J. (2014). "Magnetic facilities: Identifying the convergence settings of juvenile delinquents." *Crime and Delinquency*, 60(7), 971–998.
Bichler, G., Schmerler, K., and Enriquez, J. (2013). "Curbing nuisance motels: An evaluation of police as place regulators." *Policing: An International Journal of Police Strategies and Management*, 36(2), 437–462.
Birks, D., Townsley, M., and Stewart, A. (2012). "Generative explanations of crime: Using simulation to test criminological theory." *Criminology*, 50(1), 221–254.
Black, D.A., and Park, K. (2012). "Some problems with place-based crime policies." *Criminology and Public Policy*, 11(2), 327–334.
Block, R.L., and Block, C.R. (1995). "Space, place and crime: Hot spot areas and hot places of liquor-related crime." In J.E. Eck and D. Weisburd (eds.), *Crime and

place. *Crime Prevention Studies*, vol. 4 (pp. 145–183). Monsey, NY: Willow Tree Press.

Blokland, A.A.J., and Nieuwbeerta, P.N. (2010). "Life course criminology." In S.G. Shohan, P. Knepper, and M. Kett (eds.), *International handbook of criminology* (pp. 51–93). Boca Raton, FL: CRC Press.

Blumstein, A., and Cohen, J. (1973). "A theory of the stability of punishment." *Journal of Criminal Law and Criminology*, 64(2), 198–207.

Blumstein, A., and Moitra, S. (1979). "An analysis of the time series of the imprisonment rate in the states of the United States: A further test of the stability of punishment hypothesis." *Journal of Criminal Law and Criminology*, 70(3), 376–390.

Blumstein, A., and Wallman, J. (eds.). (2000). *The crime drop in America*. New York: Cambridge University Press.

Blumstein, A., Cohen, J., and Farrington, D.P. (1988). "Longitudinal and criminal career research: Further clarifications." *Criminology*, 26(1), 57–74.

Blumstein, A., Cohen, J., and Nagin, D. (1976). "The dynamics of a homeostatic punishment process." *The Journal of Criminal Law and Criminology*, 67(3), 317–334.

Boggs, J.S., and Rantisi, N.M. (2003). "The 'relational turn' in economic geography." *The Journal of Economic Geography*, 3(2), 109–116.

Bolt, G., Burgers, J., and Van Kempen, R. (1998). "On the social significance of spatial location; spatial segregation and social inclusion." *Journal of Housing and the Built Environment*, 13(1), 83–95.

Bottoms, A. (2009). "Disorder, order and control signals." *British Journal of Sociology*, 60(1), 49–55.

Bowers, K.J. (2014). "Risky facilities: Crime radiators or crime absorbers? A comparison of internal and external levels of theft." *Journal of Quantitative Criminology*, 30(3), 389–414.

Bowers, K.J., Johnson, S.D., and Pease, K. (2004). "Prospective hot-spotting the future of crime mapping?" *British Journal of Criminology*, 44(5), 641–658.

Bowers, K., Johnson, S., Guerette, R.T., Summers, L., and Poynton, S. (2011). "Spatial displacement and diffusion of benefits among geographically focused policing interventions." *Journal of Experimental Criminology*, 7(3), 347–374.

Braga, A.A. (2001). "The effects of hot spots policing on crime." *Annals of the American Academy of Political and Social Science*, 578, 104–125.

(2005). "Hot spots policing and crime prevention: A systematic review of randomized controlled trials." *Journal of Experimental Criminology*, 1(3), 317–342.

(2007). "The effects of hot spots policing on crime." *Campbell Systematic Reviews*, 3(1), 1–96.

Braga, A.A., and Bond, B.J. (2008). "Policing crime and disorder hot spots: A randomized controlled trial." *Criminology*, 46, 577–608.

Braga, A.A., and Clarke, R.V. (2014). "Explaining high-risk concentrations of crime in the city: Social disorganization, crime opportunities, and important next steps." *Journal of Research in Crime and Delinquency*, 51(4), 480–498.

Braga, A.A., and Weisburd, D. (2006). "Problem-oriented policing: The disconnect between principles and practice." In D. Weisburd and A.A. Braga (eds.), *Police innovation: Contrasting perspectives* (pp. 133–154). New York: Cambridge University Press.

(2010). *Policing problem places: Crime hot spots and effective prevention.* New York: Oxford University Press.
Braga, A.A., and Weisburd, D.L. (2012). "The effects of focused deterrence strategies on crime a systematic review and meta-analysis of the empirical evidence." *Journal of Research in Crime and Delinquency,* 49(3), 323–358.
Braga, A.A., Flynn, E.A., Kelling, G.L., and Cole, C.M. (2011). *Moving the work of criminal investigators towards crime control.* New Perspectives on Policing. Washington, DC: U.S. Department of Justice, National Institute of Justice.
Braga, A.A., Hureau, D.M., and Papachristos, A.A. (2011a). "An ex-post-facto evaluation framework for place-based police interventions." *Evaluation Review,* 35(6), 592–626.
Braga, A.A., Hureau, D.M., and Papachristos, A.V. (2011b). "The relevance of micro places to citywide robbery trends: A longitudinal analysis of robbery incidents at street corners and block faces in Boston." *Journal of Research in Crime and Delinquency,* 48(1), 7–32.
(2012). "Hot spots policing effects on crime." *Campbell Systematic Reviews,* 8(8).
(2014). "The effects of hot spots policing on crime: An updated systematic review and meta-analysis." *Justice Quarterly,* 31(4), 633–663.
Braga, A.A., Papachristos, A.V., and Hureau, D.M. (2010). "The concentration and stability of gun violence at microplaces in Boston, 1980–2008." *Journal of Quantitative Criminology,* 26(1), 33–53.
Braga, A.A., Weisburd, D.L., Waring, E.J., Mazerolle, L.G., Spelman, W., and Gajewski, F. (1999). "Problem-oriented policing in violent crime places: A randomized controlled experiment." *Criminology,* 37(3), 541–580.
Braga, A.A., Welsh, B.C., and Schnell, C. (2015). "Can policing disorder reduce crime? A systematic review and meta-analysis." *Journal of Research in Crime and Delinquency,* 52(4), 567–588.
Branas, C.C., Cheney, R.A., MacDonald, J.M., Tam, V.W., Jackson, T.D., and Ten Have, T.R. (2011). "A difference-in-differences analysis of health, safety, and greening vacant urban space." *American Journal of Epidemiology,* 174(11), 1296–1306.
Branas, C.C., Culhane, D., Richmond, T.S., and Wiebe, D.J. (2008). "Novel linkage of individual and geographic data to study firearm violence." *Homicide Studies,* 12(3), 298–320.
Branas, C.C., Elliott, M.R., Richmond, T.S., Culhane, D.P., and Wiebe, D.J. (2009). "Alcohol consumption, alcohol outlets, and the risk of being assaulted with a gun." *Alcoholism: Clinical and Experimental Research,* 33(5), 906–915.
Brantingham, P.J., and Brantingham P.L. (1981). *Environmental criminology.* Thousand Oaks, CA: Sage Publications.
(1984). *Patterns in crime.* New York: Macmillan.
Brantingham, P.J., and Faust, F.L. (1976). "A conceptual model of crime prevention." *Crime and Delinquency,* 22(3), 284–296.
Brantingham, P.J., and Tita, G. (2008). "Offender mobility and crime pattern formation from first principles." In L. Liu and J. Eck (eds.), *Artificial crime analysis systems: Using computer simulations and geographic information systems* (pp. 193–208). Hershey, PA: Idea Press.

Brantingham, P.J., Dyreson, D.A., and Brantingham, P.L. (1976). "Crime seen through a cone of resolution." *American Behavioral Scientist*, 20(2), 261–273.

Brantingham, P.L., and Brantingham, P.J. (1975). "Residential burglary and urban form." *Urban Studies*, 12(3), 104–125.

(1990). "Situational crime prevention in practice." *Canadian Journal of Criminology*, 32(1), 17–40.

(1993a). "Environment, routine, and situation: Toward a pattern theory of crime." In R.V. Clarke and M. Felson (eds.), *Routine activity and rational choice. Advances in Criminological Theory*, vol. 5 (pp. 259–294). New Brunswick, NJ: Transaction Publishers.

(1993b). "Nodes, paths, and edges: Considerations on the complexity of crime and the physical environment." *Journal of Environmental Psychology*, 13(1), 3–28.

(1995). "Criminality of place: Crime generators and crime attractors." *European Journal on Criminal Policy and Research*, 3(3), 5–26.

(1999). "Theoretical model of crime hot spot generation." *Studies of Crime and Crime Prevention*, 8(1), 7–26.

Brantingham, P.L., Brantingham, P.J., Vajihollahi, M., and Wuschke, K. (2009). "Crime analysis at multiple scales of aggregation: A topological approach." In D. Weisburd, W. Bernasco, and G.J.N. Bruinsma (eds.), *Putting crime in its place: Units of analysis in geographic criminology* (pp. 87–122). New York: Springer.

Brody, H., Rip, M.R., Vinten-Johansen, P., Paneth, N., and Rachman, S. (2000). "Map-making and myth-making in Broad Street: The London cholera epidemic, 1854." *The Lancet*, 356(9223), 64–68.

Brower, S. (1980). "Territory in urban settings." In I. Altman and C.M. Werner (eds.), *Human behavior and environment: Current theory and research*, vol. 4 (pp. 179–207). New York: Plenum.

Bruinsma, G.J.N. (2014). "History of criminological theories: Causes of crime." In G.J.N. Bruinsma and D. Weisburd (eds.), *The encyclopedia of criminology and criminal justice* (pp. 2137–2148). New York: Springer.

Bueermann, J. (2012). *Advancing police practice*. Presented at the Workshop on Evidence-Based Policy, Hangzhou, China.

Buerger, M., and Mazerolle, L.G. (1998). "Third-party policing: A theoretical analysis of an emerging trend." *Justice Quarterly*, 15(2), 301–328.

Bulmer, M. (1984). *The Chicago School of sociology: Institutionalization, diversity, and the rise of sociological research*. Chicago, IL: University of Chicago Press.

Burgess, E.W. (1925 [1967]). "The growth of the city: An introduction to a research project." In R.E. Park and E.W. Burgess (eds.), *The city: Suggestions for the investigation of human behavior in the urban environment* (pp. 47–62). Chicago, IL: University of Chicago Press.

(1928). "Factors determining success or failure on parole." In A.A. Bruce (ed.), *The workings of the indeterminate sentence law and parole in Illinois* (pp. 205–249). Springfield, IL: Illinois State Parole Board.

Bursik, R.J. (1988). "Social disorganization and theories of crime and delinquency: Problems and prospects." *Criminology*, 26(4), 519–552.

(2000). "The systemic theory of neighborhood crime rates." In S.S. Simpson (ed.), *Of crime and criminality: The use of theory in everyday life* (pp. 87–103). Thousand Oaks, CA: Pine Forge Press.

Bursik, R.J., and Grasmick, H.G. (1993a). "Economic deprivation and neighborhood crime rates, 1960–1980." *Law and Society Review*, 27(2), 263–284.
  (1993b). *Neighborhoods and crime: The dimensions of effective community control*. New York: Lexington Books.
Bursik, R.J. Jr., and Webb, J. (1982). "Community change and patterns of delinquency." *American Journal of Sociology*, 88(1), 24–42.
Bushway, S., and Reuter, P. (2008). "Economists' contribution to the study of crime and the criminal justice system." In M. Tonry (ed.), *Crime and Justice: A Review of Research*, vol. 37 (pp. 389–451). Chicago, IL: University of Chicago Press.
Byrne, J. (1989). "Reintegrating the concept of community into community-based corrections." *Crime and Delinquency*, 35(3), 471–499.
  (2008). "The social ecology of community corrections: Understanding the link between individual and community change." *Criminology and Public Policy*, 7(2), 263–274.
Byrne, J.M., and Sampson, R.J. (1986). "Key issues in the social ecology of crime." In J.M. Byrne and R.J. Sampson (eds.), *The social ecology of crime* (pp. 1–22). New York: Springer.
Caeti, T. (1999). *Houston's targeted beat program: A quasi-experimental test of police patrol strategies*. PhD dissertation. Huntsville, TX: Sam Houston State University.
Campbell, K.M. (2006). "Local illegal immigration relief act ordinances: A legal, policy, and litigation analysis." *Denver University Law Review*, 84, 1041–1060.
Canter, D. (1991). "Understanding, assessing, and acting in places: Is an integrative framework possible?" In T. Gärling and G.W. Evans (eds.), *Environment, cognition, and action: An integrative approach* (pp. 191–209). New York: Oxford University Press.
Caplan, J.M., Kennedy, L.W., and Miller, J. (2011). "Risk terrain modeling: Brokering criminological theory and GIS methods for crime forecasting." *Justice Quarterly*, 28(2), 360–381.
Caplan, J.M., Kennedy, L.W., and Petrossian, G. (2011). "Police-monitored CCTV cameras in Newark, NJ: A quasi-experimental test of crime deterrence." *Journal of Experimental Criminology*, 7(3), 255–274.
Carlino, G.A. (2001). "Knowledge spillovers: Cities' role in the new economy." *Business Review*, Fourth Quarter, 17–26.
Carnaghi, J., and McEwen, T. (1970). "Automatic pinging." In S.I. Conn and W.E. McMahon (eds.), *Law enforcement science and technology*, vol. 3. Chicago: Illinois Institute of Technology Research.
Chaiken, J., Lawless, M., and Stevenson, K. (1974). *The impact of police activity on crime: Robberies on the New York City subway system*. Santa Monica, CA: Rand Corporation.
Chermak, S., McGarrell, E.F., and Weiss, A. (2001). "Citizens' perceptions of aggressive traffic enforcement strategies." *Justice Quarterly*, 18(2), 365–391.
Clarke, R.V. (1980). "'Situational' crime prevention: Theory and practice." *British Journal of Criminology*, 20(2), 136–147.
  (1995). "Situational crime prevention." In M. Tonry and D.P. Farrington (eds.), *Building a safer society: Strategic approaches to crime prevention. Crime and Justice: A Review of Research*, vol. 19 (pp. 91–150). Chicago, IL: University of Chicago Press.

(1999) *Hot products: Understanding, anticipating and reducing demand for stolen goods*. Police Research Series, Paper 112, Policing and Reducing Crime Unit, Research Development and Statistics Directorate. London: Home Office.

(2000). "Situational prevention, criminology, and social values." In A. von Hirsch, D. Garland, and A. Wakefield (eds.), *Ethical and social perspectives on situational crime prevention* (pp. 97–112). Oxford, UK: Hart Publishing.

(2004). "Technology, criminology and crime science." *European Journal on Criminal Policy and Research*, 10(1), 55–63.

Clarke, R.V., and Bichler-Robertson, G. (1998). "Place managers, slumlords and crime in low rent apartment buildings." *Security Journal*, 11(1), 11–19.

Clarke, R.V., and Cornish, D.B. (1985). "Modeling offenders' decisions: A framework for research and policy." In M. Tonry and N. Morris (eds.), *Crime and Justice: A Review of Research*, vol. 6 (pp. 147–185). Chicago, IL: University of Chicago Press.

Clarke, R.V., and Eck, J.E. (2007). *Understanding risky facilities*. Problem-Solving Tool Guides, no. 6. Washington, DC: Office of Community Oriented Policing Services, U.S. Department of Justice.

Clarke, R.V., and Felson, M. (1993). "Introduction: Criminology, routine activity, and rational choice." In R.V. Clarke and M. Felson (eds.), *Routine activity and rational choice. Advances in Criminological Theory*, vol. 5 (pp. 1–14). New Brunswick, NJ: Transaction Press.

Clarke, R.V., and Weisburd, D. (1994). "Diffusion of crime control benefits: Observations on the reverse of displacement." In R.V. Clarke (ed.), *Crime Prevention Studies*, vol. 2 (pp. 165–184). Monsey, NY: Criminal Justice Press.

Cliff, A.D., and Ord, J.K. (1969). *The problem of spatial autocorrelation*. London Papers in Regional Science. London: Pion.

Clifton, W. (1987). *Convenience store robberies in Gainesville, Florida: An intervention strategy by the Gainesville Police Department*. Gainesville, FL: Gainesville Police Department.

Cloward, R.A. (1959). "Illegitimate means, anomie, and deviant behavior." *American Sociological Review*, 24(2), 164–176.

Cohen, J., Gorr, W., and Singh, P. (2003). "Estimating intervention effects in varying risk settings: Do police raids reduce illegal drug dealing at nuisance bars?" *Criminology*, 41(2), 257–292.

Cohen, L.E., and Felson, M. (1979). "Social change and crime rate trends: A routine activity approach." *American Sociological Review*, 44(4), 588–608.

Coleman, S. (2002). "A test for the effect of conformity on crime rates using voter turnout." *The Sociological Quarterly*, 43(2), 257–276.

Conrad, P., and Schneider, J.W. (2010). *Deviance and medicalization: From badness to sickness*. Philadelphia, PA: Temple University Press.

Cope, M., and Elwood, S. (eds.). (2009). *Qualitative GIS: A mixed methods approach*. Thousand Oaks, CA: Sage Publications.

Cornish, D.B, and Clarke, R.V. (eds.). (1986). *The reasoning criminal: Rational choice perspectives on offending*. New York: Springer.

(2003). "Opportunities, precipitators and criminal decisions: A reply to Wortley's critique of situational crime prevention." In M.J. Smith and D.B. Cornish (eds.), *Theory for practice in situational crime prevention. Crime Prevention Studies*, vol. 16 (pp. 41–96). Monsey, NY: Criminal Justice Press.

(2008). "The rational choice perspective." In R. Wortley and L. Mazerolle (eds.), *Environmental criminology and crime analysis* (pp. 21–47). Devon: Willan Publishing.
Corsaro, N., and McGarrell, E.F. (2009). "Testing a promising homicide reduction strategy: Re-assessing the impact of the Indianapolis 'pulling levers' intervention." *Journal of Experimental Criminology*, 5(1), 63–82.
Corsaro, N., Brunson, R.K., and McGarrell, E.F. (2013). "Problem-oriented policing and open-air drug markets: Examining the Rockford pulling levers deterrence strategy." *Crime and Delinquency*, 59(7), 1085–1107.
Crampton, J.W. (2001). "Maps as social construction: Power, communication, and visualization." *Progress in Human Geography*, 25(2), 235–252.
Crampton, J.W., Graham, M., Poorthuis, A., Shelton, T., Stephens, M., Wilson, M.W., and Zook, M. (2013). "Beyond the geotag: Situating 'big data' and leveraging the potential of the geoweb." *Cartography and Geographic Information Science*, 40(2), 130–139.
Crawford, A. (1997). *The local governance of crime: Appeals to community and partnerships*. Oxford, UK: Clarendon Press.
Criminal Justice Commission. (1998). *Beenleigh calls for service project: Evaluation report*. Brisbane: Criminal Justice Commission.
Crooks, V.A., and Andrews, G.J. (2009). *Primary health care: People, practice, place*. Burlington, VT: Ashgate Publishing, Ltd.
Crow, W.J., and Bull, J.L. (1975). *Robbery deterrence: An applied behavioral science demonstration-final report*. La Jolla, CA: Western Behavioral Sciences Institute.
Cullen, F.T. (1988). "Were Cloward and Ohlin strain theorists? Delinquency and opportunity revisited." *Journal of Research in Crime and Delinquency*, 25(3), 214–241.
(2010). "Cloward, Richard A.: The theory of illegitimate means." In F.T. Cullen and P. Wilcox (eds.), *Encyclopedia of criminological theory* (pp. 167–170). Thousand Oaks, CA: Sage Publications.
(2011). "Beyond adolescence-limited criminology: Choosing our future. The American Society of Criminology 2010 Sutherland Address." *Criminology*, 49(2), 287–330.
Cullen, F., Eck, J.E., and Lowenkamp, C.T. (2002). "Environmental corrections: A new paradigm for effective probation and parole supervision." *Federal Probation*, 66(2), 28–37.
Curman, A.S., Andresen, M.A., and Brantingham, P.J. (2015). "Crime and place: A longitudinal examination of street segment patterns in Vancouver, BC." *Journal of Quantitative Criminology*, 31(1), 127–147.
Curry, M.R. (1997). "The digital individual and the private realm." *Annals of the Association of American Geographers*, 87(4), 681–699.
Dalton, E. (2002). "Targeted crime reduction efforts in ten communities: Lessons for the Project Safe Neighborhoods." *USA Bulletin*, 50(1), 16–25.
Dalton, H. (1920). "The measurement of the inequality of incomes." *The Economic Journal*, 30(119), 348–361.
Dario, L.M., Morrow, W.J., Wooditch, A., and Vickovic, S.G. (2015). "The point break effect: An examination of surf, crime, and transitory opportunities." *Criminal Justice Studies: A Critical Journal of Crime, Law and Society*, 28(3), 257–279.

Davis, J.R., and Tunks, E. (1990–1991). "Environments and addiction: A proposed taxonomy." *The International Journal of the Addictions*, 25(S7–S8), 805–826.

DeAngelo, G. (2012). "Making space for crime: A spatial analysis of criminal competition." *Regional Science and Urban Economics*, 42(1–2), 42–51.

Dennis, R. (2015). "Don Carlos suing Twin Peaks' owners over biker gang shootout." *Waco Tribune-Herald*, May 21, 2015. http://goo.gl/WqNsEk.

DiTella, R., and Schargrodsky, E. (2004). "Do police reduce crime? Estimates using the allocation of police forces after a terrorist attack." *American Economic Review*, 94 (1), 115–133.

Dreier, P. (1996). "The struggle for our cities." *Social Policy*, 26(4), 9–24.

Duffala, D.C. (1976). "Convenience stores, armed robbery, and physical environmental features." *American Behavioral Scientist*, 20(2), 227–246.

Durkheim, E. (1893 [1984]). *The division of labour in society*. New York: Free Press.
  (1895 [1964]). *The rules of sociological method*. Edited by G.E.G. Catlin. Translated by S.A. Solovay and J.H. Mueller. New York: Free Press.

Durlauf, S.N., and Nagin, D.S. (2011). "Imprisonment and crime." *Criminology and Public Policy*, 10(1), 13–54.

Eck, J.E. (1993a). Alternative futures for policing. In D. Weisburd and C. Uchida (eds.), *Police innovation and control of the police* (pp. 59–79). New York: Springer.
  (1993b). "The threat of crime displacement." *Criminal Justice Abstracts*, 25, 527–546.
  (1994). *Drug markets and drug places: A case-control study of the spatial structure of illicit drug dealing*. PhD dissertation. College Park, MD: University of Maryland, College Park.
  (1995). "Examining routine activity theory: A review of two books." *Justice Quarterly*, 12(4), 783–797.
  (1996). "Do premises liability suits promote business crime prevention." In R.V. Clarke and M. Felson (eds.), *Business and crime prevention* (pp. 125–150). Monsey, NY: Criminal Justice Press.
  (2002). "Preventing crime at places." In L. Sherman, D. Farrington, B. Welsh, and D.L. MacKenzie (eds.), *Evidence-based crime prevention* (pp. 241–294). New York: Routledge.
  (2014). *The status of collaborative problem solving and community problem-oriented policing in Cincinnati*. Unpublished report. Cincinnati, OH: School of Criminal Justice, University of Cincinnati.

Eck, J.E., and Eck, E.B. (2012). "Crime place and pollution: Expanding crime reduction options through a regulatory approach." *Criminology and Public Policy*, 11(2), 281–316.

Eck, J.E., and Guerette, R.T. (2012). "Place-based crime prevention: Theory, evidence, and policy." In B.C. Welsh and D.P. Farrington (eds.), *The Oxford handbook of crime prevention* (pp. 354–383). New York: Oxford University Press.

Eck, J.E., and Madensen, T. (2012). "Situational crime prevention makes problem-oriented policing work." In N. Tilley and G. Farrell (eds.), *The reasoning criminologist: Essays in honour of Ron Clarke* (pp. 80–92). London: Routledge.

Eck, J.E., and Maguire, E. (2000). "Have changes in policing reduced violent crime? An assessment of the evidence." In A. Blumstein and J. Wallman (eds.), *The crime drop in America* (pp. 207–265). New York: Cambridge University Press.

Eck, J.E., and Rothman, J. (2006). "Police-community conflict and crime prevention in Cincinnati, Ohio." In J. Bailey and L. Dammert (eds.), *Public security and police reform in the Americas* (pp. 225–244). Pittsburgh, PA: University of Pittsburgh Press.

Eck, J.E., and Wartell, J. (1997). *Reducing crime and drug dealing by improving place management: A randomized experiment.* Report to the National Institute of Justice. San Diego, CA: San Diego Police Department.

——— (1998). "Improving the management of rental properties with drug problems: A randomized experiment." In L.G. Mazerolle and J. Roehl (eds.), *Civil remedies and crime prevention. Crime Prevention Studies*, vol. 9 (pp. 161–185). Monsey, NY: Criminal Justice Press.

Eck, J.E., and Weisburd, D. (1995). "Crime places in crime theory." In J.E. Eck and D. Weisburd (eds.), *Crime and place: Crime Prevention Studies*, vol. 4 (pp. 1–33). Monsey, NY: Willow Tree Press.

Eck, J.E., Chainey, S., Cameron, J., and Wilson, R. (2005). *Mapping crime: Understanding hotspots.* Washington, DC: National Institute of Justice, U.S. Department of Justice.

Eck, J.E., Clarke, R.V., and Guerette, R.T. (2007). "Risky facilities: Crime concentration in homogenous sets of establishments and facilities." In G. Farrell, K.J. Bowers, S.D. Johnson, and M. Townsley (eds.), *Imagination in crime prevention: Crime Prevention Studies*, vol. 21 (pp. 225–264). Monsey, NY: Criminal Justice Press.

Eck, J.E., Gersh, J.S., and Taylor, C. (1999). "Finding crime hot spots through repeat address mapping." In V. Goldsmith, P. McGuir, J.H. Mollenkopf, and T.A. Ross (eds.), *Analyzing crime patterns: Frontiers of practice*, (pp. 49–64). Thousand Oaks, CA: Sage Publications.

Ekblom, P. (1995). "Less crime, by design." *Annals of the American Academy of Political and Social Science*, 539, 114–129.

——— (1997). "Gearing up against crime: A dynamic framework to help designers keep up with the adaptive criminal in a changing world." *International Journal of Risk, Security and Crime Prevention*, 2(4), 249–265.

Elder, G.H. (1998). "The life course as developmental theory." *Child Development*, 69 (1), 1–12.

Elliott, D.S. (1985). "The assumption that theories can be combined with increased explanatory power: Theoretical integrations." In R.F. Meier (ed.), *Theoretical methods in criminology* (pp. 123–149). Beverly Hills, CA: Sage Publications.

Elliott, P., and Wartenberg, D. (2004). "Spatial epidemiology: Current approaches and future challenges." *Environmental Health Perspectives*, 112(9), 998–1006.

Elwood, S. (2009). "Multiple representations, significations, and epistemologies in community-based GIS." In M. Cope and S. Elwood (eds.), *Qualitative GIS: A mixed methods approach* (pp. 57–74). Thousand Oaks, CA: Sage Publications.

Epstein, J.M. (2002). "Modeling civil violence: An agent-based computational approach." *Proceedings of the National Academy of Sciences of the United States of America*, 99(Suppl. 3), 7243–7250.

Erikson, K.T. (1966). *Wayward puritans: A study in the sociology of deviance.* New York: Prentice Hall.

Evans, D.J., and Herbert, D.T. (1989). *The geography of crime.* London: Routledge.

Faris, R.E.L. (1967). *Chicago sociology 1920–1932.* San Francisco, CA: Chandler.

Farrell, G. (1995). "Preventing repeat victimization." In M. Tonry and D.P. Farrington (eds.), *Building a safer society: Strategic approaches to crime prevention. Crime and Justice: A Review of Research*, vol. 19 (pp. 469–534). Chicago, IL: University of Chicago Press.

Farrell, G., and Roman, J. (2006). "Crime as pollution: Proposal for market-based incentives to reduce crime externalities." In K. Moss and M. Stephens (eds.), *Crime reduction and the law* (pp. 135–155). London: Routledge.

Farrell, G., Phillips, C., and Pease, K. (1995). "Like taking candy: Why does repeat victimization occur?" *British Journal of Criminology*, 35(3), 384–399.

Farrell, G., Tseloni, A. Mailley, J., and Tilley, N. (2011). "The crime drop and the security hypothesis." *Journal of Research in Crime and Delinquency*, 48(2), 147–175.

Farrington, D.P., and Petrosino, A. (2001). "The Campbell Collaboration Crime and Justice Group." *Annals of the American Academy of Political and Social Sciences*, 578, 35–49.

Farrington, D.P., Lambert, S., and West, D.J. (1998). "Criminal careers of two generations of family members in the Cambridge Study in Delinquent Development." *Studies on Crime and Crime Prevention*, 7(1), 85–106.

Feeley, M.M., and Simon, J. (1992). "The new penology: Notes on the emerging strategy of corrections and its implications." *Criminology*, 30(4), 449–474.

Felson, M. (1986) "Linking criminal choices, routine activities, informal control, and criminal outcomes." In D.B. Cornish and R.V. Clarke (eds.), *The reasoning criminal: Rational choice perspectives on offending* (pp. 119–128). New York: Springer.

(1987). "Routine activities and crime prevention in the developing metropolis." *Criminology*, 25(4), 911–932.

(1995). "Those who discourage crime." In J.E. Eck and D. Weisburd (eds.), *Crime and place. Crime Prevention Studies*, vol. 4 (pp. 53–66). Monsey, NY: Willow Tree Press.

(2006). *Crime and nature*. Thousand Oaks, CA: Sage Publications.

Felson, M., and Boba, R. (2009). *Crime and everyday life*. Thousand Oaks, CA: Sage Publications.

Ferguson, A.G. (2011). "Crime mapping and the Fourth Amendment: Redrawing high-crime areas." *Hastings Law Journal*, 63, 179–232.

Forrester, D., Chatterton, M., and Pease, K. (1988). *The Kirkholt burglary prevention project, Rochdale*. London: Crime Prevention Unit, Home Office.

Fotheringham, A.S. (1985). "Spatial competition and agglomeration in urban modelling." *Environment and Planning A*, 17(2), 213–230.

Franquez, J.J., Hagala, J., Lim, S., and Bichler, G. (2013). "We be drinkin': A study of place management and premise notoriety among risky bars and nightclubs." *Western Criminology Review*, 14(3), 34–52.

Friedmann, P.D., Lemon, S.C., and Stein, M.D. (2001). "Transportation and retention in outpatient drug treatment programs." *Journal of Substance Abuse Treatment*, 21(2), 97–103.

Friedrichs, J.R., and Blasius, J.R. (2003). "Social norms in distressed neighbourhoods: Testing the Wilson hypothesis." *Housing Studies*, 18(6), 807–826.

Fyfe, N. (1991). "The police, space and society: The geography of policing." *Progress in Human Geography*, 15(3), 249–267.

Gabor, T. (1981). "The crime displacement hypothesis: An empirical examination." *Crime and Delinquency*, 27(3), 390–404.
Gau, J., and Brunson, R.K. (2010). "Procedural justice and order maintenance policing: A study of inner-city young men's perceptions of police legitimacy." *Justice Quarterly*, 27(2), 255–279.
Gelman, A., Fagan, J., and Kiss, A. (2007). "An analysis of the New York City Police Department's 'stop-and-frisk' policy in the context of claims of racial bias." *Journal of the American Statistical Association*, 102(479), 813–823.
Getis, A., and Getis, J.M. (1968). "Retail store spatial affinities." *Urban Studies*, 5(3), 317–332.
Gifford, R. (2007). "Environmental psychology and sustainable development: Expansion, maturation, and challenges." *Journal of Social Issues*, 63(1), 199–212.
Gilbert, N., and Troitzsch, K. (2005). *Simulation for the social scientist*. New York: McGraw-Hill.
Gilboy, J.A. (1997). "Implications of 'third-party' involvement in enforcement: The INS, illegal travelers, and international airlines." *Law and Society Review*, 31(3), 505–530.
Gini, C. (1912). *Variabilità e mutabilità*. Bologna, Italy: C. Cuppini.
Glyde, J. (1856). "Localities of crime in Suffolk." *Journal of the Statistical Society of London*, 19(2), 102–106.
Goldstein, H. (1990). *Problem-oriented policing*. New York: McGraw-Hill.
Goodchild, M.F. (2009). "What problem? Spatial autocorrelation and Geographic Information Science." *Geographical Analysis*, 41(4), 411–417.
Gottfredson, D.C., Wilson, D.B., and Najaka, S.S. (2002). "School-based crime prevention." In L. Sherman, D. Farrington, B. Welsh, and D.L. MacKenzie (eds.), *Evidence-based crime prevention* (pp. 56–164). New York: Routledge.
Gottfredson, M.R., and Hirschi, T. (1990). *A general theory of crime*. Stanford, CA: Stanford University Press.
  (1995). "National crime control policies." *Society*, 32(2), 30–36.
Grannis, R. (1998). "The importance of trivial streets: Residential streets and residential segregation." *American Journal of Sociology*, 103(6), 1530–1564.
Green, L. (1995). "Cleaning up drug hot spots in Oakland, California: The displacement and diffusion effects." *Justice Quarterly*, 12(4), 737–754.
  (1996). *Policing places with drug problems*. Thousand Oaks, CA: Sage Publications.
Greenwood, P., Chaiken, J. and Petersilia, J. (1977). *The investigation process*. Lexington, MA: Lexington Books.
Greider, T., and Garkovich, L. (1994). "Landscapes: The social construction of nature and the environment." *Rural Sociology*, 59(1), 1–24.
Groff, E.R. (2007a). "Simulation for theory testing and experimentation: An example using routine activity theory and street robbery." *Journal of Quantitative Criminology*, 23(2), 75–103.
  (2007b). "Situating simulation to model human spatio-temporal interactions: An example using crime events." *Transactions in GIS*, 11(4), 507–530.
  (2011). "Exploring 'near': Characterizing the spatial extent of drinking place influence on crime." *Australian and New Zealand Journal of Criminology*, 44(2), 156–179.
Groff, E.R., and LaVigne, N. (2001). Mapping an opportunity surface of residential burglary. *Journal of Research in Crime and Delinquency*, 38(3), 257–278.

Groff, E.R., Ratcliffe, J.H., Haberman, C.P., Sorg, E.T., Joyce, N.M., and Taylor, R.B. (2015). "Does what police do at hot spots matter? The Philadelphia policing tactics experiment." *Criminology*, 53(1), 23–53.

Groff, E.R., Weisburd, D., and Morris, N. (2009). "Where the action is at places: Examining spatio-temporal patterns of juvenile crime at places using trajectory analysis and GIS." In D. Weisburd, W. Bernasco, and G.J.N. Bruinsma (eds.), *Putting crime in its place: Units of analysis in spatial crime research* (pp. 61–86). New York: Springer.

Groff, E.R., Weisburd, D., and Yang, S.M. (2010). Is it important to examine crime trends at a local "micro" level?: A longitudinal analysis of street to street variability in crime trajectories. *Journal of Quantitative Criminology*, 26(1), 7–32.

Grove, L., Farrell, G., Farrington, D.F., and Johnson, S.D. (2012). *Preventing repeat victimization: A systematic review*. Stockholm: Swedish National Council for Crime Prevention.

Grubesic, T.H., and Mack, E.A. (2008). "Spatio-temporal interaction of urban crime." *Journal of Quantitative Criminology*, 24(3), 285–306.

Guerette, R.T., and Bowers, K.J. (2009). "Assessing the extent of crime displacement and diffusion of benefits: A review of situational crime prevention evaluations." *Criminology*, 47(4), 1331–1368.

Guerry, A.-M. (1833). *Essai sur la statistique morale de la France: Precede d'un rapport a l'Academie de sciences*. Paris: Chez Crochard.

(1864). *Statistique morale de la France et de l'Angleterre comparee avec la statistique morale de la France*. Paris: J.-B. Bailliere et fils.

Guo, J.Y., and Bhat, C.R. (2007). "Operationalizing the concept of neighborhood: Application to residential location choice analysis." *Journal of Transport Geography*, 15(1), 31–45.

Hakim, S., and Rengert, G.F. (eds.) (1981). *Crime spillover*. Beverly Hills, CA: Sage Publications.

Harada, Y., and Shimada, T. (2006). "Examining the impact of the precision of address geocoding on estimated density of crime locations." *Computers and Geosciences*, 32(8), 1096–1107.

Harcourt, B.E. (2001). *Illusion of order: The false promise of broken windows policing*. Cambridge, MA: Harvard University Press.

Hardey, M. (2007). "The city in the age of web 2.0: A new synergistic relationship between place and people." *Information, Communication and Society*, 10(6), 867–884.

Harvey, L. (1987). *Myths of the Chicago School of sociology*. Aldershot: Avebury.

Hawkins, J.D., Herrenkohl, D.J.T., Farrington, D.P., Brewer, D., Catalano, R.F., and Harachi, T.W. (1998). "A review of predictors of youth violence." In R. Loeber and D.P. Farrington (eds.), *Serious and violent juvenile offenders: Risk factors and successful interventions* (pp. 106–146). Thousand Oaks, CA: Sage Publications.

Hayward, M.D., Miles, T.P., Crimmins, E.M., and Yang, Y. (2000). "The significance of socioeconomic status in explaining the racial gap in chronic health conditions." *American Sociological Review*, 65(6), 910–930.

Heft, H. (2001). *Ecological psychology in context: James Gibson, Roger Barker, and the legacy of William James's radical empiricism*. Mahwah, NJ: Lawrence Erlbaum Associates Publishers.

Hesseling, R. (1994). "Displacement: A review of the empirical literature." In R.V. Clarke (ed.), *Crime Prevention Studies*, vol. 3 (pp. 197–230). Monsey, NY: Criminal Justice Press.

Hibdon, J. (2013). *Crime hot spots in suburbia: A case study*. Paper presented at the Annual Meeting of the American Society of Criminology, Atlanta, GA.

Hickman, M.J., and Reaves, B.A. (2003). *Local police departments, 2000*. Washington, DC: Bureau of Justice Statistics, U.S. Department of Justice.

Hill, L.G., Maucione, K., and Hood, B.K. (2007). "A focused approach to assessing program fidelity." *Prevention Science*, 8(1), 25–34.

Hindelang, M.J. (1976). "With a little help from their friends: Group participation in reported offending behaviour." *British Journal of Criminology*, 16(2), 109–125.

Hipp, J.R. (2007). "Block, tract, and levels of aggregation: Neighborhood structure and crime and disorder as a case in point." *American Sociological Review*, 72(5), 659–680.

Hipp, J.R., and Boessen, A. (2013). "Egohoods as waves washing across the city: A new measure of 'neighborhoods.'" *Criminology*, 51(2), 287–327.

Hipp, J.R., Jannetta, J., Shah, R., and Turner, S. (2009). "Parolees' physical closeness to health service providers: A study of California parolees." *Health and Place*, 15(3), 679–688.

Hipp, J.R., Petersilia, J., and Turner, S. (2010). "Parolee recidivism in California: The effect of neighborhood context and social service agency characteristics." *Criminology*, 48(4), 947–979.

Hirschi, T. (1989). "Exploring alternatives to integrated theory." In S.F. Messner, M.D. Krohn, and A.E. Liska (eds.), *Theoretical integration in the study of deviance and crime: Problems and prospects* (pp. 37–50). Albany, NY: State University of New York Press.

(1993). "Review: Administrative criminology." *Contemporary Sociology*, 22(3), 348–350.

Hirschman, A.O. (1945). *National power and the structure of foreign trade*. Berkeley, CA: University of California Press.

Hope, T. (1994). "Problem-oriented policing and drug market locations: Three case studies." In R.V. Clarke (ed.), *Crime Prevention Studies*, vol. 2 (pp. 5–32). Monsey, NY: Criminal Justice Press.

Hunter, A.J. (1979). "The urban neighborhood: Its analytical and social contexts." *Urban Affairs Quarterly*, 14(3), 267–288.

Hunter, R.D. (1988). *Environmental characteristics of convenience store robberies in the state of Florida*. Paper presented at the Annual Meeting of the American Society of Criminology, Chicago.

Innes, M. (2004). "Signal crimes and signal disorders: notes on deviance as communicative action." *The British Journal of Sociology*, 55(3), 335–355.

Jacobs, J. (1961). *The death and life of great American cities*. New York: Vintage Books.

(1969). *The economy of cities*. New York: Vintage Books.

Jacobson, J. (2004). *The ecological context of substance abuse treatment outcomes: Implications for NIMBY disputes and client placement decisions*. Santa Monica, CA: Rand Corporation.

Janetta, J. (2009). Statement to the House of Representatives Oversight and Government Reform Subcommittee on federal workforce, postal service, and the District of Columbia. September 22.

Jeffery, C.R. (1971). *Crime prevention through environmental design*. Beverly Hills, CA: Sage Publications.
— (2009). "Potential uses of computational methods in the evaluation of crime reduction activity." In J. Knuttson and N. Tilley (eds.), *Evaluating crime prevention. Crime Prevention Studies*, vol. 24 (pp. 175–217). Monsey, NY: Criminal Justice Press.
— (2010). "A brief history of the analysis of crime concentration." *European Journal of Applied Mathematics*, 21(4–5), 349–370.
Johnson, S.D. (2008). "Repeat burglary victimisation: A tale of two theories." *Journal of Experimental Criminology*, 4(3), 215–240.
Johnson, S.D., and Bowers, K.J. (2004a). "The burglary as a clue to the future: The beginnings of prospective hot-spotting." *European Journal of Criminology*, 1(2), 237–255.
— (2004b). "The stability of space-time clusters of burglary." *British Journal of Criminology*, 44(1), 55–65.
— (2010). "Permeability and burglary risk: Are cul-de-sacs safer?" *Journal of Quantitative Criminology*, 26(1), 89–111.
Johnson, S.D., Bernasco, W., Bowers, K.J., Elffers, H., Ratcliffe, J., Rengert, G., and Townsley, M. (2007). "Space-time patterns of risk: A cross national assessment of residential burglary victimization." *Journal of Quantitative Criminology*, 23(3), 201–219.
Johnson, S.D., Birks, D., McLaughlin, L., Bowers, K., and Pease, K. (2007). *Prospective mapping in operational context*. London: Home Office.
Johnson, S.D., Bowers, K.J., and Hirschfield, A.F.G. (1997). "New insights into the spatial and temporal distribution of repeat victimisation." *British Journal of Criminology*, 37(2), 224–241.
Johnson, S.D., Summers, L., and Pease, K. (2009). "Offender as forager? A direct test of the boost account of victimization." *Journal of Quantitative Criminology*, 25(2), 181–200.
Johnson, L.T., Taylor, R.B., and Ratcliffe, J.H. (2013). "Need drugs, will travel? The distances to crime of illegal drug buyers." *Journal of Criminal Justice*, 41(3), 178–187.
Joiner, T.M., and Mansourian, J.A. (2009). Integrating social disorganization and routine activity theories: A look at urban crime in Morristown, New Jersey. Unpublished report, presented to the Morristown Police Department (NJ). Boston, MA: Northeastern University.
Jorgensen, B.S., and Stedman, R.C. (2006). "A comparative analysis of predictors of sense of place dimensions: Attachment to, dependence on, and identification with lakeshore properties." *Journal of Environmental Management*, 79(3), 316–327.
Juran, J.M. (1951). *Quality control handbook*. New York: McGraw-Hill.
Kautt, P.M., and Roncek, D.W. (2007). "Schools as criminal 'hot spots' primary, secondary, and beyond." *Criminal Justice Review*, 32(4), 339–357.
Kearns, R., and Moon, G. (2002). "From medical to health geography: Novelty, place and theory after a decade of change." *Progress in Human Geography*, 26(5), 605–625.
Kearns, R.A., and Joseph, A.E. (1993). "Space in its place: Developing the link in medical geography." *Social Science and Medicine*, 37(6), 711–717.
Kelling, G.L., and Coles, C.M. (1996). *Fixing broken windows: Restoring order and reducing crime in our communities*. New York: Touchstone.

Kelling, G.L., Pate, A., Dieckman, D., and Brown, C. (1974). *The Kansas City preventive patrol experiment: A technical report.* Washington, DC: Police Foundation.

Kempf, K.L. (1993). "The empirical status of Hirschi's control theory." In F. Adler and W.S. Laufer (eds.), *New directions in criminological theory. Advances in Criminological Theory*, vol. 4 (pp. 143–185). New Brunswick, NJ: Transaction Publishers.

Kennedy, L.W., Caplan, J.M., and Piza, E. (2011). "Risk clusters, hot spots, and spatial intelligence: Risk terrain modeling as an algorithm for police resource allocation strategies." *Journal of Quantitative Criminology*, 27(3), 339–362.

Kent, J., Leitner, M., and Curtis, A. (2006). "Evaluating the usefulness of functional distance measures when calibrating journey-to-crime distance decay functions." *Computers, Environment and Urban Systems*, 30(2), 181–200.

Kleiman, M., and Young, R. (1995). "The factors of production in retail drug dealing." *Urban Affairs Review*, 30(5), 730–748.

Knigge, L., and Cope, M. (2006). "Grounded visualization: Integrating the analysis of qualitative and quantitative data through grounded theory and visualization." *Environment and Planning A*, 38(11), 2021–2037.

Knox, G. (1964). "Epidemiology of childhood leukaemia in Northumber and Durham." *British Journal of Preventive & Social Medicine*, 18(1), 17–24.

Koch, P.N., Simpson, T.W., Allen, J.K., and Mistree, F. (1999). "Statistical approximations for multidisciplinary design optimization: The problem of size." *Journal of Aircraft*, 36(1), 275–286.

Kochel, T.R. (2011) "Constructing hot spots policing: Unexamined consequences for disadvantaged populations and for police legitimacy." *Criminal Justice Policy Review*, 22(3), 350–374.

(2013). *Hot spots policing community impact: Police legitimacy, collective efficacy, and perceptions of crime and safety.* Presented at the Annual Meeting of the American Society of Criminology, Atlanta, GA.

Koper, C.S. (1995). "Just enough police presence: Reducing crime and disorderly behavior by optimizing patrol time in crime hot spots." *Justice Quarterly*, 12(4), 649–672.

(2014). "Assessing the practice of hot spots policing survey results from a national convenience sample of local police agencies." *Journal of Contemporary Criminal Justice*, 30(2), 123–146.

Kornhauser, R. (1978). *Social sources of delinquency: An appraisal of analytic models.* Chicago, IL: University of Chicago.

Krieger, N., Chen, J.T., Waterman, P.D., Soobader, M.-J., Subramanian, S.V., and Carson, R. (2002). "Geocoding and monitoring of U.S. socioeconomic inequalities in mortality and cancer incidence: Does the choice of area-based measure and geographic level matter? The Public Health Disparities Geocoding Project." *American Journal of Epidemiology*, 156(5), 471–482.

Kubrin, C.E., and Stewart, E.A. (2006). "Predicting who reoffends: The neglected role of neighborhood context in recidivism studies." *Criminology*, 44(1), 171–204.

Kwan, M.-P. (2007). "Affecting geospatial technologies: Toward a feminist politics of emotion." *The Professional Geographer*, 29(1), 22–34.

(2012). "How GIS can help address the uncertain geographic context problem in social science research." *Annals of GIS*, 18(4), 245–255.

La Vigne, N.G. (2007). *Mapping for community-based prisoner reentry efforts: A guidebook for law enforcement and their partners*. Washington, DC: Police Foundation.

Laub, J.H. (2004). "Life course of criminology in the United States: The American Society of Criminology 2003 Presidential Address." *Criminology*, 42(1), 1–26.

Laub, J.H., and Sampson, R.J. (2003). *Shared beginnings, divergent lives: Delinquent boys to age 70*. Cambridge, MA: Harvard University Press.

Lawton, B.A., Taylor, R.B., and Luongo, A.J. (2005). "Police officers on drug corners in Philadelphia, drug crime, and violent crime: Intended, diffusion, and displacement impacts." *Justice Quarterly*, 22(4), 427–451.

Laycock, G. (2005). "Defining crime science." In M. Smith and N. Tilley. (eds.), *Crime science: New approaches to preventing and detecting crime* (pp. 3–24). Cullompton: Willan.

LeBeau, J. L. (1987). "The methods and measures of centrography and the spatial dynamics of rape." *Journal of Quantitative Criminology*, 3(2), 125–141.

Levitt, S.D., and Venkatesh, S.A. (2000). "An economic analysis of a drug-selling gang's finances." *The Quarterly Journal of Economics*, 115(3), 755–789.

Lewis, G.M. (1998). *Cartographic encounters: Perspectives on Native American mapmaking and map use*. Chicago, IL: University of Chicago Press.

Lewis, D.A., and Salem, G. (1986). *Fear of crime: Incivility and production of a social problem*. Piscataway, NJ: Transaction Publishers.

Lipovetsky, S. (2009). "Pareto 80/20 law: Derivation via random partitioning." *International Journal of Mathematical Education in Science and Technology*, 40(2), 271–277.

Lipsky, M. (1980). *Street-level bureaucracy: Dilemmas of the individual in public services*. New York: Russell Sage Foundation.

Lipsey, M., and Wilson, D.B. (2001). *Practical meta-analysis*. Thousand Oaks, CA: Sage Publications.

Logan, J.R., and Molotch, H.L. (2007). *Urban fortunes: The political economy of place*. Berkeley, CA: University of California Press.

Lorenz, M.O. (1905). "Methods for measuring the concentration of wealth." *Publications of the American Statistical Association*, 9(70), 209–219.

Loveday, B. (1999). Government and accountability of the police. In R.I. Mawby (ed.), *Policing across the world: Issues for the twenty-first century* (pp. 132–150). New York: Routledge.

Low, S., and Altman, I. (1992). "Place attachment: A conceptual inquiry." In S. Low and A. Irwin (eds.), *Place attachment* (pp. 1–12). New York: Plenum.

Lum, C. (2009). *Translating police research into practice. Ideas in American Policing*. Washington, DC: Police Foundation.

Lum, C., Koper, C., and Telep, C.W. (2011). "The Evidence-Based Policing Matrix." *Journal of Experimental Criminology*, 7(1), 3–26.

Lynch, J.P., and Addington, L.A. (2007). *Understanding crime statistics: Revisiting the divergence of the NCVS and UCR*. New York: Cambridge University Press.

Lynch, K. (1960). *The image of the city*. Cambridge, MA: MIT Press.

Madensen, T.D. (2007). *Bar management and crime: Toward a dynamic theory of place management and crime hot spots*. PhD dissertation. Cincinnati, OH: University of Cincinnati.

Madensen, T.D., and Eck, J.E. (2008). "Violence in bars: Exploring the impact of place manager decision-making." *Crime Prevention and Community Safety*, 10(2), 111–125.

— (2013). "Crime places and place management." In F. Cullen and P. Wilcox (eds.), *Oxford handbook of criminological theory* (pp. 544–578). New York: Oxford University Press.

Maguire, M. (2000). "Policing by risks and targets: Some dimensions and implications of intelligence-led crime control." *Policing and Society: An International Journal*, 9(4), 315–336.

Maguire, E.R., and Mastrofski, S.D. (2000). "Patterns of community policing in the United States." *Police Quarterly*, 3(1), 4–45.

Maltz, M.D. (1995). "Criminality in space and time: Life course analysis and the microecology of crime." In J.E. Eck and D. Weisburd (eds.), *Crime and place. Crime Prevention Studies*, vol. 4 (pp. 315–347). Monsey, NY: Criminal Justice Press.

— (2009). "Waves, particles, and crime." In D. Weisburd, W. Bernasco, and G. Bruinsma (eds.), *Putting crime in its place: Units of analysis in geographic criminology* (pp. 123–142). New York: Springer.

Martin, R., and Sunley, P. (2003). "Deconstructing clusters: Chaotic concept or policy panacea?" *Journal of Economic Geography*, 3(1), 5–35.

Mason M., Cheung I., and Walker L. (2004). "Substance use, social networks and the geography of urban adolescents." *Substance Use and Misuse*, 39(10–12), 1751–1777.

Mastrofski, S.D., Weisburd, D., and Braga, A.A. (2010). "Rethinking policing: The policy implications of hot spots of crime." In N. Frost, J. Freilich, and T. Clear (eds.), *Contemporary issues in criminal justice policy: Policy proposals from the American Society of Criminology conference* (pp. 251–264). Belmont, CA: Wadsworth.

Matthews, R. (1993). *Kerb-crawling, prostitution, and multiagency policing*. Crime Prevention Unit Series, Paper 43. London: Home Office.

Mattson, M., and Rengert, G. (1995). "Danger, distance, and desirability." *European Journal on Criminal Policy and Research*, 3(3), 70–78.

May, K.O. (1952). "A set of independent necessary and sufficient conditions for simple majority decision." *Econometrica*, 20(4), 680–685.

Mayhew, H. (1851). *London's underworld. Being selections from "Those that will not work," the 4th vol. of "London labour and the London poor."* London: Spring Books.

Mayhew, P., Clarke, R.V., Sturman, A., and Hough, M. (1976). *Crime as opportunity*. Home Office Research Study, vol. 34. London: Home Office, H.M. Stationary Office.

Mazerolle, L.G., and Ransley, J. (2006). *Third party policing*. New York: Cambridge University Press.

Mazerolle, L.G., and Roehl, J. (1998). "Civil remedies and crime prevention: An introduction." In L.G. Mazerolle and J. Roehl (eds.), *Civil remedies and crime prevention. Crime Prevention Studies*, vol. 9 (pp. 1–18). Monsey, NY: Criminal Justice Press.

Mazerolle, L.G., Kadleck, C., and Roehl, J. (1998). "Controlling drug and disorder problems: The role of place managers." *Criminology*, 36(2), 371–404.

Mazerolle, L.G., Price, J.F., and Roehl, J. (2000). "Civil remedies and drug control: A randomized field trial in Oakland, California." *Evaluation Review*, 24(2), 212–241.

McCann, E.J. (2002). "The cultural politics of local economic development: Meaning-making, place-making, and the urban policy process." *Geoforum*, 33(3), 385–398.

McMillan, D.W., and Chavis, D.M. (1986). "Sense of community: A definition and theory." *Journal of Community Psychology*, 14(1), 6–23.

Mears, D., Wang, X., Hay, C., and Bales, W. (2008). "Social ecology and recidivism: Implications for prisoner reentry." *Criminology*, 46(2), 301–340.

Meinig, D.W. (1979). *The interpretation of ordinary landscapes: Geographical essays*. New York: Oxford University Press.

Mencken, F.C., and Barnett, C. (1999). "Murder, nonnegligent manslaughter and spatial autocorrelation in mid-South counties." *Journal of Quantitative Criminology*, 15(4), 407–422.

Merriam-Webster (2015). Merriam-Webster online dictionary. Accessed May 25, 2015. www.merriam-webster.com.

Merzel, C., and D'Afflitti, J. (2003). "Reconsidering community-based health promotion: Promise, performance, and potential." *American Journal of Public Health*, 93(4), 557–574.

Mesch, G.S., and Manor, O. (1998). "Social ties, environmental perception, and local attachment." *Environment and Behavior*, 30(4), 504–519.

Messner, S.F., Anselin, L., Baller, R.D., Hawkins, D.F., Deane, G., and Tolnay, S.E. (1999). "The spatial patterning of county homicide rates: An application of exploratory spatial data analysis." *Journal of Quantitative Criminology*, 15(4), 423–450.

Miethe, T.D. (1991). "Citizen based crime control activity and victimization risks: An examination of displacement and free rider effects." *Criminology*, 29(3), 419–440.

Miethe, T.D., Stafford, M.C., and Long, J.S. (1987). "Social differentiation in criminal victimization: A test of routine activities/lifestyle theories." *American Sociological Review*, 52(2), 184–194.

Millie, A. (2008). "Anti-social behaviour, behavioural expectations and an urban aesthetic." *British Journal of Criminology*, 48(3), 379–394.

Moffitt, T.E. (1993). "Adolescence-limited and life-course-persistent antisocial behavior: A developmental taxonomy." *Psychological Review*, 100(4), 674–701.

Mohler, G.O., Short, M.B., Brantingham, P.J., Schoenberg, F.P., and Tita, G.E. (2011). "Self-exciting point process modeling of crime." *Journal of the American Statistical Association*, 106(493), 100–108.

Monk, K. (2012). *How central business districts manage crime and disorder: A case study in the processes of place management in downtown Cincinnati*. PhD dissertation. Cincinnati, OH: University of Cincinnati.

Moore, G.T. (1979). "Knowing about environmental knowing: The current state of theory and research on environmental cognition." *Environment and Behavior*, 11(1), 33–70.

Moore, M.H. (1995). "Public health and criminal justice approaches to prevention." In M. Tonry and D.P. Farrington (eds.), *Building a safer society: Strategic approaches to crime prevention. Crime and Justice: A Review of Research*, vol. 19 (pp. 237–262). Chicago, IL: University of Chicago Press.

Morenoff, J.D., Sampson, R.J., and Raudenbush, S.W. (2001). "Neighborhood inequality, collective efficacy, and the spatial dynamics of urban violence." *Criminology*, 39(3), 517–558.
Morgan, F. (2001). "Repeat burglary in a Perth suburb: Indicator of short-term or long-term risk?" In G. Farrell and K. Pease (eds.), *Repeat victimization. Crime Prevention Studies*, vol. 12 (pp. 83–118). Monsey, NY: Criminal Justice Press.
Nagin, D.S. (1999). "Analyzing developmental trajectories: A semiparametric, group-based approach." *Psychological Methods*, 4(2), 139–157.
⎯⎯ (2013). "Deterrence in the twenty-first century." In M. Tonry (ed.), *Crime and Justice: A Review of Research*, vol. 42 (pp. 199–263). Chicago, IL: University of Chicago Press.
Nagin, D.S., and Pogarsky, G. (2001). "Integrating celerity, impulsivity, and extralegal sanction threats into a model of general deterrence: Theory and evidence." *Criminology*, 39(4), 865–892.
National Criminal Intelligence Service (2000). *National intelligence model*. London: NCIS.
National Research Council. (1993). *Understanding and preventing violence*, vol. 1. Panel on the Understanding and Control of Violent Behavior. A.J. Reiss, Jr. and J.A. Roth (eds.). Washington, DC: National Academies Press.
⎯⎯ (2004). *Fairness and effectiveness in policing: The evidence*. Committee to Review Research on Police Policy and Practices. Committee on Law and Justice, Division of Behavioral and Social Sciences and Education. W. Skogan and K. Frydl (eds.). Washington, DC: National Academies Press.
Newman, O. (1972) *Defensible space*. New York: Macmillan.
Nisbett, R.E., and Cohen, D. (1996). *Culture of honor: The psychology of violence in the South*. Boulder, CO: Westview Press.
North, D.C. (1990). *Institutional change and economic performance*. Cambridge: Cambridge University Press.
Oberwittler, D., and Wikström, P.H. (2009). "Why small is better: Advancing the study of the role of behavioral contexts in crime causation." In D. Weisburd, G. Bruinsma, and W. Bernasco (eds.), *Putting crime in its place: Units of analysis in geographic criminology* (pp. 35–59). New York: Springer.
Openshaw, S. (1984). *The modifiable areal unit problem. Concepts and Techniques in Modern Geography*, vol. 38. Norwick, UK: Geo Books.
Ouimet, M. (2000). "Aggregation bias in ecological research: How social disorganization and criminal opportunities shape the spatial distribution of juvenile delinquency in Montreal." *Canadian Journal of Criminology*, 42(2), 135–156.
Overman, H.G. (2004). "Can we learn anything from economic geography proper?" *Journal of Economic Geography*, 4(5), 501–516.
Oxford English Dictionary. (2010). *Oxford English dictionary*. 3rd ed. Oxford: Oxford University Press.
Pain, R., MacFarlane, R., Turner, K., and Gill, S. (2006). "When, where, if, and but: Qualifying GIS and the effect of streetlighting on crime and fear." *Environment and Planning A*, 38(11), 2055–2074.
Palmquist, R.B. (2005). "Property value models." In K.G. Maler and J.R. Vincent (eds.), *Handbook of environmental economics: Valuing economic changes* (pp. 763–819). San Diego, CA: Elsevier.

Pareto, V. (1909). *Manuel d'économie politique. Oeuvres completes*, vol. 7. Geneva, Switzerland: Droz.

Park, R.E., and Burgess, E.W. (1924). *Introduction to the science of sociology*. 2nd ed. Chicago, IL: University of Chicago Press.

Pauly, G.A., and Finch, S.J. (1967). "Computer mapping: A new technique in crime analysis." In Illinois Institute of Technology Research Institute (ed.), *Law enforcement science and technology: Proceedings of the First National Symposium on Law Enforcement Science and Technology* (pp. 739–749). Washington, DC: Thompson Book Company.

Pavlovskaya, M. (2009). "Non-quantitative GIS." In M. Cope and S. Elwood (eds.), *Qualitative GIS: A mixed methods approach* (pp. 13–37). Thousand Oaks, CA: Sage Publications.

Pavlovskaya, M.E. (2006). "Theorizing with GIS: A tool for critical geographies?" *Environment and Planning A*, 38(11), 2003–2020.

Payne, T. (2010). *Does changing ownership change crime? An analysis of apartment ownership and crime in Cincinnati*. PhD dissertation. Cincinnati, OH: University of Cincinnati.

Payne, T.C. (2015). "Reducing excessive police incidents: Do notices to owners work?" *Security Journal*, 28(1), 1–18.

Payne, T., and Eck, J.E. (2007). *Who owns crime?* Presented at the Annual Meeting of the American Society of Criminology, Atlanta, GA.

Payne, T., Gallagher, K., Eck, J.E., and Frank, J. (2013). "Problem framing in problem solving: A case study." *Policing: An International Journal of Police Strategies and Management*. 36(4), 670–682.

Pease, K. (1998). *Repeat victimization: Taking stock*. Home Office Police Research Group. Crime Detection and Prevention Series, Paper 90. London: Home Office.

 (2001). "What to do about it? Let's turn off our minds and GIS." In A. Hirschfield and K. Bowers (eds.), *Mapping and analysing crime data* (pp. 225–236). London: Taylor and Francis.

Peterson, W.J. (1986). "Deterrence and compellence: A critical assessment of conventional wisdom." *International Studies Quarterly*, 30(3), 269–294.

Petrosino, A., Boruch, R., Soydan, H., Duggan, L., and Sanchez-Meca, J. (2001). "Meeting the challenge of evidence-based policy: The Campbell Collaboration." *Annals of the American Academy of Political and Social Science*, 578, 14–34.

Pierce, G., Spaar, S., and Briggs, L. (1988). *The character of police work: Strategic and tactical implications*. Boston, MA: Center for Applied Social Research, Northeastern University.

Piquero, A.R., and Mazerolle, P. (eds.). (2001). *Life-course criminology: Contemporary and classic readings*. Belmont, CA: Wadsworth.

Piquero, A.R., Farrington, D.P., and Blumstein, A. (2007). *Key issues in criminal career research: New analyses of the Cambridge Study in Delinquent Development*. Cambridge: Cambridge University Press.

Piza, E.L. (2012). *Identifying the best context for CCTV camera deployment: An analysis of micro-level features*. PhD dissertation. Newark, NJ: Rutgers University.

Pong, R.W., and Pitblado, J.R. (2001). "Don't take 'geography' for granted! Some methodological issues in measuring geographic distribution of physicians." *Canadian Journal of Rural Medicine*, 6(2), 103–112.

Pratt, T.C., and Cullen, F.T. (2005). "Assessing macro-level predictors and theories of crime: A meta-analysis." In M. Tonry (ed.), *Crime and Justice: A Review of Research*, vol. 32 (pp. 373–450). Chicago, IL: University of Chicago Press.

Putnam, R. (2001). "Social capital: Measurement and consequences." *Canadian Journal of Policy Research*, 2(1), 41–51.

Quetelet A. (1831 [1984]). *Research on the propensity for crime at different ages.* Cincinnati, OH: Anderson Publishing.

(1842). *A treatise in man.* Edinburgh, Scotland: Chambers.

Rapoport, A. (1982). *The meaning of the built environment.* Beverly Hills, CA: Sage Publications.

Rasmussen, D.W., Benson, B.L., and Sollars, D.L. (1993). "Spatial competition in illicit drug markets: The consequences of increased drug law enforcement." *The Review of Regional Studies*, 23(3), 219–236.

Ratcliffe, J.H. (2004a). "Geocoding crime and a first estimate of a minimum acceptable hit rate." *International Journal of Geographical Information Science*, 18(1), 61–72.

(2004b). "The hotspot matrix: A framework for the spatio-temporal targeting of crime reduction." *Police Practice and Research*, 5(1), 5–23.

(2006). "A temporal constraint theory to explain opportunity-based spatial offending patterns." *Journal of Research in Crime and Delinquency*, 43(3), 261–291.

(2012). "The spatial extent of criminogenic places: A changepoint regression of violence around bars." *Geographical Analysis*, 44(4), 302–320.

Ratcliffe, J.H., and Breen, C. (2011). "Crime diffusion and displacement: Measuring the side effects of police operations." *Professional Geographer*, 63(2), 230–243.

Ratcliffe, J.H., and McCullagh, M.J. (1998). "Aoristic crime analysis." *International Journal of Geographical Information Science*, 12(7), 751–764.

(1999). "Hotbeds of crime and the search for spatial accuracy." *Geographical Systems*, 1(4), 385–398.

Ratcliffe, J.H., and Rengert, G.F. (2008). "Near repeat patterns in Philadelphia shootings." *Security Journal*, 21(1–2), 58–76.

Ratcliffe, J.H., Taniguchi, T., and Taylor, R.B. (2009). "The crime reduction effects of public CCTV cameras: A multi-method spatial approach." *Justice Quarterly*, 26(4), 746–770.

Ratcliffe, J.H., Taniguchi, T., Groff, E.R., and Wood, J.D. (2011). "The Philadelphia foot patrol experiment: A randomized controlled trial of police patrol effectiveness in violent crime hotspots." *Criminology*, 49(3), 795–831.

Reaves, B.A. (2010). *Local police departments, 2007.* Washington, DC: Bureau of Justice Statistics, U.S. Department of Justice.

Reiss, A.J. Jr. (1981). "Towards a revitalization of theory and research on victimization by crime." *Journal of Criminal Law and Criminology*, 72(2), 704–713.

(1986). "Why are communities important in understanding crime?" In A.J. Reiss and M. Tonry (eds.), *Communities and crime. Crime and Justice: A Review of Research*, vol. 8 (pp. 1–33). Chicago, IL: University of Chicago Press.

(1988). "Co-offending and criminal careers." In M. Tonry and N. Morris (eds.), *Crime and Justice: A Review of Research*, vol. 10. (pp. 117–170). Chicago, IL: University of Chicago Press.

Reiss, A.J. Jr., and Farrington, D.P. (1991). "Advancing knowledge about co-offending: Results from a prospective longitudinal survey of London males." *Journal of Criminal Law and Criminology*, 82(2), 360–395.

Relph, E. (1976). *Place and placelessness*. London: Pion.
Rengert, G.F. (1980). "Spatial aspects of criminal behavior." In D. E. Georges-Abeyie and K. D. Harries (eds.), *Crime: A spatial perspective* (pp. 47–57). New York: Columbia University Press.
(1981). "Burglary in Philadelphia: A critique of an opportunity structure model." In P. Brantingham and P. Brantingham (eds.), *Environmental criminology* (pp. 189–201). Beverly Hills, CA: Sage Publications.
(1986). *Crime spillovers from Atlantic City gambling*. Paper presented at the Middle States Division of the Association of American Geographers, New York.
(1997). "Auto theft in central Philadelphia." In R. Homel (ed.), *Policing for prevention: Reducing crime, public intoxication and injury. Crime Prevention Studies*, vol. 7 (pp. 199–220). Monsey, NY: Criminal Justice Press.
Rengert, G.F., and Groff, E. (2011). *Residential burglary: How the urban environment and our lifestyles play a contributing role*. Springfield, IL: Charles Thomas.
Rengert, G.F., and Lockwood, B. (2009). "Geographic units of analysis and the analysis of crime." In D. Weisburd, W. Bernasco, and G.J.N. Bruinsma (eds.), *Putting crime in its place: Units of analysis in geographic criminology* (pp. 109–122). New York: Springer.
Rengert, G.F., and Lowell, R. (2005). "Combating campus crime with mapping and analysis." *Police Foundation Crime Mapping News*, 7(1), 1–5.
Rengert, G.F., and Pelfrey, W.V. (1997). "Cognitive mapping of the city center: Comparative perceptions of dangerous places." In D. Weisburd and T. McEwen (eds.), *Crime mapping and crime prevention. Crime Prevention Studies*, vol. 8 (pp. 193–217). Monsey, NY: Criminal Justice Press.
Rengert, G.F., Mattson, M., and Henderson, K. (2001). *Campus security: Situational crime prevention in high-density environments*. Monsey, NY: Criminal Justice Press.
Rengert, G.F., Ratcliffe, J.H., and Chakravorty, S. (2005). *Policing illegal drug markets: Geographic approaches to crime reduction*. Monsey, NY: Criminal Justice Press.
Reppetto, T. (1976). "Crime prevention and the displacement phenomenon." *Crime and Delinquency*, 22(2), 166–177.
Reynald, D.M. (2010). "Guardians on guardianship: Factors affecting the willingness to supervise, ability to detect potential offenders, and willingness to intervene." *Journal of Research in Crime and Delinquency*, 47(3), 358–390.
(2011). "Factors associated with guardianship of places: Assessing the relative importance of the spatio-physical and sociodemographic contexts in generating opportunities for capable guardianship." *Journal of Research in Crime and Delinquency*, 48(1), 110–142.
Rice, K.J., and Smith, W.R. (2002). "Socioecological models of automotive theft: Integrating routine activity and social disorganization approaches." *Journal of Research in Crime and Delinquency*, 39(3), 304–336.
Rich, T., and Shively, M. (2004). *A methodology for evaluating geographic profiling software: Final report*. Cambridge, MA: Abt Associates Inc.
Richter, C.F. (1935). "An instrumental earthquake magnitude scale." *Bulletin of the Seismological Society of America*, 25(1), 1–32.
Ridgeway, G. (2007). *Analysis of racial disparities in the New York Police Department's stop, question, and frisk practices*. Santa Monica, CA: RAND Corporation.

Robinson, W.S. (1950). "Ecological correlations and the behavior of individuals." *American Sociological Review*, 15(3), 351–357.
Roncek, D.W. (1999). "Schools and crime." In V. Goldsmith, P.G. McGuire, J.H. Mollenkopf, and T.A. Ross (eds.), *Analyzing crime patterns: Frontiers of practice* (pp. 153–166). Thousand Oaks, CA: Sage Publications.
Roncek, D.W., and Bell, R. (1981). "Bars, blocks and crimes." *Journal of Environmental Systems*, 11(1), 36–47.
Roncek, D.W., and Faggiani, D. (1985). "High schools and crime: A replication." *Sociological Quarterly*, 26(4), 491–505.
Roncek, D.W., and LoBosco, A. (1983). "The effect of high schools on crime in their neighborhoods." *Social Science Quarterly*, 64(3), 598–613.
Roncek, D.W., and Mair, P. (1991). "Bars, blocks and crimes revisited: Linking the theory of routine activities to the empiricism of hot spots." *Criminology*, 29(4), 725–753.
Roncek, D.W., and Pravatiner, M. (1989). "Additional evidence that taverns enhance nearby crime." *Sociology and Social Research*, 73(4), 185–188.
Rosenbaum, D.P. (2006). "The limits of hot spots policing." In D. Weisburd and A.A. Braga (eds.), *Police innovation: Contrasting perspectives* (pp. 245–263). New York: Cambridge University Press.
Rossmo, D.K. (1999). *Geographic profiling*. Boca Raton, FL: CRC Press.
Ryden, K.C. (1993). *Mapping the invisible landscape: Folklore, writing, and the sense of place*. Iowa City: University of Iowa Press.
Sampson, R., Eck, J.E., and Dunham, J. (2009). "Super controllers and crime prevention: A routine activity explanation of crime prevention success and failure." *Security Journal*, 23(1), 37–51.
Sampson, R.J. (1986). "Crime in cities: The effects of formal and informal social control." In A.J. Reiss and M. Tonry (eds.), *Communities and crime. Crime and Justice: A Review of Research*, vol. 8 (pp. 271–311). Chicago, IL: University of Chicago Press.
(1993). "Linking time and place: Dynamic contextualism and the future of criminological inquiry." *Journal of Research in Crime and Delinquency*, 30(4), 426–444.
(1995). "The community." In J. Wilson and J. Petersilia (eds.), *Crime* (pp. 193–216). San Francisco, CA: Institute for Contemporary Studies Press.
(2008). "Moving to inequality: Neighborhood effects and experiments meet social structure." *American Journal of Sociology*, 114(1), 189–231.
(2010). "Collective efficacy theory." In F.T. Cullen and P. Wilcox (eds.), *Encyclopedia of criminological theory* (pp. 802–812). Thousand Oaks, CA: Sage Publications.
(2012). *Great American city: Chicago and the enduring neighborhood effect*. Chicago, IL: University of Chicago Press.
Sampson, R.J., and Groves, W.B. (1989). "Community structure and crime: Testing social-disorganization theory." *American Journal of Sociology*, 94(4), 774–802.
Sampson, R.J., and Laub, J.H. (1993). *Crime in the making: Pathways and turning points through life*. Cambridge, MA: Harvard University Press.
(2003). "Life course desisters? Trajectories of crime among delinquent boys followed to age 70." *Criminology*, 41(3), 555–592.
Sampson, R.J., and Raudenbush, S.W. (1999). "Systematic social observation of public spaces: A new look at disorder in urban neighborhoods." *American Journal of Sociology*, 105(3), 603–651.

Sampson, R.J., and Wilson, W.J. (1995). "Toward a theory of race, crime, and urban inequality." In J. Hagan and R.D. Peterson (eds.), *Crime and inequality* (pp. 37–54). Stanford, CA: Stanford University Press.

Sampson, R.J., Raudenbush, S.W., and Earls, F. (1997). "Neighborhoods and violent crime: A multilevel study of collective efficacy." *Science*, 277(5328), 918–924.

Sampson, R.J., Morenoff, J.D., and Gannon-Rowley, T. (2002). "Assessing 'neighborhood effects': Social processes and new directions in research." *Annual Review of Sociology*, 28, 443–478.

Schaefer, L.W. (2013). *Environmental corrections: Making offender supervision work*. PhD dissertation. Cincinnati, OH: University of Cincinnati.

Schaefer, L., Cullen, F., and Eck, J.E. (2015). *Environmental corrections: A new paradigm for supervising offenders in the community*. Thousand Oaks, CA: Sage Publications.

Scherdin, M.J. (1986). "The halo effect: Psychological deterrence of electronic security systems." *Information Technology and Libraries*, 5(3), 232–235.

Schmerler, K. (2005). *Disorder at budget motels*. Problem-Specific Guides, no. 30. Washington, DC: Office of Community Oriented Policing Services, U.S. Department of Justice.

Schmitt S., Phibbs C., and Piette J. (2003). "The influence of distance on utilization of outpatient mental health aftercare following inpatient substance abuse treatment." *Addiction Behavior*, 28(6), 1183–1192.

Shaw, C.R., Zorbaugh F.M., McKay, H.D., and Cottrell L.S. (1929). *Delinquency areas: A study of the geographical distribution of school truants, juvenile delinquents, and adult offenders in Chicago*. Chicago, IL: University of Chicago Press.

Shaw, C.R., and McKay, H.D. (1942 [1969]). *Juvenile delinquency and urban areas. A study of rates of delinquency in relation to differential characteristics of local communities in American cities*. Rev. ed. Chicago, IL: University of Chicago Press.

Shaw, C.R., and Myers, E.D. (1929). *The juvenile delinquent*. Springfield: Illinois Association for Criminal Justice.

Shaw, J. (1995). "Community policing against guns: Public opinion of the Kansas City Gun Experiment." *Justice Quarterly*, 12(4), 695–710.

Sheptycki, J. (2009). "Policing, intelligence theory and the new human security paradigm: Some lesson from the field." In P. Gill, S. Marrin, and M. Phythian (eds.), *Intelligence theory: Key questions and debates* (pp. 166–185). New York: Routledge.

Sherman, L.W. (1990). "Police crackdowns: Initial and residual deterrence." In M. Tonry and N. Morris (eds.), *Crime and Justice: A Review of Research*, vol. 12 (pp. 1–48). Chicago, IL: University of Chicago Press.

(1995). "Hot spots of crime and criminal careers of places." In J.E. Eck and D. Weisburd (eds.), *Crime and place. Crime Prevention Studies*, vol. 4 (pp. 35–52). Monsey, NY: Criminal Justice Press.

(2007). "The power few: Experimental criminology and the reduction of harm." *Journal of Experimental Criminology*, 3(4), 299–321.

Sherman, L.W., and Eck, J.E. (2002). "Policing for crime prevention." In L.W. Sherman, D.P. Farrington, B.C. Welsh, and D.L. MacKenzie (eds.), *Evidence-based crime prevention* (pp. 295–329). New York: Routledge.

Sherman, L.W., and Rogan, D. (1995a). "Deterrent effects of police raids on crack houses: A randomized controlled experiment." *Justice Quarterly*, 12(4), 755–782.

(1995b). "Effects of gun seizures on gun violence: 'Hot spots' patrol in Kansas City." *Justice Quarterly*, 12(4), 673–694.
Sherman, L.W., and Weisburd, D. (1995). "General deterrent effects of police patrol in crime 'hot spots': A randomized, controlled trial." *Justice Quarterly*, 12(4), 625–648.
Sherman, L.W., Buerger, M., and Gartin, P. (1989). *Beyond dial-a-cop: A randomized test of Repeat Call Policing (RECAP)*. Washington, DC: Crime Control Institute.
Sherman, L.W., Gartin, P., and Buerger, M.E. (1989). "Hot spots of predatory crime: Routine activities and the criminology of place." *Criminology*, 27(1), 27–55.
Sherman, L., Gottfredson, D.L., MacKenzie, D. Eck, J.E., Reuter, P., and Bushway, S. (1997). *Preventing crime: What works, what doesn't, what's promising*. Washington, DC: U.S. Department of Justice, National Institute of Justice.
Sherman, L., Farrington, D.P., Welsh, B., and MacKenzie, D.L. (2002). *Evidence-based crime prevention*. New York: Routledge.
Simpson, E.H. (1949). "Measurement of diversity." Nature, 163, 688.
Skogan, W. (1990). *Disorder and decline: Crime and the spiral of decay in American neighborhoods*. New York: Free Press.
Skogan, W.G., and Annan, S. (1994). "Drugs and public housing: Toward an effective police response." In D. MacKenzie and C.D. Uchida (eds.), *Drugs and crime: Evaluating public policy initiatives* (pp. 129–148). Thousand Oaks, CA: Sage Publications.
Spelman, W., and Brown, D. (1984). *Calling the police: Citizen reporting of serious crime*. Washington, DC: U.S. Government Printing Office.
Spicer, V., Reid, A.A., Ginther, J., Seifi, H., and Dabbaghian, V. (2012). "Bars on blocks: A cellular automata model of crime and liquor licensed establishment density." *Computers, Environment, and Urban Systems*, 36(5), 412–422.
St. Jean, P.K.B. (2007). *Pockets of crime: Broken windows, collective efficacy, and the criminal point of view*. Chicago, IL: University of Chicago Press.
Stahler, G., Mazzella, S., Mennis, J., Chakravorty, S., Rengert, G., and Spiga, R. (2007). "The effect of individual, program, and neighborhood variables on continuity of treatment among dually diagnosed individuals." *Drug and Alcohol Dependence*, 87(1), 54–62.
Stavins, R. (2007). "Market-based environmental policies: What can we learn from U.S. experience?" In J. Freeman and C.D. Kolstad (eds.), *Moving to markets in environmental regulation: Lessons from twenty years of experience*. New York: Oxford University Press.
Stedman, R.C. (2002). "Toward a social psychology of place: Predicting behavior from place-based cognitions, attitude, and identity." *Environment and Behavior*, 34(5), 561–581.
Stevens, A., and Coupe, P. (1978). "Distortions in judged spatial relations." *Cognitive Psychology*, 10(4), 422–437.
Stokols, D. (1983). "Editor's introduction: Theoretical directions of environment and behavior research." *Environment and Behavior*, 15(3), 259–272.
(1987). "Conceptual strategies of environmental psychology." In D. Stokols and I. Altman (eds.), *Handbook of environmental psychology* (pp. 41–70). New York: John Wiley and Sons.
Stokols, D., and Altman, I. (eds.) (1987). *Handbook of environmental psychology*. New York: John Wiley and Sons.

Stoks, F.G. (1981). *Assessing urban public space environments for danger of violent crime*. PhD dissertation. Seattle: University of Washington.
Summers, L., Johnson, S., and Rengert, G.F. (2010). "The use of maps in offender interviewing." In W. Bernasco (ed.), *Offenders on offending: Learning about crime from criminals* (pp. 246–272). Cullompton: Willan.
Sutherland, E.H. (1924). *Principles of criminology*. Chicago, IL: University of Chicago Press.
  (1947). *Principles of criminology: A sociological theory of criminal behavior*. New York: J.B. Lippincott Company.
Sviridoff, M., Sadd, S., Curtis, R., and Grinc, R. (1992). *The neighborhood effects of street-level drug enforcement: Tactical narcotics teams in New York*. New York: Vera Institute of Justice.
Taniguchi, T.A., Ratcliffe, J.H., and Taylor, R.B. (2011). "Gang set space, drug markets, and crime around drug corners in Camden." *Journal of Research in Crime and Delinquency*, 48(3), 327–363.
Taniguchi, T.A., Rengert, G.F., and McCord, E.S. (2009). "Where size matters: Agglomeration economies of illegal drug markets in Philadelphia." *Justice Quarterly*, 26(4), 670–694.
Taxman, F.S. (2008). "No illusions: Offender and organizational change in Maryland's Proactive Community Supervision efforts." *Criminology and Public Policy*, 7(2), 275–302.
Taylor, B., Koper, C.S., and Woods, D.J. (2011). "A randomized controlled trial of different policing strategies at hot spots of violent crime." *Journal of Experimental Criminology*, 7(2), 149–181.
Taylor, R.B. (1987). "Toward an environmental psychology of disorder: Delinquency, crime, and fear of crime." In D. Stokols and I. Altman (eds.), *Handbook of environmental psychology* (pp. 951–986). New York: John Wiley and Sons.
  (1997). "Social order and disorder of street blocks and neighborhoods: Ecology, microecology, and the systemic model of social disorganization." *Journal of Research in Crime and Delinquency*, 34(1), 113–155.
  (1998). "Crime and small-scale places: What we know, what we can prevent, and what else we need to know." In R.B. Taylor, G. Bazemore, B. Boland, T.R. Clear, R.P.J. Corbett, J. Feinblatt, G. Berman, M. Sviridoff, and C. Stone (eds.), *Crime and place: Plenary papers of the 1997 Conference on Criminal Justice Research and Evaluation* (pp. 1–22). Washington, DC: National Institute of Justice, U.S. Department of Justice.
  (2001). *Breaking away from Broken Windows: Baltimore neighborhoods and the nationwide fight against crime, grime, fear, and decline*. Boulder, CO: Wakefield Press.
  (2010). "Hot spots do not exist, and four other fundamental concerns about hot spots policing." In N. Frost, J. Freilich and T. Clear (eds.), *Contemporary issues in criminal justice policy: Policy proposals from the American Society of Criminology conference* (pp. 271–278). Belmont, CA: Wadsworth.
  (2012). "Defining neighborhoods in space and time." *Cityscape: A Journal of Policy Development and Research*, 14(2), 225–230.
Taylor, R.B., and Harrell, A.V. (1996). *Physical environment and crime*. Washington, DC: National Institute of Justice, U.S. Department of Justice.

Taylor, R.B., Gottfredson, S.D., and Brower, S. (1984). "Block crime and fear: Defensible space, local social ties, and territorial functioning." *Journal of Research in Crime and Delinquency*, 21(4), 303-331.

Telep, C.W., and Weisburd, D. (2012). "What is known about the effectiveness of police practices in reducing crime and disorder?" *Police Quarterly*, 15(4), 331-357.

Telep, C.W., Mitchell, R.J., and Weisburd, D. (2014). "How much time should the police spend at crime hot spots?: Answers from a police agency directed randomized field trial in Sacramento, California." *Justice Quarterly*, 31(5), 905-933.

Telep, C.W., Weisburd, D., Gill, C.E., Teichman, D., and Vitter, Z. (2014). "Displacement of crime and diffusion of crime control benefits in large-scale geographic areas: A systematic review." *Journal of Experimental Criminology*, 10(4), 515-548.

Thompson, C.Y., and Fisher, B. (1996). "Predicting household victimization utilizing a multi-level routine activity approach." *Journal of Crime and Justice*, 19(2), 49-66.

Tillyer, M.S., and Eck, J.E. (2011). "Getting a handle on crime: A further extension of routine activities theory." *Security Journal*, 24(2), 179-193.

Tita, G.E., Petras, T.L., and Greenbaum, R.T. (2006). "Crime and residential choice: A neighborhood level analysis of the impact of crime on housing prices." *Journal of Quantitative Criminology*, 22(4), 299-317.

Tobler, W.R. (1970). "A computer movie simulating urban growth in the Detroit region." *Economic Geography*, 46, 234-240.

Townsley, M. (2009). "Spatial autocorrelation and impacts on criminology." *Geographical Analysis*, 41(4), 452-461.

Townsley, M., Homel, R., and Chaseling, J. (2000). "Repeat burglary victimization: Spatial and temporal patterns." *Australian and New Zealand Journal of Criminology*, 33(1), 37-63.

(2003). "Infectious burglaries: A test of the near repeat hypothesis." *British Journal of Criminology*, 43(3), 615-633

Trasler, G. (1993). "Conscience, opportunity, rational choice, and crime." In R.V. Clarke and M. Felson (eds.), *Routine activity and rational choice. Advances in Criminological Theory*, vol. 5 (pp. 305-322). New Brunswick, NJ: Transaction Publishers.

Tremblay, P. (1986). "Designing crime." *British Journal of Criminology*, 26(3), 234-253.

Treves, V. (2005). *Towards a law enforcement techologies complex: Situating Compstat in neo-liberal penality.* Master's thesis. New York: Hunter College.

Trowbridge, C.C. (1913). "On fundamental methods of orientation and 'imaginary maps.'" *Science*, 38(990), 888-896.

Tunstall, H.V.Z., Shaw, M., and Dorling, D. (2004). "Places and health." *Journal of Epidemiology and Community Health*, 58(1), 6-10.

Tversky, B. (1993). "Cognitive maps, cognitive collages, and spatial mental models." In A.U. Frank and I. Campari (eds.), *Spatial information theory a theoretical basis for GIS* (pp. 14-24). New York: Springer.

Tyler, T.R. (1990). *Why people obey the law.* New Haven, CT: Yale University Press.

(2004). "Enhancing police legitimacy." *The Annals of the American Academy of Political and Social Science*, 593, 84-99.

Unger, D.G., and Wandersman, A. (1983). "Neighboring and its role in block organizations: An exploratory report." *American Journal of Community Psychology*, 11(3), 291-300.

U.S. Census Bureau. (2006). "Current housing reports, Series H150/05," *American Housing Survey for the United States: 2005*. Washington, DC: U.S. Government Printing Office.

Veysey, B.M., and Messner, S.F. (1999). "Further testing of social disorganization theory: An elaboration of Sampson and Groves's 'Community structure and crime.'" *Journal of Research in Crime and Delinquency*, 36(2), 156–174.

Vold, G.B., Bernard, T.J., and Snipes, J.B. (2002). *Theoretical criminology*. 5th ed. New York: Oxford University Press.

Warburton, A.L., and Shepherd, J.P. (2006). "Tackling alcohol related violence in city centres: Effect of emergency medicine and police intervention." *Emergency Medicine Journal*, 23(1), 12–17.

Webb, J. (1996). *Direct line Homesafe*. Lincolnshire, UK: Janice Webb Research.

Webster, N. (1936). *Webster's universal unabridged dictionary*, vol. 2. New York: World Syndicate Publishing Company.

Weisburd, D. (2002). "From criminals to criminal contexts: Reorienting crime prevention research and policy." In E. Waring and D. Weisburd (eds.), *Crime and social organization. Advances in Criminological Theory*, vol. 10 (pp. 197–216). New Brunswick, NJ: Transaction Publishers.

(2008). *Place-based policing: Ideas in American Policing*. Washington, DC: Police Foundation.

(2014). *Crime at street segments in Tel Aviv-Jaffa: A longitudinal study*. Funded proposal to the Israel Science Foundation.

(2015a). "The law of crime concentrations and the criminology of place." *Criminology*, 53(2), 133–157.

(2015b). "Small worlds of crime and criminal justice interventions: Discovering crime hot spots." In M. Maltz and S. Rice (eds.), *Envisioning criminology: Researchers on research as a process of discovery* (pp. 261–267). New York: Springer.

Weisburd, D., and Amram, S. (2014). "The law of concentrations of crime at place: The case of Tel Aviv-Jaffa." *Police Practice and Research*, 15(2), 101–114.

Weisburd, D., and Braga, A.A. (2013). "The importance of legitimacy in hot spots policing." *Community Policing Dispatch*, 6(9), http://cops.usdoj.gov/html/dispatch/09-2013/the_importance_of_legitimacy_in_hot_spots_policing.asp.

Weisburd, D., and Britt, C. (2007). *Statistics in criminal justice*. 3rd ed. New York: Springer.

Weisburd, D., and Eck, J.E. (2004). "What can the police do to reduce crime, disorder, and fear?" *Annals of the American Academy of Political and Social Science*, 593, 42–65.

Weisburd, D., and Green, L. (1994). "Defining the street-level drug market." In D.L. MacKenzie and C.D. Uchida (eds.), *Drugs and crime: Evaluating public policy initiatives* (pp. 61–76). Thousand Oaks, CA: Sage Publications.

(1995a). "Measuring immediate spatial displacement: Methodological issues and problems." In J.E. Eck and D. Weisburd (eds.), *Crime and place. Crime Prevention Studies*, vol. 4 (pp. 349–361). Monsey, NY: Willow Tree Press.

(1995b). "Policing drug hot spots: The Jersey City drug market analysis experiment." *Justice Quarterly*, 12(4), 711–735.

Weisburd, D., and Lum, C. (2005). "The diffusion of computerized crime mapping in policing: Linking research and practice." *Police Practice and Research*, 6(5), 419–434.

Weisburd, D., and Mazerolle, L.G. (2000). "Crime and disorder in drug hot spots: Implications for theory and practice in policing." *Police Quarterly*, 3(3), 331–349.

Weisburd, D. and McEwen, T. (eds.). (1997). *Crime mapping and crime prevention. Crime Prevention Studies*, vol. 8. Monsey, NY: Criminal Justice Press.

Weisburd, D., and Piquero, A.R. (2008). "How well do criminologists explain crime? Statistical modeling in published studies." In M. Tonry (ed.), *Crime and Justice: A Review of Research*, vol. 37 (pp. 453–502). Chicago, IL: University of Chicago Press.

Weisburd, D., and Telep, C.W. (2012). "Spatial displacement and diffusion of crime control benefits revisited: New evidence on why crime doesn't just move around the corner." In N. Tilley and G. Farrell (eds.), *The reasoning criminologist: Essays in honour of Ronald V. Clarke* (pp. 142–159). New York: Routledge.

(2014). "Hot spots policing: What we know and what we need to know." *Journal of Contemporary Criminal Justice*, 30(2), 200–220.

Weisburd, D., Bernasco, W., and Bruinsma, G.J.N. (eds.). (2009). *Putting crime in its place: Units of analysis in geographic criminology*. New York: Springer.

Weisburd, D., Bruinsma, G.J.N., and Bernasco, W. (2009). "Units of analysis in geographic criminology: Historical development, critical issues, and open questions." In D. Weisburd, W. Bernasco, and G.J.N. Bruinsma (eds.), *Putting crime in its place: Units of analysis in geographic criminology* (pp. 3–31). New York: Springer.

Weisburd, D., Bushway, S., Lum, C., and Yang, S.-M. (2004). "Trajectories of crime at places: A longitudinal study of street segments in the city of Seattle." *Criminology*, 42(2), 283–321.

Weisburd, D., Gill, C., and Wooditch, A. (2014). *Smart Police Initiative action plan: Brooklyn Park. Grant 2013-DB-BX-0030*. Washington, DC: Bureau of Justice Assistance, U.S. Department of Justice.

Weisburd, D., Groff, E.R., and Yang, S.-M. (2012). *The criminology of place: Street segments and our understanding of the crime problem*. New York: Oxford University Press.

Weisburd, D., Groff, E.R., Jones, G., Cave, B., Amendola, K., and Emison, R. (2014). *Transforming unallocated patrol time to crime prevention: Experimental evidence of the importance of dosage in general deterrence in police patrol*. Presented at the Center for Evidence-Based Crime Policy Annual Symposium, Arlington, VA.

(2014). "Understanding and controlling hot spots of crime: The importance of formal and informal social controls." *Prevention Science*, 15(1), 31–43.

Weisburd, D., Hinkle, J.C., Famega, C., and Ready, J. (2011). "The possible 'backfire' effects of hot spots policing: An experimental assessment of impacts on legitimacy, fear and collective efficacy." *Journal of Experimental Criminology*, 7(4), 297–320.

Weisburd, D., Lawton, B., and Ready, J. (2013). "Staking out the next generation of studies of the criminology of place: Collecting prospective longitudinal data at crime hot spots." In R. Loeber and B.C. Welsh (eds.), *The future of criminology* (pp. 236–243). New York: Oxford University Press.

Weisburd, D., Lawton, B., Ready, J., Haviland, A., Cave, B., and Nelson, M. (2014). *Preliminary survey findings from the Baltimore NIH Crime and Community Health Study*. Presented at the American Society of Criminology Conference, Chicago, IL.

Weisburd, D., Maher, L., and Sherman, L. (1992). "Contrasting crime general and crime specific theory: The case of hot spots of crime." In F. Adler and W.S. Laufer (eds.), *Advances in criminological theory* (pp. 45–70). NewBrunswick,NJ: Transaction Press.

Weisburd, D., Morris, N.A., and Groff, E.R. (2009). "Hot spots of juvenile crime: A longitudinal study of arrest incidents at street segments in Seattle, Washington." *Journal of Quantitative Criminology*, 25(4), 443–467.

Weisburd, D., Telep, C.W., and Lawton, B.A. (2014). "Could innovations in policing have contributed to the New York city crime drop even in a period of declining police strength? The case of stop, question and frisk as a hot spots policing strategy." *Justice Quarterly*, 31(1), 129–153.

Weisburd, D., Wyckoff, L.A., Ready, J., Eck, J.E., Hinkle, J.C., and Gajewski, F. (2006). "Does crime just move around the corner? A controlled study of spatial displacement and diffusion of crime control benefits." *Criminology*, 44(3), 549–592.

Welsh, B.C. and Farrington, D.P. (2010). *The future of crime prevention: Developmental and situational strategies*. Washington, DC: National Institute of Justice, U.S. Department of Justice.

Welsh, B.C., Braga, A.A., and Sullivan, C.J. (2014). "Serious youth violence and innovative prevention: On the emerging link between public health and criminology." *Justice Quarterly*, 31(3), 500–523.

Wicker, A.W. (1987). "Behavior settings reconsidered: Temporal stages, resources, internal dynamics, context." In D. Stokels and I. Altman (eds.), *Handbook of environmental psychology* (pp. 613–653). New York: Wiley-Interscience.

Wikström, P.-O.H. (2010). "Explaining crime as moral actions." In S. Hitlin and S. Vaisey (eds.), *Handbook of the sociology of morality* (pp. 211–240). New York: Springer.

Wikström, P.-O.H., Ceccato, V., Hardie, B., and Treiber, K. (2010). "Activity fields and the dynamics of crime." *Journal of Quantitative Criminology*, 26(1), 55–87.

Wikström, P.-O.H., Oberwittler, D., Treiber, K., and Hardie, B. (2012). *Breaking rules: The social and situational dynamics of young people's urban crime*. Oxford: Oxford University Press.

Wilcox, P., and Eck, J.E. (2011). "Criminology of the unpopular: Implications for policy aimed at payday lending facilities." *Criminology and Public Policy*, 10(2), 473–482.

Wilcox, P., Land, K.C., and Hunt, S.A. (2003). *Criminal circumstance: A dynamic multi-contextual criminal opportunity theory*. New York: Walter de Gruyster.

Wilcox, P., Madensen, T.D., and Tillyer, M.S. (2007). "Guardianship in context: Implications for burglary victimization risk and prevention." *Criminology*, 45(4), 771–803.

Wilcox, P., Quisenberry, N., Cabrera, D.T., and Jones, S. (2004). "Busy places and broken windows? Toward defining the role of physical structure and process in community crime models." *The Sociological Quarterly*, 45(2), 185–207.

Wilson, D.B. (2001). "Meta-analytic methods for criminology." *Annals of the American Academy of Political and Social Science*, 578, 71–89.

Wilson, J.Q., and Kelling, G. (1982). "Broken windows: The police and neighborhood safety." *Atlantic Monthly*, 249(3), 29–38.

Winslow, C.E.A. (1920). "The untilled fields of public health." *Science*, 51(1306), 23–33.

Wolff, M. and Asche, H. (2009). "Exploring crime hotspots: Geospatial analysis and 3D mapping." In M. Schrenk, V. Popovich, D. Engelke and P. Elisei (eds.), *Cities 3.0-smart, sustainable, and integrative* (pp. 147–156). Sitges, Spain: Competence Center of Urban and Regional Planning.

Wolfgang, M.E., Figlio, R.M., and Sellin, T. (1972). *Delinquency in a birth cohort.* Chicago, IL: University of Chicago Press.

Wolfgang, M.E., Thornberry, T.P., and Figlio, R.M. (1987). *From boy to man, from delinquency to crime.* Chicago, IL: University of Chicago Press.

Wood, J., and Shearing, C. (2007). *Imagining security.* Cullompton: Willan.

Wooditch, A., Lawton, B., and Taxman, F.S. (2013). "The geography of drug abuse epidemiology among probationers in Baltimore." *Journal of Drug Issues,* 43(2), 231–249.

Worden, R., Bynum, T., and Frank, J. (1994). "Police crackdowns on drug abuse and trafficking." In D. MacKenzie and C.D. Uchida (eds.), *Drugs and crime: Evaluating public policy initiatives* (pp. 95–113). Thousand Oaks, CA: Sage Publications.

Wortley, R. (2001). "A classification of techniques for controlling situational precipitators of crime." *Security Journal,* 14(4), 63–82.

Yen, I.H., and Kaplan, G.A. (1999). "Neighborhood social environment and risk of death: Multilevel evidence from the Alameda County study." *American Journal of Epidemiology,* 149(10), 898–907.

Zhu, L., Gorman, D.M., and Horel, S. (2004). "Alcohol outlet density and violence: A geospatial analysis." *Alcohol and Alcoholism,* 39(4), 369–375.

Zimring, F.E. (2006). *The great American crime decline.* New York: Oxford University Press.

Zipf, G.K. (1949). *Human behavior and the principle of least effort.* Cambridge, MA: Addison-Wesley.

Zorbaugh, H.W. (1929). *The gold coast and the slum: A sociological study of Chicago's near north side.* Chicago, IL: University of Chicago Press.

Index

Agglomeration 37, 80, 138
Aggregation problem 94
Aspatial crime patterns 89
Assault 18, 37, 79
Auto theft 18, 36, 92, 116, 155

Back cloth 150
Balbi, Adriano 11
Barker, Roger 72–3
Behavior setting 10–11, 53–4, 70–3, 83, 96, 128
Benefits, diffusion of 4, 66, 83, 92, 113, 122–3, 135–8
Boost model 43
Bounded rationality 44
Broken windows policing 126
Broken windows theory 2, 52, 59, 79
Brunswik, Egon 72
Bueerman, Jim 110
Burgess, Ernest 2, 12, 50
Burglary 36, 38, 84, 102–4
Business improvement district (BID) 66

Chicago School of Sociology 2, 6, 12, 44, 50, 68
Closed-circuit television (CCTV) 50, 56, 100
  viewshed 100–1
Cognitive mapping 73–4
Collective efficacy 51, 54, 58–61, 67, 73, 77, 82, 134, 158, 161
Community corrections 113, 133–4, 138, 156
Compellence 65
Compstat 154

Computational criminology 96
Computer simulations 108–10
  agent-based modeling 35, 109, 152
  cone of resolution 93, 95
Control of access 46, 48–50, 64, 114, 144
Crime, *see also* Auto theft; Homicide; Hot spots of crime; Rape; Robbery
  density 42, 92
  facilitation 56, 118
  general theory 70
  generation 48, 55–6, 80, 142
  mapping 6–8, 12, 33, 86, 92, 105, 151, 153
  pattern theory 44, 56, 87, 148, 150
  and place 3–9, 11, 13, 16–17, 30, 37, 42, 52, 69, 77–8, 81, 138, 141, 147–8, 150, 152, 157
  spatial patterns 88
  spillover 34, 83, 90, 95, 111
  variability 8, 13, 28–30, 52, 54, 60–1
Crime attractor 48, 56, 142
Crime concentration 14, 16–33, 41, 49, 54, 76, 95, 116, 141, 143–4, 146, 154–6
Crime coupling 29–30, 138, 149
Crime data 8–9, 23, 91, 111, 118, 151, 153
  address data 6–9, 12, 18, 75, 145, 151–2
  XY coordinates 8–9
Crime prevention through environmental design (CPTED) 127
Criminality (individual offending) 2, 42, 44, 50–2, 54, 68, 70, 149, 155
Criminology
  computational 96
  environmental 8, 14

197

Criminology (cont.)
    of place, see Crime, and place
    standard 42

Deterrence 64, 116–17, 127, 138, 158
Diffusion of benefits 4, 66, 83, 92, 113, 122–3, 135–8
Discouragement 138
Disorder 15, 46, 49, 52, 54, 58–61, 66, 79, 82, 84, 113–18, 120, 122–4, 127–31, 135, 137–8
Disorganization 2, 6, 14, 42, 43, 50–4, 58, 60–1, 65, 67–8, 73, 114–15, 149
Displacement 92, 113, 120, 122–3, 135–8, 156–7
Domestic disturbances/violence 20, 38
Drug enforcement 81, 117
Durkheim, Emile 17, 27, 50, 142–4

Ecological fallacy 12, 93
Edge effects 93–4
Environmental criminology 8, 14
Environmental psychology 72

Facilities 3, 9, 20–3, 35, 37, 40, 47, 53, 66, 76, 80, 103, 127–8, 130, 143
Family structure 51
Friendship networks 51, 59

General strain theory 71
Geographic context 6, 45, 52, 75, 92
Geographic profiling 87, 111
Geographic information systems (GIS) 8–9, 35, 39, 88, 96–101
    three-dimensional GIS 98
    two-dimensional GIS 98
Glyde, John 11, 13, 18
Group-based trajectory modeling 29
Guardianship/guardian(s) 6, 45, 48–50, 55–6, 61–7, 69, 80, 84, 114, 134, 145
Guerry, Andre-Michel 2, 11, 87, 93

Handlers 45, 65, 67
Heuristics 44
Homicide 125, 155
Hot products 48
Hot spots of crime 3, 13, 18–20, 28, 30–4, 36, 41–3, 53, 60–1, 64, 76–7, 83, 87, 94, 98, 101, 104, 110, 113–39, 142–4, 150, 153–4, 156–8

policing 3–6, 27, 64, 87, 102, 110, 113, 115, 117–18, 120–1, 135, 137–8, 141, 153–4, 156, 158

Informal social control 48–9, 52, 54, 58–9, 64–7, 73, 82, 145, 158
Institutional-cultural theory 83–4
Interactional networks 14

Juran, Joseph Moses 141, 143
Juvenile delinquency 6, 11, 50, 59, 74, 151

Kernel density estimation 92, 94, 104
Knowledge spillover 83–4

Landlord training 47, 65
Larceny(ies) 37
Law of crime concentrations of places 20–6, 28–9, 41, 141, 143–4
Legal authority 49, 57, 127, 146
Lewin, Kurt 72
Life course theory 70–1
Lighting 16, 50, 56, 72, 87, 117, 128
London cholera epidemic 75, 77
Lynch, Kevin 74

Market theory 80–1
    factors of production 81
    agglomeration 37, 80
McKay, Henry 2, 12, 50–1, 58–9
Meta-analysis 120, 122–5, 136
Microcommunities 53, 96
Microgeographic units 3, 6–9, 10–11, 12–15, 16, 23, 29, 34, 52–3, 73
Microplaces 1, 9, 14, 16, 17–18, 28, 29–34, 35, 40, 53, 61, 67, 75–7, 80, 83, 84, 96, 110, 151
Minneapolis Hot Spots Patrol Experiment 3, 8, 18, 116, 121
Mutual trust 58, 59

Natural areas 50
Neighborhood 1, 2, 12, 14, 30–4, 37, 39, 42, 44, 50–3, 54, 58–60, 66, 71, 81, 93, 102–3, 127, 130, 134, 135, 137, 145, 154, 155
Neighborhood organizations 42
New geographies 95–6, 101, 110
New public management 88
Nightingale, Florence 75

Index

Offender search theory 45
Offenders 2, 6, 10, 12, 28, 38, 42–5, 49–50, 52, 55–7, 69–70, 71, 72, 75, 77, 80, 81, 84, 88, 92, 101, 114, 117, 120, 124–5, 127, 130–5, 138, 140, 142, 145, 148–9, 151–2
Opportunity perspective/theory 44, 48, 52, 56, 79, 147
Organization, of space 46, 48, 144
Organization of space, regulation of conduct, control of access, and acquisition of resources (ORCA) 46, 47–8, 144

Pareto, Vilfredo 141, 143
Pareto principle 141, 143
Park, Robert 2, 12, 50
Permutation approach 102
Place management (place managers) 9, 14, 38–9, 45–50, 56–8, 61–7, 114, 127–32, 134, 138, 144–6, 156–7
Police 3, 6, 9, 28, 37, 46, 49–50, 52, 64–5, 74, 79, 89–91, 93–4, 99, 102, 108, 110–11, 113, 115–17, 119–20, 122–30, 135–8, 146, 151–4, 156–7
Population density 58
Population heterogeneity model 14, 43, 51
Poverty 6, 11, 35, 50, 58–60
Prevention perspective 78
Problem-oriented policing 79, 117–19, 121, 123–6, 156–7
Property rights 49, 144
Proprietary places 46, 57, 64, 66, 146
Prospective crime mapping 105
Proximal places 57, 65–6
Psychology, environmental 72
Public health 77
Public housing 53, 60, 74, 129

Quetelet, Adolphe 2, 11, 87, 93

Rape 20, 131
Raster cells (raster surface) 99
Rational choice perspective 44–5, 79, 87, 109, 148
Rationality, bounded 44
Regulation, of conduct 46, 48–9, 144
Regulatory approaches 131–2, 157
Repeat victimization 20, 30, 33, 38, 48–9, 103
  boost 38
  Flag explanation 38
Residential stability 50–1, 91

Resources, acquisition of 46, 49, 144
Risk terrain modeling 35, 105
Risky facility 56
Robbery 6, 16, 18, 30, 60, 80, 84, 104, 145, 155
Routine activity theory 45, 56, 69, 75, 87, 103, 114, 124, 146, 149

Sampson, Robert 51, 58, 60, 69
Scale problem 94
Scientific methods scale 119
Seattle, Washington 13, 20, 25–6, 28–30, 53, 60–1
Section 8- 53
Self-exciting point process 107
Shared expectations 51
Shaw, Clifford 2, 6, 12, 50–1, 58–9, 151–2
Situational action theory 70, 148
Situational crime prevention 3, 45, 77–9, 87, 114, 118, 136, 141, 146, 148
Situations 1, 35–41, 45, 49, 52, 58, 69–71, 77–8, 81, 97, 109, 118, 138, 143, 149, 156, 158
Snow, Jon 75
Social cohesion 51, 58–9
Social disorganization perspective/theory 2, 6, 14, 42–3, 50–4, 58, 60–1, 65, 67–8, 73, 114–15, 147, 149
Social geography 76
Social networks 51
Space 16–17, 35–7, 39–40, 45–7, 50, 52, 55–7, 65–6, 71, 77, 83–4, 90, 93, 95, 98, 102, 104–9, 111, 123, 134, 144, 155
Space-time budget 71
Spatial autocorrelation 91–2, 152
Spatial crime patterns 88
Spatiotemporal hotspots 102
Spatiotemporal routines 45
Standard criminology 42
State dependence model 14, 43
Street segment 52–3, 57, 60–1, 64–6, 71, 73, 76, 80, 93, 95–6, 101–3, 116, 126, 153
Structure 12, 45, 50, 58, 80, 92, 128
Super controller(s) 65, 146
Sutherland, Edwin 5
Systemic theory 51

Targets 28, 38, 44–5, 48–50, 55–6, 61, 64–5, 67, 69, 80, 104, 114, 135, 137, 142, 145
Teenagers 10, 51, 59, 128
Temporal contagion model 43

Territoriality 82
Terrorist attack 89
Terry stops 124
Theoretical integration 52, 61, 147
Third-party policing 65, 129
Thomas, William 2, 12
Tobler's first law of geography 40, 95

Victimization, *see* Repeat victimization
Victims 6, 20, 23, 30, 33, 38, 45, 48–9, 60, 77, 79, 103–4, 116, 131, 142, 145, 155

Willingness to intervene 51, 58–9
Wirth, Louis 2, 12